Jorg Schlagheck

Destinations are Fake

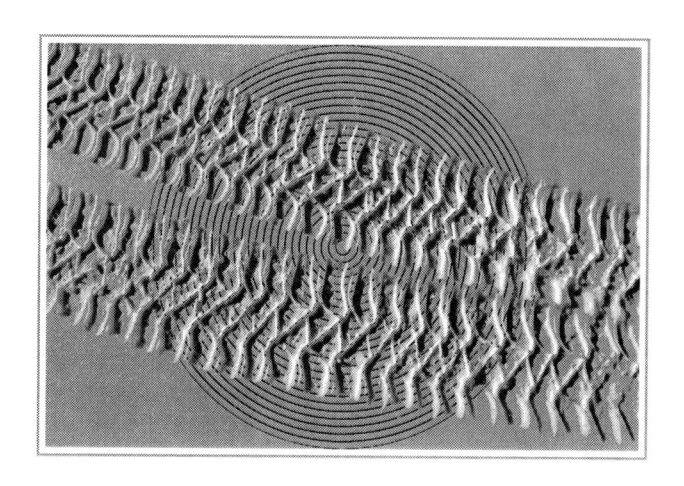

secreativ press

Copyright © 2017 by Jorg Schlagheck

All rights reserved. No part of this publication may be reproduced, distributed, or transmitted in any form or by any means, including photocopying, recording, or other electronic or mechanical methods, without the prior written permission of the publisher, except in the case of brief quotations embodied in critical reviews and certain other noncommercial uses permitted by copyright law. For permission requests, write to the author at the email address below.

Secreativ Press
secreativ.com

jorgschlagheck@gmail.com

Ordering Information:
Quantity sales. Special discounts are available on quantity purchases by corporations, associations, and others. For details, contact the publisher through secreativ.com.

For orders by bookstores and wholesalers; please contact Ingram Sparks Tel: (800) 800-8000; Fax: (800) 800-8001 or visit www.bigbooks.com.

Printed in Canada

ISBN 978-0-9959459-0-6

ISBN 978-0-9959459-2-0 (electronic book)

Destinations are Fake

Introduction

Have you ever tried to travel more than a few hundred kilometers, or miles away from your home without a destination and on your own power? Perhaps you are wondering what would be the point, or you might even simply dismiss it as silly, nothing but a waste of time. You might also be intrigued by the idea.

This book is about long distance bicycle touring. It is also very personal. The fall of 1982 was a rough time for me. I had broken my left femur in a motorcycle accident. It required a bone transplant from my hipbone and a 12" long metal plate along with 14 screws to mend one of the largest bones in my body. After the operation the leg became septic. At that point my outlook was very bleak. The complete loss of my left leg was a looming possibility. For over a decade after the operation I struggled with occasional flare-ups of osteomyelitis that not only restricted me physically, but also took a huge mental toll. Even after successful treatment of the infection in the 1990's, my leg was never as strong as it had once been. Throughout the 2000's I made a living as a highway driver, which led to a very unhealthy lifestyle. While I was doing fine financially and fulfilling a dream of free travel, the occupation had a very negative impact on my wellbeing. It all came crashing down in the summer of 2009. I had chronic back pain, was diagnosed with low HDL cholesterol and was going through a divorce, all at the same time. I credit an old bicycle with saving my life.

Before I discovered bicycle touring late in in 2009, I had been a trucker for almost nine years. At the beginning this had been like a dream come true. I had always felt the travel bug inside me and had chosen the occupation for that reason. After a number of years however, I became disillusioned. I kept getting sent to all sorts of exciting US-destinations, by my dispatchers, but could have been replaced by a robot the minute this technology would have become available. The objective of the trip was always to get the cargo to its destination, while I got to ride along and see all the interstate highways, truck stops and some industrial parks along the way. After a few years it didn't even matter where I was going any more. Destinations had become nothing more than words on a bill of lading. I was feeling cheated because I was totally excluded from all of the attractions that usually draw people. All I got was a brief glimpse of the landscapes that people often talk about. More often than not, I was wondering what it looked like beyond those exit ramps I didn't get to take with my truck. What was there to see, down those trails I couldn't go? Over the years I had seen parts of 48 states and nine Canadian provinces, but did I know any of them at all? 2009 was the turning point for me. My divorce and was adding more stress to my already unhealthy way of life. I realized that I had already lost pretty much everything that had ever meant anything to me. It was time to think about leaving the trucking business behind, if I didn't want to become a statistic.

  I went to Cuba twice that year. Both were discounted trips to lower end tourist traps that had access to beautiful beaches, unlimited cheap booze and tobacco, and lots of company who were much like myself. Ironically most of my fellow vacationers were also Canadians. Ordinary folks, whose lives back home were anything, but exciting. Like me, they had come to Cuba for an escape from the cold weather and the daily grind. Once at the destination they tended to do a little exploring around safe places, but aside from that they didn't do much besides drinking rum and smoking tobacco all day, while getting a sunburn on top of it all. Don't get me wrong, Cuba was a fantastic experience and the escape was exactly what I needed at the time, but after round number two I was done. This was no longer the way I wanted to travel. I realized that I had missed much of what Cuba had to offer, simply because I had been distracted by booze and the kind of company that goes along with it. Getting drunk on a beautiful beach without any responsibilities felt great and even the new friends I had made seemed to become more awesome the more we all drank. But I always ended up back home afterwards, with a huge hangover, more depressed than before.

On a positive note, the trips had given me just enough glimpse of Latin culture to pique my curiosity. I became upset with myself for having spent most of the time with intoxicated tourists, instead of exploring more of the surroundings and making more connections with Cubans, whose lives were very different from my own. It motivated me to learn more about Latin culture. I made the resolve to travel south again, mingle with locals and speak their language.

There had been a few unforgettable days during my stays in Cuba. One truly stands out in my memory. Inspired by a local man who was hauling coconuts on a bicycle, some 25 kilometers one way, each day, I had rented a bicycle. It was my way of escaping the tourist traps for a day. I cycled to a nearby town that had no tourist attractions at all, not even a hotel, as far as I know. Cardenas (the name of the town) was my destination, but the 25-kilometer ride it took to get there was every bit as exciting as the little town itself. I was moving on my own power through unknown territory, at a pace that was perfect to optimize my experience. It was like a dream and though I hadn't ridden a bicycle in years, the primitive, one speed bike seemed to move almost effortless toward new sights that my fellow vacationers back at the hotel bar would probably never get to see. I was seeing a small part of the real Cuba, the non-destination that almost nobody considered worthy of exploring.

Commercial tourist destinations are hugely overrated, or even fake, when the journey is what stays with us forever. Think about all the places you pass over when taking a flight on an airplane! Have you ever wondered what you may have missed?

The idea took a while to grow even after the cycling day in Cuba, but the seed had been planted in my mind. Months later, I rediscovered the bicycle as a mode of transportation. Gradually my rides grew longer and at some point I had an epiphany: I had to explore foreign lands by bicycle.

I have to admit that planning isn't my strength. So when I first set out on my quest to go to Mexico, I was so ill prepared that some bike experts laughed at me. It didn't hold me back from cycling to the Buffalo NY airport (from Parry Sound ON) to catch a flight to Orlando. From there I cycled almost every day, until I eventually reached Cancun. Six months later I was a different person when I returned to Buffalo, and eventually Ontario. I had lost weight, my back pain was gone and my left leg was stronger than it had been in almost three decades. The tour had many interesting twists and turns. I learned about bicycle touring the hard way, but there are no regrets.

In order to share my stories and what I've learned, I've written this book. The title "Destinations are Fake" came to me because in bicycle touring it is completely irrelevant where you are headed. The focus is entirely on the journey. We get to experience those "non destinations" we usually fly over or browse by in our vehicles, first hand. The discoveries are so plentiful that no single destination could possibly match that. Soon you realize that those dream destinations that are trying to lure you to spend a lot of money in a really short time are nothing but fake. Not only are they trying to rob you of your hard earned money, they're also denying you an authentic experience. I'm hoping to inspire you and many others to try touring by bicycle.

Bicycles are an amazing invention. They are so much more than a kid's toy, a sport article or a cheap way to get to the store. As you will see, you can go just about anywhere on your own power.

Why aren't more people exploring foreign countries by bicycle? Many of us are locked into an occupation that simply doesn't allow enough time to travel that way. We have to decide between riding the bike and spending time in nice places. The choice is often influenced by the travel industry that is in the business of marketing tourist destinations. Cycling can also be a dangerous activity, mainly due to the lack of suitable roads, trails and bike lanes.

With this book I'm hoping to address those issues and contribute to making bicycle touring a mainstream activity. I hope to show through my adventures, how time spent riding a bicycle is never wasted. If you value your life, you'll want to live it to the fullest. Have you ever wondered what exactly that means? Bicycle touring has a lot to offer, above and beyond recreation. To discover what I mean by that you will have to get on your bike and try it. Let's forget about destinations and start off locally. For some of you this will be enough incentive to venture out further and further, while others will be content with the shorter rides. Your imagination is the limit. Over time, cycling will get safer as our infrastructure adapts due to growing demand. Efforts are already underway to build trails that connect provinces, states and countries. An example is the Trans Canada Trail. Even if large portions of the trail are not yet accessible by bicycle, it is a step in the right direction. With enough support, some day we will have a network of safe cycling routes that spans the globe. Bicycle touring will capture the mainstream and the result will be a better society.

Chapter 1

The Miracle

Why bicycles are such an amazing invention

Do you remember the feeling that overcame you when you mastered riding a bicycle for the very first time in your life? At the time I'm writing this I am 52 years old, yet I still clearly remember riding my first real bicycle, probably about 47 years ago. Not only was it a huge step up from the tricycle I had owned prior, it was a major step of growing up. All of a sudden I was a big kid. I was fast. Sure, at first it took some getting used to the seating position on the bike, but soon I was hooked by the speed I was able to achieve on my own power. It was nothing short of mind boggling for my five-year-old brain. To this day I can point at the scar above my left eyelid that remains from the gash I suffered when I failed to pace myself and crashed, head first, against a curb. The accident could have been much worse, but my parents had bought me a helmet, which made me think I was invincible for a very short while. I learned the hard way, but thanks to the bike, new adventures came within reach. I was no longer limited to spending hours in the driveway without going anywhere. Instead was bombing around all over the neighborhood.

Over the next couple of years the little kid's bike got a lot of use. It took a beating, and it was amazing that my parents were able to resell it after I eventually outgrew it and pretty well wore it out. Even though that little blue and red bike is long gone, it will always exist in my memory and have a special place in my heart. As I changed over the years, so did my bikes. First came a bigger kid's bike with 24-inch wheels, later a men's bike with 26-inch ones. My favorite bike as a boy was a purple, three-speed bike that came with fenders and even a rack. That bike quickly became my mode of everyday transportation around the town we lived in. That's not to say that riding wasn't fun any more; I remember installing a fully mechanical speedometer once, which my dad helped me with. Of course it was a challenge to go faster and faster. Today I understand that even as kid of eight or nine years old I was already training my body to perform and it never seemed like work at all. I loved the feeling of pushing myself past new limits. At first it seemed like a huge achievement to reach 35 km/hour for short distances, but that barrier was broken shortly after. Later I reached 40 and even 45. Riding the bike long and hard always gave me a sense of accomplishment.

To this day, nothing can replace the feeling of riding a bike at high speed on my own physical power. Even so many years later, I simply can't get over the magic that makes bicycles move so well. Let me explain! Imagine having to walk a certain distance, say 10 kilometers. How long would it take? Probably more than a couple of hours! How about running? That would certainly cut off a good chunk of time, but it is pretty hard. Now add a load, like thirty pounds of awkwardly shaped metal to the fun! Yes, carry it! Do you see where I'm going with this? Moving yourself, let alone thirty pounds of anything, without external power, over long distances is hard work. Doing so at 20, 30 or even 40 km/hour is nothing short of a miracle. This miracle weighs about thirty pounds (your load) and is accessible to almost anyone. Bicycles are, without a doubt, one of the greatest inventions of all times.

Today however, too many people might never even think of walking 10 kilometers, let alone carrying anything for even half that distance. We have cars for that, don't we? Why work so hard if we can just drive? Unfortunately this attitude is all too common in today's era of instant results. Most of us don't think twice about using their automobile for transportation, because there is always a destination on their mind that takes priority over the journey it takes to get there. The cost to our society is not apparent to most, who are caught up in an ongoing rat race of ever growing commutes and tight schedules.

Let's examine some of the key differences between automobiles and bicycles! How much does an average car weigh, about 3,000 pounds? Just starting the engine sets a complex combination of parts in motion. The battery that supplies the power to start your engine is essentially a toxic mess, made up of lead and acid, contained in a plastic box. The starter that turns the engine over would be powerful enough to propel your bicycle to breakneck speed within seconds and to keep it going for hours. In a car however, it just manages to turn over the engine. This engine cannot run without fuel and more electrical power to ignite it. All of this is controlled by carefully designed mechanisms and electronics that took decades to develop and huge factories to build. Bicycles by comparison, are brilliantly simple. A car costs upwards of $ 10,000 and typically wears out in ten years. A decent bicycle on the other hand, can be had for as little as $ 300 and, with some basic TLC, will last decades. Cars burn gasoline and need a number of other toxic fluids just to make them function. Bicycles occasionally need a few drops of lubricant in a few places. Cars are powerful, they can reach speeds well in excess of 100 km/h, which is sometimes more than a human can safely control. Traffic accidents involving cars happen every day, often bearing disastrous consequences for those involved.

As a mode of transportation cars may be superior to bicycles for long distances, but at what price? More energy and resources are used to move that car itself than the person who is using it, which is just the opposite of efficient. In my example above I challenged you to carry 30 pounds of awkwardly shaped metal, because that is what an average bicycle weighs. Guess what; you can ride that 30 pound thing and reach your destination, with some minor effort, in just a little bit more time than it would take by car, especially in an urban area where it might allow shortcuts that are not accessible to motorized vehicles. Besides being fast, light, clean and efficient, bikes also take up little space and can go almost anywhere a person could walk. Anyone with two arms and legs can learn to ride a bicycle. The way it makes getting around easier despite packing extra weight, is nothing short of magic. Then there is the fact that a bicycle cannot stand up on it's own when parked, but is easily balanced while in motion. Minimal contact with the road makes for optimum efficiency and also allows for traveling on narrow trails. How much better can it get? Why is it then that bicycles are generally not taken seriously as a mode of transportation in North America? Throughout my entire life, starting with the kid's bike I mentioned above, I have always owned at least one bicycle. However, there were times when they collected dust in the garage. When I was 16, I couldn't wait to get a license for a scooter. Back in those days the stinky exhaust and the noise of the little engine didn't bother me. At first it was simply fun to ride faster, but eventually even more speed seemed necessary because of how busy my life had become. There always seemed to be a shortage of time. A motorcycle replaced the scooter when I was 18, which was replaced by my first car after I had learned the hard way that cars offered better protection in an accident. I had broken my left femur in a collision with an automobile. The injury took years to recover from, perhaps in part because at that time it never even entered my mind to ride the bike as a means of physiotherapy, except for the stationary version at a gym, which simply isn't the same as riding a real one.

      Bike rides became less frequent as my life got busier. This trend continued after moving from Germany to Canada in 1987. In North America, the infrastructure is designed for cars and trucks. There are sidewalks for pedestrians, to cover short distances, but for anything more than a kilometer or two, which is considered walking distance, most people are driving or using public transit. Even for those who own a bike, it is often dangerous to use it. Where would you ride in an urban setting? On the road you'd take your chances, mostly because they're congested with big heavy cars that are as hard as the steel they're made from and powerful enough to do serious damage in a collision. A minor fender bender could change your life forever, or worse, end it. Unfortunately this still happens quite regularly in major cities. On the sidewalk on the other hand you and your bike become a danger to pedestrians, besides suffering a terrible ride that is constantly interrupted by curbs and other obstacles.

While many countries in Europe have always had bicycle lanes and trails, America is lagging behind in that department. In any major city, a huge amount of space is designated for cars. The impact this has on our way of life can hardly be considered positive. Cars emit toxic exhaust, make noise and are dangerous. In some cities the gridlock is so bad that at certain times even walking can be faster than driving. Many of us have become addicted to their motorized vehicles, which commonly represent one of their biggest expenses in life. However, there still is hope for the bicycle. In recent years a trend toward cycling appears to be underway, as more people look for a way to reduce their carbon footprint while improving their health and save money at the same time. Can riding a bicycle improve your health? At this point I would like to invite you to take a look at any statistic you can find on obesity. Compare European Countries, the Netherlands for example, where cycling for transportation is relatively common and a good bicycle infrastructure exists, to Canada or the USA. I would bet my dollar, that obesity is less of a problem in Europe. I'm not going to bore you with numbers to prove my point. I'm just hinting that cycling is intense exercise that promotes a healthy body weight. Who does not want to loose a few pounds these days? An entire industry is dedicated to that goal and doing rather well financially, while generally failing to deliver the goods. Diets and exercise plans work for a period of time, but people usually fall off the wagon and gain back the weight. What if I told you I had a sure fire way for you to loose weight and keep it off for good? Sounds pretty good now doesn't it? There is no doubt that cycling can do that for you. I would even go further and suggest that heart attacks and strokes could be all but eliminated, if people started using bikes for transportation whenever possible. Unfortunately, due to a lack of safe roads and trails for bikes, more accidental deaths and injuries could be the flip side of the same coin. This needs to change. Despite the many dangers, the trend towards more and more cycling appears to be strong and here to stay. While much of it is due to recreational activities, more and more people ride bikes for everyday transportation and experience the benefits first hand. I have personally rediscovered the benefits of cycling for my transportation needs a few years ago. Let me tell you what they are:

- Physical exercise without spending extra time at a recreational facility.

- More time spent outdoors has health benefits all by itself.

- Substantial savings. Bicycles don't burn gasoline, are cheap to buy and maintain.

- A more relaxed pace of life. The ride to work, for example, can become an enjoyable activity, rather than a stressful commute in rush-hour traffic.

- No need to look for parking spots in dense urban areas. A bike fits almost anywhere!

- Bicycles are quiet and have zero emissions; they are easy on the environment.

- A feeling of general wellbeing and accomplishment, almost a high, often follows long bike rides.

The formula is simple: The more you ride your bike, the more you benefit! Of course there are times when cycling is not a good option. Canadian winter comes to mind. Cycling on ice and snow is not as much fun and can be extremely dangerous. Some hardcore cyclists will go all the way and make it through the entire winter, no matter how cold it gets or how much snow and ice is obstructing the roads, but that is hardly something I would advocate for everyone. Quite the contrary, a long winter of cycling in poor conditions can spoil your fun in the activity permanently, unless of course you're already hooked. Then you might be hardcore and the bicycle may be the only option imaginable. You may then invest in a set of studded tires or even a winter bike, which means an older bicycle that is nothing fancy, but can take a beating. Either way, even in Canada there are always three seasons that are perfect for cycling. There is hope that, in the near future the trend towards bicycle use will grow strong enough to cause the addition of new infrastructure, built specifically and exclusively for bicycles. This book is an effort to contribute to this trend. Like a popular saying goes; if I can even persuade one person to rediscover their bicycle, either as a recreational piece of equipment, or better yet, a means of every day transportation, then I have accomplished at least part of my mission. Bicycles are ideal for transportation, at least within a certain range. This range varies as each of us has different capabilities and sense of time, but usually grows as one becomes accustomed to regular bike rides. Of course there is an underlying dream that is much bigger. A bicycle can take you almost anywhere without ever running out of fuel. The fact that it does this at a slower pace than many of us demand in today's world is not a disadvantage, but a major part of the true beauty of cycling. You will understand when you get to the end of this book. Destinations are Fake. What truly matters is your journey.

Chapter 2

Rediscovering the Bicycle

My personal story

Throughout much of my adult life I was a car guy. At times there was not one car in my driveway, but four or five, most of them not running too well. One of my dreams was to rebuild a cool old car to new glory. As a result I ended up with a big collection of automotive tools and built my own garage. I even went back to school and took an entire program toward becoming an auto-mechanic. I loved cars! Going back to my growing up years in Germany, I had good reasons to switch from two wheels to four. Somebody I had known well had died in a collision with a car. The boy, a teenager at the time, had been on his way home, riding his bicycle one evening, without proper reflectors or lighting. The impact had killed him on the spot; wiped him out for eternity.

I myself had suffered a severely fractured femur, from a relatively minor motorcycle accident, also a collision with a car. The incident kept me in the hospital for 10 weeks in one initial stretch, then in and out for the next two years. It had turned out to be quite a detour for what was supposed to be my way home from swimming practice! Still limping, I took ownership of my shiny orange VW Passat, the first one in a line of used cars that I would own over the next three decades. I can't deny that it was a special treat to drive my first own car. At the time it made perfect sense; my bones were no longer out on the road for other motorists to hit and break. The vehicle served me well for about four years, living in Germany. I even discovered long distance travel across parts of Europe. Driving was fun and definitely gave me a sense of freedom. It was around the same time that I started dreaming of becoming a long haul trucker some day. The dream eventually materialized and shaped my life in a big way. There was a downside however. The responsibilities that came with owning a car were quite the opposite of true freedom. A lot of my meager apprenticeship wages went straight into the gas tank, insurance was high for young drivers and my used car always needed something. I quickly learned about overdrawing my bank account. Whenever the car broke down I had to get creative, first in obtaining affordable parts, then in teaching myself how to do the repair. The costs were out of my range, but there always seemed to be a way. I was hooked on driving and doing exactly what addicts do; find a way to get their fix. At the age of 23, funded by insurance money from my motorcycle accident, I went on to explore Canada by car for six months. I bought an old (1970) Pontiac Acadian in Toronto and drove it, first to Montreal, and then around in a big loop of Northern Quebec and Ontario to the Western Provinces, all the way out to the West Coast and eventually Alaska. It was the trip of a lifetime and actually cost relatively little. Gas prices in Canada during the mid 1980's were very affordable. The car had cost only a few hundred dollars and was big enough to live in for a while. The backseat was not the most comfortable, but it was okay to sleep on. Food was cheap too. I had a good size cooler that I kept well stocked with groceries and there were two-dollar breakfast specials wherever I went. I had been involved in competitive triathlon back home, and owned a nice road bike, which I carried in the trunk during the entire trip. I remember using that bike once or twice to get exercise and explore, but didn't really find it worth the trouble of handling it. Driving was more fun. Canadian highways were endless and wide open for me to enjoy. A year later my life changed drastically as a result of this trip. I had met someone special in Montreal, fallen in love and stayed in touch. After exchanging letters for a while and exploring parts of Europe together in that orange Passat, we got married and I moved to Montreal. The fun of driving a cool old car across the country still fresh in my memory, I was now being introduced to a daily commute in rush hour traffic. It meant joining a long queue of vehicles across the Champlain Bridge every morning and every evening. I never thought twice about my new routine, it quickly became a way of life. Soon my bicycle became a dust collector.

There was a brief period in the mid 1990's when I discovered the occasional bike ride as a way to get some exercise, but to ride to work or do serious bike tours? It seemed unthinkable! Who had the time? My wife and I had started a family and the responsibilities were many. A lot of my time went into maintaining our vehicles, because we absolutely needed them to get around. After moving to Brampton, Ontario, in 1998, I finally fulfilled my old dream and became a truck driver. It was another adventure and, for some time, felt like retirement from actual working. My "career" as a professional highway-driver lasted nine years in total. I soon decided to buy my own truck, a used Peterbilt that I ended up driving more than a million miles over a period of eight years. My trips took me across most of Canada and to 48 US states. The travel bug was alive and well in me. Trips that most drivers would have considered grueling work were just plain fun. Even when layovers were involved I considered them a chance to explore. I was finally making money doing what I loved; driving on the open road! Nine years later, the trucking lifestyle had taken its toll; my marriage was over and my body was in rough shape. A physical revealed low levels of HDL-cholesterol, the good stuff. What was worse, I was barely able to crawl out of bed in the morning! There was a constant pain in my spine that often radiated through my entire right arm, even to the point of numbing my fingertips. Driving the truck had become painful, especially since I needed my right arm to shift through the 13 gears. Every time I had to operate the shifter it felt like my arm was suffering some kind of tear that kept getting worse and more painful. Trips that would have been fun before seemed like hard work now. There were ever looming deadlines. Finally, in early 2009, a time when the trucking industry had taken a dive, I realized that it cost more and more to operate the truck, while earnings were on a steady decline. Brutally long hours behind the wheel were necessary just to keep up with schedules. Anyone who has been around truck stops every now and then will know that most truck-drivers in their later years don't exactly represent an image of good health. While I always thought of myself as being in good shape and even worked out whenever time would allow, I was clearly headed downhill, both physically and mentally. In February of 2009 my truck needed a set of tires that would have cost over $ 3,000 brand new. At the time I was reluctant to spend the money. Somehow I could not see myself driving the truck for too much longer. A tire dealer introduced me to another option. He said that he could have my old tires retreaded at a much lower cost than what it would take to replace them. The downside would be that would need my tires for an entire week, so I would loose considerable revenue. I didn't think twice. I needed a break. With a few clicks on my laptop a trip to Cuba was booked. I roughly spent the money I was saving on tires, which seemed like a brilliant idea.

    A few days later I found myself in a paradise of palm trees, sunshine, cheap rum and cigarettes and women in bikinis. I was newly single, depressed and longing for adventure. It was on this trip, over rum and late night skinny-dipping in the ocean, that I met a woman I almost immediately developed a crush on. Marianne (not her real name) was everything my ex wife was not. She appeared open minded, was good looking without being pretty, and adventurous, like myself. She was also a heavy drinker and smoker. Without a doubt, this all helped fuel a stormy fling between us. We spent days together exploring the beaches and the town of Varadero, and nights drinking rum and enjoying each other's company.

    Reality hit me hard when I found myself back in my truck on a trip to Wisconsin a week later. Never in my life had I consumed so much alcohol, nor had I ever been a smoker. The hangover seemed to linger on and turned into depression. I hated dark highways and blowing snow, but that was exactly what my life looked like. I had learned long before, that in trucking the destination never meant a whole lot, but now even the journeys had become unbearable. It was no more than a few weeks later that my dispatcher informed me about a shutdown in one of the paper-mills I was hauling for, and that there would not be any loads for about a week. Once again I decided to search the Internet for a cheap trip to Cuba and lucked out immediately on a last minute deal. The trip I booked was all-inclusive and cost only about half the amount of money my previous trip had set me back. I even emailed Marianne, but she only responded with a one liner, informing me she couldn't afford to go.

Once again I spent a week in the sunshine, consumed way too much booze and met a bunch of people. Ironically, most of them were from Canada. About half way through the week however, I had enough of the numbed out feeling and decided to rent a bicycle to get some exercise. Inspired by a local coconut-vendor, who made his living hauling coconuts on his bicycle daily, over a distance of 25 kilometers. He was from a town called Cardenas that was relatively close to Varadero, the tourist area. I decided to do some exploring by bike and ended up riding the 50 kilometers, to Cardenas and back that day. The ride was challenging, but it was, without a doubt, the highlight of my vacation. I remember getting back to my hotel after dark, planning to end the day at the bar, but passing out on my bed instead. I slept like a log till the next morning.

To this day, I credit this ride for my rediscovery of cycling. However, after the day of exploring I was back to drinking and smoking with my buddies at the hotel. Booze was free, and my time in Cuba limited, so I had to take advantage. The stay in paradise passed quickly.

I returned to my truck the following week, sober, hurting and with an assignment to haul something, somewhere. Life was back to what I had come to consider normal, but it was no longer satisfying. It took all my courage to finally quit the trucking business three months later. The final straw was a decrease in pay due to the difficult economic situation of 2009. I turned my back on what had been my way of life for close to a decade. Without a long-term plan for the future, I decided to cancel my contract and put the truck up for sale. The next few months were pivotal. Both my daughters were now grown up and taking major trips to Europe. I wanted to travel too, but Europe was where I had grown up and my curiosities were elsewhere. In part because of my trips to Cuba, I had become interested in Latin America. I already knew some Spanish from listening to tapes during long hours in the truck and my first attempts to speak it on trips to Texas and in Cuba. To equip myself with something to earn a living during a long-term stay, I enrolled into a basic course on how to teach English as a second language. After three weekends I was a certified ESL-teacher.

At first I was thinking of buying or building a small camping trailer that I could pull with my car. I was thinking of traveling to Mexico and spend the winter, check out the country and escape at least an entire Canadian winter. My car was a nicely equipped Buick Lesabre. I had always enjoyed the smooth ride on long distances, especially compared to my transport truck. For a while I drove the car a lot, but soon I realized how much gasoline cost. I was unemployed and without income, so there had to be another way. There was another way. With more time on my hands than before, I started fixing up an old bicycle that was rusting away in the shed at home. It had actually belonged to my ex wife, but was too big for her. Nobody had ridden it for about ten years. I decided to give it some new tires, lubricant and all around maintenance. The idea was to ride it around town to save on gas money. The bike didn't need much and within a few days it resembled a brand-new one. I started riding it only to the gym at first. Three kilometers each way were easy to do, but each trip felt like a small accomplishment and allowed me to skip most of my cardio. Riding the bike seemed not practical for the longer distances right away. Cycling was actually painful, especially on sidewalks and rough roads. My spine was still battered from the effects of driving the truck for so many years and I was starting to wonder if it was ever going to recover. This almost worried me to the point of giving up cycling again for good, but I simply wasn't ready to accept a permanent handicap. At first I considered getting massages or seeing a chiropractor, but that would have cost money, so it was put off. Instead I continued cycling with a pain in my back. The rides made me feel good in every other way. I don't know exactly at what point my back stopped hurting, but it eventually did. The increased blood circulation from cycling probably helped it heal. Over time my rides became longer and longer. Errands that didn't require transporting something heavy or awkward, no matter how far I'd have to go, were tackled by bicycle. Any necessary trip had suddenly become a reason for a bike ride. I felt better than I had in years. To this day I tend to recommend riding a bicycle as a universal remedy. The human body is extremely well suited for cycling. It is an intense form of exercise, yet gentle on the bones and joints.

    As my rides gradually got longer and longer, my car started to collect dust. I was truly enjoying life in a whole new way. The slower pace suited me well and I was getting back in shape. Sure, errands were taking longer, but the feeling of accomplishment that consistently followed every major bike ride had totally won me over. Soon I was a committed cyclist.

    At that point even my travel plans began to change. Research on the Internet revealed that some people went on months long bike tours. I began to study everything I could find about bicycle touring. What type of bikes were people using? What did they take along on their trips? Even stories going into the details of how they managed to pack everything they needed onto a bicycle captured my attention completely. I already mentioned that I'm curious by nature, so it might not surprise you at this point that I simply had to try bicycle touring for myself.

    Along with the truck, my car went up for sale. I was still set on spending the following winter in Mexico. How was I going to get there? A new idea had taken over!

Chapter 3

Possibilities

Preparing for a tour

Bicycles can go pretty much anywhere. Your bike will go as far as you, the rider, can take it. The only fuel is the food you eat. Simply put, the more calories you eat, the further you can ride. Think about this for a moment! How many of us struggle with obesity these days? Switching to your bike for a daily commute is probably the best way to address a weight problem and promote good health. Spending about an hour riding a bicycle each day, consistently, will make a huge difference in physical, as well as mental well being. The possibilities do not end there. Once you start seeing your stored fat reserves as fuel, rather than useless blubber, you can think about traveling long distances to spend this stored energy. While it takes some conditioning to get to this point, any bike ride longer than about twenty minutes will be fueled out of your stored fat directly, because your body generally does not have enough glycogen reserves to last beyond that.

For some, regular bike rides around town, for commuting or other purposes, are all they'll ever do and desire. For others however, cycling can become a way of life. Can you imagine kissing your car goodbye to do all your traveling by bike? How about going on tour and covering hundred or more kilometers almost every day for weeks or even months? A tour of that nature can be life changing. With relatively modest amounts of money in the bank, it is even possible to go around the world.

Traveling long distances by bicycle is far from mainstream and after my rediscovery of the bicycle for transportation it sure captured my imagination. I began to read whatever I could find about bicycle touring. Websites such as "Crazy Guy on a Bike" and "Ken Kifer's Bike Pages" are excellent sources of information and very inspirational, just to name a few. Do your own searches; the list is always growing! In my case, I was planning my own bike tour before I knew it.

How do you plan for a major bike tour? Despite all the information available on the Internet, it still took a lot of guesswork to come up with even a very basic plan. I was interested in exploring Mexico, a country I knew little about. To my surprise I was not able to find a lot of information about cycling across Mexico. What I found was not exactly encouraging. Another question was what kind of equipment to choose. Would a regular hybrid bike with 700c size wheels be up to the challenge? Could I take my bicycle, which worked really well to get around town, on a months long trip across the continent? Could it safely be loaded with everything needed for the tour? Or would this require a touring specific bike? It is easy to get lost in the planning phase.

No matter how much research you do about the regions you want to visit, nothing ever remains the same for long, anywhere. You might come across somebody's journal of a bike tour from a couple of years ago, but it can only provide limited information. One of the ideas of a big bike tour is adventure, exploring new places and experiencing the unexpected. I found it helpful to read about Mexico and look at maps, but out of all I was learning the only thing truly relevant was, that there were towns, connected by roads. Nearly every piece of information beyond that was someone else's subjective experience, often tainted with opinions. Even official travel sites often distort reality to prove a point. In the case of Mexico the information was generally on the negative side. Crime seemed to be the main concern along with corrupt police and, at the time, the swine flu. Yes, I had some reservations about going to Mexico by bicycle on my own. However, the ultimate decision was easy; my curiosity and desire for endless bike rides without a set destination were stronger than my fear. I also really had no idea how to plan the details of the trip, so I didn't. All I knew was that I was going to Mexico to explore the country. Everything else would somehow fall into place. You can call this faith.

When it comes to equipment however, some planning is inevitable. To be on the road for weeks at a time requires at least a suitable bike in good condition, the right clothes, a way of carrying luggage and perhaps camping gear. Let's discuss the bike first.

A touring specific bicycle, brand new from a bike store, will cost upwards of $ 1,000. The big question I was facing was weather I needed one or not. Reading about touring bikes and their characteristics helped me make my decision. Here are some key points you will find over and over:

- For touring, your bike should have a steel frame.

- The bike should have a geometry that allows the installation of racks. Ideally it will have eyelets at the dropouts (the pair of slots that hold the axles, front and back).

- A longer wheelbase with long chain-stays (the tubes that go from the bottom bracket, where the cranks are attached, to the rear axle) makes for a more stable ride with a load.

- Rear suspensions are generally not useful for riding with a load.

- The bike should fit you well and be comfortable.

- The bike should have gears that allow you to pedal uphill with all your gear loaded up on the bike, without killing yourself.

If your bike meets those requirements and is in good working order, you are probably good to tour. A regular bicycle is good to carry a load of around 300 pounds, including the rider. Even for a heavy guy of over 200 pounds, that allows for a lot of luggage. Most bike manufacturers offer touring specific bikes that will surpass many of the specifications above. They are also expensive. If money is not an object, then go ahead and knock yourself out! However, a touring bike with all the bells and whistles is not necessarily the right choice for every tour. I will discuss the reasons later.

For my first bicycle tour, I decided to use the bike I already had. It was by no means the perfect fit, but was good enough to carry a load and provide for a fairly comfortable ride. For anyone interested, the bike was a mid 1990's "Minelli Mojave". It had 700 series tires, was equipped with plastic fenders and a rear rack. I purchased and installed a low rider front rack for panniers and swapped the wheels for higher quality ones.

With the bike ready to go, it was time to decide what else was needed for the tour. The best and most common way to carry luggage on a bike are panniers. I bought four: two really large ones for the rear and two smaller ones for the front. The handlebars were outfitted with a fairly large handlebar bag, intended to hold my maps, travel documentation and camera.

There were other necessities. Let's walk through them one by one:

Camping gear

- While not everyone might plan on sleeping outdoors, it has the potential to save a ton of money, especially on longer trips. You carry your own bedroom, ready to set up anywhere, at least in theory (more on that later). Look for a small tent that fits into a very small bag and doesn't weigh much. Ideally, all your camping gear should fit into one of the large panniers. I like dome tents that you can set up anywhere, even on a concrete pad. However, right before my first bike tour I had no idea and bought a very basic two-person tent for $ 35.

- To sleep comfortably you will also need some kind of padding. I bought a regular air mattress. I liked how compact it was when deflated. The downsides were that it was very small, had no built in pillow and was prone to leaks. While it might be tempting to buy a better, more comfortable pad or mattress, let me remind you; space is limited!

- On my first trip I was using a duffle bag packed with dirty clothes for a pillow; not a great idea! Small inflatable or compressible pillows are available and probably a good investment.

- Last not least, when it comes to sleeping, you will need a blanket or a sleeping bag. I recommend the latter as it can double as either. Mine was a very light down filled one, which was perfect. Sometimes feathers might come out and after washing it requires thorough drying, followed by a good shake to loosen up the feathers. Sleeping bags with synthetic insulation might be an even better choice. Unless you'll be riding in truly cold climate, don't go crazy on the insulation! You'll likely be warm enough anyways.

Another question to ponder is whether or not you are planning to cook your own food, even just occasionally, along the way. A cooking pot can double as a food bowl to eat from and a simple fork and spoon combination can go a long way. Remember; you'll have to haul all this stuff. Focus on the essentials! To cook food you will need fire, for which a small camping stove might come in handy. When shopping for mine, I didn't find anything I liked and decided to build a simple alcohol stove. Instructions for this can be found on websites such as "Instructables".

A good pocketknife comes in handy for any touring cyclist. It has many applications besides cutting food, some of which you won't even think of until they come up. This leads me to more essentials.

Tools.

No matter how good your bike is, at some point you'll have to repair it. If nothing else, somewhere along the way you are bound to get a flat tire. Let's start with the tools you need to get you rolling again: To remove your wheel you may need a wrench, usually 15 millimeter (not applicable for quick release axles). I have found is useful to carry a small adjustable wrench for that purpose. Next you will have to remove the tire from the wheel, which requires a set of tire levers. To patch an inner tube you'll need a patch kit. A pair of long nose pliers is useful to pull a nail or a piece of wire out of the tire, so you won't get another flat right away. No tire is good without air in it, so you'll also need a pump.

To make your own, complete list of tools, imagine it breaking down your bike and visualize the steps it would take to get it back on the road! Quite obviously it makes a lot of sense to choose a bike that is rather simple. For example, index shifters for changing gears and ten speed rear cassettes are nice ideas, but when it comes to touring they simply add more potential something to go wrong.

Here is a generic list of essential tools that will be useful for most bikes:

- 10" adjustable wrench
- Air pump
- Tire levers
- Patch kit
- Metric Allen key set
- Combination wrenches 8, 9 and 10 millimeter
- Socket drivers 8, 9 and 10 millimeter
- Screwdrivers: Phillips and flat tip
- Side cutters
- Long nose pliers
- Vice grips (small)
- Spoke wrench

Those are just some of the things to get you moving again in case something basic goes wrong. It is not a complete list and some riders will want to ad bicycle specific tools:

- Cone wrenches (to adjust or dismantle front and rear axles)
- Bottom bracket wrenches (adjust or dismantle bottom bracket)
- Headset wrenches (in case the headset requires adjusting)
- A chain breaker (to deal with of chain or derailleur problems)
- A spoke wrench (for dealing with wheel problems)

To carry all of those may seem like unnecessary weight, but only until you need them! Even with all those tools it is still possible to get stuck pushing the bike, but the odds are in your favor. If worse comes to worse; bike shops can help. Hopefully you won't be stuck too far from one! Even nasty breakdowns can usually be resolved. Keep in mind that your tour is not about getting to a destination, but a journey in which challenges add to the adventure. Bicycle touring is not for the faint of heart. Before we move on to clothing and other luggage, top off your toolkit with some lubricant and a couple of rags! You will have to keep your chain and the cables of your bike lubricated. There is controversy in the cyclist community, over what to use. I like 3 in 1 oil mixed with some graphite powder. The idea is that the 3 in 1 oil is light enough to make it penetrate the inside of the chain rollers and cable housings, while the graphite powder is a dry lubricant that will last and thereby prolong the life of those parts. Bicycle specific lubricants are also available. Whatever you decide to use, it is important to wipe off the excess oil when done, because otherwise dirt will stick to it and sabotage your efforts.

You've probably filled half a pannier with tools by now, might as well keep going and throw in a couple of spare tubes for your tires and spare cables for breaks and gear shifters! How about brake pads and a couple of spokes? One last look! Does your bike have any small parts that could fail and might be hard to find where you're going? Perhaps it makes sense to pack a spare!

Now that you've covered your bicycle's needs, move on to your own; the clothing list! I won't bore you with my own or preach what you should wear. There are too many different options, preferences and climate considerations. Some riders like bicycle shorts and - jerseys, others ride in cut off jeans and t-shirt. Whatever you like, take a few of each, to last at least four days or so. Personally I like short sleeve shirts with buttons and a collar for hot weather. They allow for very good ventilation and the collar can protect your neck from sunburn. When it cools off and starts to rain, I put on a windbreaker. The fabric it's made from is water repellant fabric, but not watertight. A hoodie is good to have if it gets colder, so are some gloves. Beyond that, just take whatever you think you'll need for the trip. I colder weather, choose fabrics that will keep your body dry, rather than cotton. You will probably fill up those panniers pretty fast, so cut down on stuff and only take the bare essentials. Your ride will be better as a result.

Other things to take are your camera, perhaps a phone or a laptop, flashlight, bike helmet, safety vest, maps, LED lights for the bike, water bottles and a can opener. Again, I'm not claiming this list is complete. It is just there to assist you in making up your own. A fully loaded bike can be heavy, so it is best to stick to the basics.

Loading up the bike can take some experimenting. Usually your rear rack will be the one best suited to support serious weight, so the heavy stuff, like tools and camping gear should go there. Clothes may be bulky, but are usually light. Due to the fragile nature of many typical front racks (I broke two already), I would try to pack some of those in the front panniers.

Finally, take the bike for a test ride! Does it feel all right? How about climbing the toughest hill in your area, can you make it all the way up? You will have to ride like this for many hours each day, so make sure it is still something you can handle with relative ease! It should go without saying that a certain level of conditioning is required to go on any major tour. If you are new to riding long distances, don't stop at preparing your gear and your bike! Your body will need some preparation as well. This can be as simple as taking your bike to work several times a week and perhaps throwing in a longer ride on the weekend. You don't need to be a super athlete, but the stronger you are as a cyclist, the more fun it will be to break out into unknown territory.

Not sure where to go on your first major tour? In the next chapter I will share some highlights of my first few days of touring, starting from a little cabin I called home after my divorce, In Central Ontario, Canada.

Chapter 4

My humble beginnings

In late October of 2009, after months of dreaming and considerable preparation, I was finally ready to start my first major bicycle tour. The original idea had been to ride the bike across southern Ontario, to the US border, then all the way to Mexico. The plan changed a bit due to the sometimes-harsh climate of Canadian fall. What was I going to do when sub zero temperatures and snow finally caught up with me? Even at a pace of 100 kilometers per day, which seemed possible before ever trying it out on a smaller tour, it would have taken me weeks to get into a warmer climate. It had never been my intention to wait until October to get going, but life doesn't always go as planned. With Thanksgiving already passed, I was thankful that I was finally going on tour at all.

I have to admit that I wasn't looking forward to cycling on snowy highways and sleeping in my tent during cold nights. Hotels were certainly an option, at least occasionally for the extra cold nights, but my budget might not have lasted the entire winter. Perhaps there was a way to take the bike on a plane to somewhere south, where weather wasn't such an issue. Before I set out on my tour I was living in a tiny cabin, 30 kilometers away from the next town and had Internet access only at a public library, but that was all I needed to search for options. After researching some airline and travel sites I found a really sweet deal on a flight from Buffalo, NY, to Orlando, FL. It was booked with only a few clicks, including a return five and a half months later; all of it without cancellation insurance. Suddenly it was do or die; my tour was a reality. I either had to make it to Buffalo in time to board the plane, or I could stay in my unheated cabin near Parry Sound, Ontario and freeze to death; not a hard decision! Just to get to Buffalo would take four or five days. This alone meant more cycling than I had ever done in my life. With the deadline looming I had to get organized, and get going.

    The day of my planned departure came. Somehow it almost seemed impossible to get going. I had developed a routine of cooking, washing myself sitting by the fire and keeping busy with things I can't even remember, that could easily fill an entire day. It was a very enjoyable way of living, but it spoiled my plans for an early departure before I even realized it. Was there something trying to keep my back in this cabin? I knew I loved my place at the lake and would certainly miss it, but I was also looking ahead at winter and the cycling adventure of a lifetime.

    Just to have breakfast, pack my things and get the cabin cleaned up for my return next spring, took more than half a day. It was around 3 pm when I finally hit the road. The first twenty kilometers were very familiar, but after that I had to take a route that was new to me, in order to stay off the main highway that was off limits for bicycles. The weather was good and there was no traffic. Riding the heavily loaded bike felt much different from what I was used to, but finally being on the road was exciting all by itself. At some point strong emotion hit me like a load of bricks; I was totally free to go anywhere the bike could take me! For most of the afternoon I was running on pure adrenaline, faster than I thought possible. Beautiful fall colors were everywhere and the sun was shining. I was leaving my old life behind to start a new adventure.

    Reality set back in when the sun started going down. A cold wind was now blowing from the wrong direction and my energy was starting to run low. I decided to stop for a bit, look at the map and decide where to spend the night. The original plan had been to stealth camp; pitch my tent somewhere nobody would notice. I had no idea where this would be safe. Besides, I was hungry and not well stocked with food. Finally I decided to make it to Gravenhurst, the next town along my route, and find the cheapest motel to crash. Darkness beat me to my destination and I was grateful for the wide shoulder on the perfectly smooth country road. My bike was equipped with a small flashing light and I was wearing a reflective vest, but riding in the dark did not feel safe at all. The temperature had dropped considerably and my hands were feeling numb despite the leather gloves I was wearing. After what seemed like an eternity, I eventually arrived in Gravenhurst. Shivering from the cold I started searching for a hotel. The town was not familiar to me, except for a small part just off the main highway. Now I found myself downtown, desperate to find a place with a warm shower and a bed, as well as a store to buy some food. I was exhausted by the time I finally found a place that had a nice room at a comparatively low rate of $ 69. My fingers were frozen to the point where I could barely pull the credit card out of my wallet. My hands were shaking as I handed it to the front desk clerk.

It took a long hot shower and a big meal at a fast food outlet across the street to make me feel human again. Walking back to the hotel gave me a chance to reflect on the first day of touring. Obviously, Mexico was a long way off! Had I overestimated my capacity for cycling? Even if I did, I'd definitely make it to Buffalo and my flight to Florida, where winter wouldn't be a problem. I was content and fell asleep quickly that night.

The next morning started with picture perfect sunshine. I found out that the temperature the evening before had been around -7 degrees Celsius, which was definitely on the chilly side for October. On the other hand, cold nights like that one could happen any time again, until I reached Orlando. Rain and even snow were also possible. Shortly after starting my ride that morning, all my worries were forgotten. It turned out to be another beautiful and warm fall day. For the first time I realized that even minor hills were quite a challenge with a fully loaded bike. Perhaps I had packed too much? The terrain of Southern Ontario is actually very flat by comparison, but some hills are miles long, yet barely noticeable by eye. The best strategy I found for climbing long hills was to gear down, pace myself, and look down on the pavement. Looking too far ahead just seemed to give the impression of standing still, much like on a stationary bike on the highest setting. Just seeing my tires move past potholes and cracks in the road made a big difference, even if this was purely psychological.

    The day went by uneventful with a few stops for food and to get oriented. The ride took me to somewhere south of Barry, Ontario. Once again the darkness was catching up to me faster than anticipated. There were open fields on both sides of the country road I was on. A voice inside my head was criticizing me for continuing past Barry, where I could have found a hotel easily. However, another part of me was arguing that my budget was at stake here and I had to make up for the money the hotel for the previous night had cost me. The temperature was much milder than the night before. There was no excuse to spend another seventy or eighty bucks just for comfort's sake. Finally I found a wooded area, decided to check it out, and discovered a well-hidden spot of grass, just big enough for my tent. It wasn't exactly what I had envisioned for my first night of stealth camping, but it was already dark and I was too tired to keep going, Still arguing with myself (this tends to happen when you're traveling by yourself), I pitched the tent under the beam of my little LED-light that was attached to my handlebars and I had positioned just so. It couldn't have been much later than 6 o'clock by the time I was done. Once again I was tired enough to fall asleep fast, at least at first. Some time later I woke up again. Dogs were barking, somewhere not too far away. Did they sense my presence? The sheer thought of a pack of dogs or coyotes discovering my tent and sneaking up on me was enough to keep me tossing and turning. Once again I was arguing with myself about why I had chosen to stealth camp. Long after it was dead quiet outside, I finally fell asleep again.

I woke up early the next morning. My sleeping bag was warm and cozy and at first I didn't feel like getting up. Then however, I realized where I was. Suddenly I was wide-awake. It was time to get busy and back on the road. I ate a few slices of bread along with Italian salami and washed it down with water for a quick breakfast. A coffee would have been nice, but it had to wait until I reached some place that would serve it.

The first real task of the day was to take down the camp and pack everything back onto the bike. It was pretty easy to do in the daylight and took just minutes. Soon I hopped on my bike and hit the road. Just a hundred meters or so down the road I noticed a driveway. There were two signs that caught my eyes: "Beware of the Dogs" warned the first one. Another one revealed that I had spent the night on the property of a dog breeder. Laughing at myself I picked up speed. What an initiation to stealth camping! None-the-less, I felt good about having spent the night in relative comfort, without spending a dime. The next time I would have to pick my campsite a bit more carefully.

Later that day, somewhere on the outskirts of greater Toronto, I was dealing with an entirely different problem. I had stopped for lunch at a fast food restaurant. The bike stood outside, supported by the kickstand that I had always liked because it allowed me to park pretty much anywhere. I was sitting by the window enjoying a burger while trying to keep an eye on the unlocked bike, when suddenly I almost choked on a big bite. There was a crashing sound. The bike had tipped over. The kickstand had collapsed under the heavy weight. No big deal, was my first thought. Why worry about it and interrupt a perfectly good meal?

When I finally got outside and inspected the bike, the heavily bent kickstand really started to bother me. I began to see a problem that could last the duration of the tour. But there was hope; I would just have to straighten that kickstand and bend it a bit further, to a perfect angle, so that it would almost balance the bike. My first attempts revealed that it was quite sturdy. Why mess with this now? I decided to take advantage of the nice weather and keep riding. I would simply get back to the minor problem later. Perhaps the bike was just too heavy now and I had to get used to other ways of parking it. I'm not sure why I didn't stick with this decision, as it certainly would have been the smart way. A few miles further down the road however, the perfectionist voice in my head was nagging. I was arguing with myself once again. This was only my third day on the road by myself, yet it already felt like more than one person was going on tour. In an effort to resolve the issue I stopped once again at a little strip mall. I was convinced that a firm push, with my right foot, right at the tip of the kickstand would do the trick. Before I realized that this was a bad idea, my rear wheel was bent beyond repair.

To assess the damage, I had to get my luggage off the bike, turn it upside down and remove the wheel. Focused, but still angry with myself, I wasted no time. There was nothing left to loose regarding the wheel; it was toast! Even pushing the bike would have been impossible now. In a desperate effort to straighten it at least to the point of being able to turn it within its mounts, I found a curb that was about five inches high. Holding the outside of the rim on opposite sides with my hands I pressed the hub against the curb with considerable force. The aluminum rim started to move, back toward its original shape. There was a glimmer of hope, so I kept pushing, checking the wheel for straightness now and then between pushing some more. Eventually, while still severely deformed, the wheel fit back into the frame, rotating without rubbing on anything except the brakes. At the very least I was going to be able to push the bike to a shop! A few people had seen me struggle and were now watching curiously. "Is there a bike shop nearby?" I asked. Nobody seemed to know, but they all encouraged me to check a strip mall several kilometers further toward Toronto. I thanked my audience and started pushing the bike down the road. Then it dawned on me; if I was able to push the bike without much effort, then I could perhaps ride it really carefully! After unhooking the rear brake-cable nothing was rubbing at all. I hopped on and started riding, first slowly, then a bit faster. Little by little I wobbled my way to Brampton, my former home, where I would interrupt the trip for a few days to take care of some personal things besides getting a brand new rear wheel.

"You're crazy!" the bike shop owner was lecturing me while his mechanic was curiously watching. "What are you trying to do?" My answer must have convinced both of them that I was completely nuts. "I'm going to Mexico" -I told them. What followed was an argument between myself and two bike experts about the suitability of my rickety old bicycle for serious touring. I stood my ground, more out of stubbornness, than confidence. Perhaps those guys had a point. So far, I had ridden the better part of three days, perhaps around 250 kilometers, and here I was with a broken wheel! An hour later and around $ 80 lighter, I left the bike shop with a new, better rear wheel and a center mounted kickstand. At first I was not impressed. The wheel had a quick release axle. The first set of railroad tracks I crossed after leaving the shop caused the axle to shift within the slots of the rear dropouts (my bike had stamped dropouts which are relatively thin). Once again I had to unload the bike entirely to center the new rear wheel. The quick release axle was not getting a very good grip on the left side dropout, the non-drive side. Where the old kickstand had been mounted and had provided some additional metal for the axle to hold onto, the dropout alone was insufficient. After considerable frustration I found a simple, yet effective remedy without having to return to the bike shop. A knurled washer, inserted between the quick release and the dropout helped secure the axle in place sufficiently. Later I checked into a motel and attended an event at the public library of my former hometown. This event had been part of the reason for delaying the departure of the trip, but it turned out to be worth it. I had won a photo contest the library had sponsored during the summer. My entry had been one of the pictures I had taken on my first trip to Cuba, showing a group of students waving from a yellow bus. The price was $ 500. The only way to collect was to attend. After celebrating with wine and cheese I returned to my motel with the check in my pocket.

Almost a week later and completely recuperated from my adventures, I finally left Brampton with only two days to spare before my flight out of Buffalo. Making the distance in time was not the only challenge. I still had to cross the US border, which meant a potential delay. Since I didn't have a map of upstate New York, I also had no idea how to get to the Buffalo airport, more potential delays!

To make things go smoothly I already had a hotel room pre-booked near the airport. From there a free shuttle was going to take me to the terminal the following morning.

The ride to Buffalo went smoothly. I ended up spending another night in an inexpensive motel near St. Catharines and crossed the border the following morning at Niagara Falls. The crossing was simple and it felt funny to occupy a car lane with my bicycle at the control booth. I probably stunned the customs officer with some of my responses to his standard questions. The officer appeared to be in his mid thirties and I probably made his day. At least that was the feeling I got when his questions gradually turned more informal and revealed his plain curiosity about bicycle touring. Perhaps this man has already toured on a bicycle himself by the time I'm writing this.

South of the border I first got lost for a bit, but then found a store that was selling maps. As a trucker I had been familiar with the major highways of the region for years, but cycling was another matter. The trip along the Niagara River revealed a beauty that I had never known existed. Who needs a destination at all, if one can find beauty in ordinary places and enjoy it at a dreamlike pace from the comfort of a bicycle seat? Even finding my way through the outskirts of Buffalo and to the Day's Inn at the airport was unforgettable. With the map it was relatively easy to navigate. I finally checked into my room some time late in the afternoon.

I was excited and exhausted at the same time. Was I ready for my flight the next morning? There was another challenge. The bike would have to be prepared according to airline regulations. It would have to be to be packed in a suitable box, which of course, I didn't have.

Chapter 5

Bikes and Airplanes

Time to get creative

To be perfectly honest with you, taking a bicycle on board a plane is never truly my first choice. Unless you are crossing oceans, there is probably a path to cover the distance by riding that bike and I can guarantee you that it will be far more interesting than four or five hours cramped in a seat next to strangers in a hurry to get somewhere, watching movies in substandard picture and sound quality. Actually, the title of this book, "Destinations are Fake", tries to make that point. By taking your bike on a flight, you are skipping a major part of your journey, even if you have a specific tour in mind, like traveling along beaches or through rainforest. Here is an honest confession: The original plan for my own first major bike tour did not include a flight. I was simply running away from winter and made it my excuse for finding a shortcut. To this day I'm still wondering what kind of adventures I might have had in US States, such as Ohio, Missouri or Oklahoma. Unless I take another tour I will never find out. The point here is that every region has its perks and it is up to us to find out what they are. Often we tend to think we know an area, due to the fact that we've traveled though it on major highways. Of course this cannot possibly be accurate. The best bike route usually isn't on major highways, but far more scenic. Having said that, in reality we often have reasons to fly. Some of us simply can't spare enough time to cycle the whole distance, while others (like me) are not thrilled with cold weather. Lastly there are oceans we cannot conquer on bicycles. This book is on bicycle touring and uses my first tour as an example on how to ease into the activity. As you already know, this tour included a flight.

Arriving at my hotel in Buffalo felt like a major accomplishment. I wasn't hungry because I had checked into a burger joint somewhere not too far from the airport, but I was exhausted from the ride and really tempted to spend the rest of my day in the cozy room watching TV, stretched out on the bed. Of course this wasn't an option if I wanted to take my bike on the flight to Orlando the next morning, Tired as I was, I had no time to relax. The bike had to be packed into a suitable container and, as mentioned previously; I didn't have a box or any other alternative packaging material. What was worse, I didn't even know where to obtain any of it on a short notice. I found a solution that night that was kind of awkward in hindsight, but sufficient to get my bike on the plane the next day. By no means was it the perfect approach. Even today I'm still learning something new every time I take a flight with a bicycle in my luggage. Airlines are not exactly the most helpful in general. Sure, they will tell you what you need to do to get your bike on board, but then they will gladly charge you up to $ 250 in extra fees, which is only one way. If your touring bike is like mine, it is probably barely worth that much money, especially when you're also planning to take it home on a return flight. What is the best solution?

Why is there a problem taking your bike on a flight?

Pretty much any bicycle is considered an oversize article by the airlines. With ever increasing fees, even for regular luggage, your bicycle is a prime opportunity to charge you extra. They will take advantage, not just a bit, but a lot. Even if money is not an issue, or if you can find an airline that does not charge an arm and a leg, there are still regulations to follow that vary broadly. For example, I have once boarded a Jet Blue flight with the bicycle completely wrapped in stretch wrap and nothing else, without paying a fee, yet the next day Continental airlines refused to accept the same package and forced me to buy a box for my connecting flight. To top it off I was also charged a fee of over $ 100. The problems are also not limited to the flight alone, but even a transfer from the airport to a nearby hotel will often cost significantly more with a bicycle box in your luggage.

What are the regulations for taking a bike on board?

The most reliable way to find out is to read your airline's website or contact it directly. You will find information on how to prepare your bicycle, the maximum size of luggage and the extra charges for exceeding those dimensions. The most common options are bike boxes for one time use, and special bags or hard shell cases, sold by bicycle manufacturers.

Is there a way around paying extra luggage fees for the bike?

In the past I have found airlines that didn't charge extra for taking bicycles. As of April 2010, Jet Blue was one of them. As mentioned above, it is necessary to read the updated conditions on the website of your airline. However, if you can dismantle your bike to the point where it fits into a regular size suitcase, the airline has no grounds to charge extra money for carrying it, as long as the weight is within regulations too. Perhaps your bike has a small frame size. In this case it might be worth shopping for a cheap, but large suitcase. Make sure you take some key measurements! Also keep in mind that you cannot take this suitcase on the ride with you, so you might have to give it away or find someone to hold it for you until your return flight, assuming it departs from the same airport. A large bicycle frame does not fit into any suitcase with regular dimensions no matter what you do, with one exception. Special couplings that allow you to take your bicycle frame apart do exist.

They are called S&S Couplers. Unfortunately they have to be built into a bicycle frame by a professional frame builder. This alone can be quite pricey, but should make it possible to fit your bike into regular luggage. Ask yourself how often you will be taking your bike on flights. S&S couplers may be a viable option for frequent flyers. Of course, sticking a touring bike into a suitcase is never an easy task. You will have to strip your frame to bare bones and find ways to fit all other parts around it, some of which will require extra padding. At your destination you will have to unpack all the goodies and reassemble everything; not a terrible process for experienced bike mechanics, but considerable trouble for the average cyclist.

Another option worth mentioning is a folding bike. Brompton makes a great one that is geared toward touring. It is an exceptional high quality bike that many swear by. Some have taken it on 1000-mile trips without any issues at all. The nice thing about it is that it folds several times and can fit into your standard size carry on luggage. At a purchase price of around $ 2,000 a Brompton does not come cheap. Other alternatives are available and I would encourage anyone who likes the idea to do some more research into it.

What is the most common way to prepare a bike for a flight?

You can get a bike box, often for free, at any bicycle store. New bikes arrive in such boxes, which is why stores end up with plenty of them. New bikes are not assembled when they are shipped to the distributors, so your bike won't fit into such a box, unless it is first taken apart. This can be a bit tricky, but it becomes easier with practice. Often it is enough to remove the front wheel, handlebars and seat-post assembly, which then have to be packed into the same box, using some padding, packing tape and/or zip ties. Most often this can be done without disconnecting any of the cables. Larger bikes are more of a challenge to fit into a box. It is a good idea to use extra padding on fragile parts. Luggage handlers at the airport may not be as careful as you would like to see.

Is taking your bike on a flight worth it?

This is a good question. First off, ask yourself if riding your bike instead of flying to your destination is an option! Unfortunately, most often that could take months and most of us have lives that simply don't allow for that much time off from their jobs. Still, there are other ways. Buying a mid range bicycle at the destination is worth considering. Sometimes a decent bike can be found for around the same price it would cost to take your bike along (return flight is charged separately). After your trip you can resell the bike and get some of your money back. If you're planning to tour a so-called third world country, chances are that you would have a hard time finding parts for your state of the art European or North American bike. A locally purchased bike will not have that problem. Parts will be cheap and available. Further, bike shops in the area will be familiar with this type of bike. The downside is that you may not find a bike of good quality that fits your body size. A poorly suited bike can spoil your tour! It boils down to personal preference and what kind of tour you are planning. After having done one tour on a locally purchased bike in Panama, I now prefer to pay the premium to take my own bike with me from home. I like knowing that the ride will be comfortable and that the bike is suited to the challenge.

How did I manage on my first flight from Buffalo to Orlando?

Even with the help of a friendly front desk clerk at the hotel, it was quite an adventure to find a bicycle store in Buffalo. Of course I was too cheap to take a cab to get there so I rode my bike, thinking it would be a piece of cake to haul all the packaging material back to the hotel. Let me just tell you that I learned something the hard way that evening. Finding a bike shop was easy enough and the bike box was free. The challenge was to ride back to the hotel with it. I was trying to hold the large box with my right hand, while controlling the handlebars with my left. It was very windy which made it hard to steer. At times it felt like I was sailing, which is not good idea on public roads. During the ride I also realized that the box alone wouldn't be enough to pack the bike, so I made one more stop at Home Depot to get stretch-wrap and tape. It took quite a while to wobble my way back to the hotel, switching between pushing and riding the bike, whichever seemed safe, moment to moment.

Of course, getting back to the hotel after dark was just half the battle. It took the better part o the night to get the bike into the box. I had to get creative to fit everything in there, especially since my bike had racks and fenders. As it turned out, I even had to cut one end of the box and then tape it back together in order to fit the rear wheel and fender. Today I know that not every airline would accept the package I eventually came up with, but I got lucky that time. The large roll of stretch-wrap I had bought came in handy. It even helped me transform my four panniers into one piece of luggage, remotely resembling a suitcase.

Boarding the plane was a breeze the next day. To my luck, an airline employee helped me with the automated check in. Despite of an official $ 100 fee according to the airline's website, staff at Delta Airlines gave me a break and only charged $ 50 for an extra bag. Freebies of this kind are rare. Perhaps it was good karma.

As is common with cheap flights, I had one connection in Cincinnati and it took the entire day to get to Orlando, where I had booked another, really cheap room. As it turned out, the hotel was not close to the airport. The money I had saved on the booking went towards a twenty-minute ride in a van taxi. It was already dark when I arrived in Orlando, but that was in part because the sun sets early in November, even in Florida. After my arrival I checked into the room, changed into shorts and a loose shirt and hit a nearby Waffle House for a greasy dinner. The weather was perfect, warm and humid just like summer.

Even though I was dead tired, I immediately unpacked and reassembled the bike after returning from supper. It proved to be much easier than packing it. A test ride on the wrap around balcony of the hotel (not actually recommended) and finally around the parking lot assured that I was ready to continue my tour the next day, in Florida, the Sunshine State.

Chapter 6

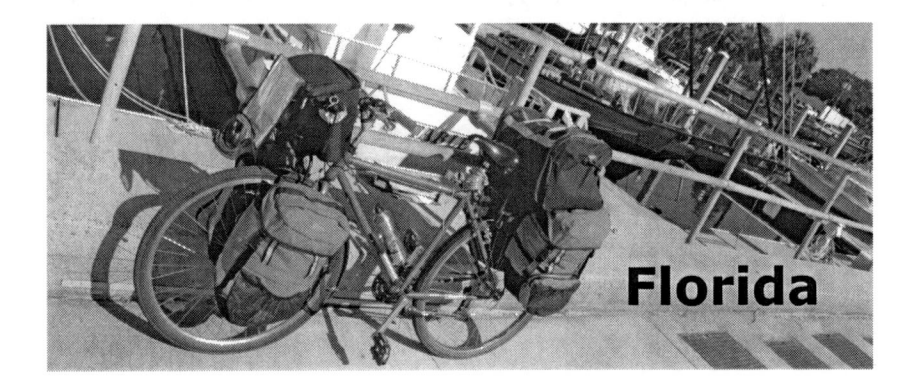

Florida

Living the dream

I woke up early the next morning without having to rely on an alarm clock. The weather outside was beautiful, even by Florida standards. It was the first of November, but it felt more like July, especially from a Canadian perspective. I already knew where the Waffle House was. Their breakfast menu was just about right for my appetite. I had a fully loaded omelet with hash browns and toast, along with what had to be half a gallon of black coffee, probably not the smartest way to ensure good nutrition and hydration. By twelve o'clock, checkout time of the hotel, I was ready to leave Orlando on my bicycle. My first step was trying to find a tourist-information to pick up a free map, which was not a very difficult task in Orlando. Soon I managed to figure out a decent route out of the city and toward the gulf coast. The idea was to ride along the Gulf of Mexico all the way around and eventually cross the border into Mexico. There were five US-states along my way, starting with a part of Florida that I was vaguely familiar with because of my trucking experience.

The first day of cycling in the warm climate and sunshine was physically challenging. My exposed skin was getting burnt despite wearing a thick layer sunscreen and I simply could not quench my thirst. When I arrived in Clermont late in the afternoon to take my first major break of the day, aside from a quick stop to buy groceries on the outskirts of Orlando, I was soaked in sweat and exhausted enough to quit. It was the excitement of being on tour in Florida, along with a good deal of stubbornness that convinced me to keep going. The decision was by no means rational, but fueled by adrenaline. Perhaps it was even dangerous; the pounding sunshine turned into a colorful sunset, with darkness following not far behind. I ended up riding my bike on a major highway in the dark my first night. Wasn't the daylight supposed to last a bit longer this far south? There was no choice but to keep going, once again relying on my safety vest and the little flashing light for visibility. I did not even bother checking how far I had left to go in order to find a safe place to spend the night. My vague destination was the intersection of interstate 75 and the road I was on, US-98. According to my map this was just outside of Brooksville. There was supposed to be a state park with camping facilities in the area. When I finally reached the interstate, I couldn't find the park. Wondering if I had passed it, I turned around and backtracked for a few miles, then took the only nearby turnoff going north. It was a spooky looking dirt road that took me past a few houses and ended up at a fence and a pile of sand. I was way beyond tired and just standing there wondering what to do next. The air was clear, but comfortably warm. I paused for a while and told myself that there was absolutely no reason to worry. Due to the warmth I was better off here than back home in Canada, even if I had to sleep in a ditch. Still, I was clearly out of my comfort zone, by myself in the dark in this unfamiliar place, having neither a firm destination, nor a place to call home. Even the stars and the moon looked different here.

After a slow ride back to the interstate and some asking around at a gas station, I finally found the state park. Unfortunately it was too late. The gate had long been closed. A sign with the words "Park closes at Sunset" was confirming that. I had made it this far just to find the park closed? Desperate for a break I started snooping around the gate. There had to be a way in for my bike and me. I would just pitch my tent and worry about registering in the morning, but it proved difficult to find my way around, let alone a suitable camping spot in the dark. My inner voices were arguing and eventually I decided to turn around. There were some hotels along the interstate, a short walk away. I made an effort to locate the most economical one and rented a room. After a very long shower I fell asleep in what felt like the most comfortable bed on earth.

Getting up was a tough the next morning. I definitely felt the aftereffects of the past three days and my butt was sore to top it off. Eleven o'clock was checkout time and I wasn't ready a minute too early. Repacking my bike even seemed like quite a chore, but who was I to complain?

The weather outside was beautiful again. Once I hopped back on my bike I felt good, except for some discomfort were my butt was rubbing on the seat. Florida's US-98 proved to be a very good route for cycling, mostly due to light traffic and the shoulder that resembled a bicycle lane most of the way. After having spent about 50 bucks on lodging I was now intent stretching my budget. Aside from my morning coffee I managed to feed myself sufficiently from the grocery reserves I had bought the day before. Dry salami, bread, tomatoes and bagged salad mix were part of the menu, great for making sandwiches, but prone to going rancid in the heat. A huge bag of trail mix was the other main staple, a high- energy food that was going to prove perfect for touring throughout my trip.

My second day of cycling in Florida took me to Crystal River, a scenic little town. By the time I got there it was late afternoon, time to look for a place to crash. Determined that I wasn't going to spend another $ 50 on a hotel, I asked a police officer about places to camp, but didn't get the answer I had hoped for. I could ask at the fire station, he implied. I decided to move on for a while longer and keep my eyes open. There had to be a quiet place where nobody would bother me, somewhere on the outskirts of town. I found such a place just a short distance away. A dirt road ran parallel to the highway for a short stretch, but eventually made a slight turn. It was easy to access off the highway, so I decided to follow it. Soon I came to a fork in the road and found a place right between the two ways that looked perfect for my tent. I was able to get into the bush just far enough to keep me hidden. Of course I was nervous about camping in a place I didn't know, but it was going to get dark shortly and I didn't think anyone was going to disturb me. Falling asleep was a different story. What if I was wrong and somebody would have a problem with my invasion? What if that somebody wasn't human, but a snake? Stealth camping can be a bit nerve wrecking that way. Eventually fatigue overwhelmed me and I passed out.

When I woke up later I realized that it was very bright inside my tent. Where was I? Slowly things came back together. I had found a "free" campsite! It was quiet all around me, but had I slept through the whole night? Thinking it was broad daylight outside, I decided to get an early start and leave the campsite before anyone would even notice I was there. I rolled over once and got up. Without wasting time I took down my tent and packed up all my things. It was only after everything was back on my bicycle, ready to roll, that I checked my watch to see what time it was. The darn watch couldn't possibly be right. Was it really 1:30 am? The light that was surrounding me was bright, but completely lacking the colors that usually accommodate a sunrise. It was coming from the full moon. How could it have fooled me like that?

For a few minutes I stood there wondering what to do. What were the options? Perhaps I could have set up camp all over again. It probably would have meant spending a few hours awake in my tent. The moonlight was brighter than I had ever seen in my life. Perhaps it was enough for a safe ride? A brief calculation revealed that it was a Monday. Most people had to get up early and go to work, so there was little chance of encountering drunk drivers on the road. My thoughts drifted to memories of what Monday mornings had been like for me, most of my life. Being somewhere in Florida under a moonlit sky with a fully loaded bicycle and no other responsibilities beat all of those memories by a mile and a half. It didn't matter what day, or even what time it was. I could go cycling any time I wanted. Starting my day in the middle of the night suddenly seemed like a great idea.

The empty road was more than a bit spooky at first, but it was reasonably well lit by the moonlight. For miles I was completely alone. Somewhere in the distance was an amber flashing light. Whenever I thought I was getting close to it, it disappeared for a while, only to appear again after the next hump in the straight road. There were no cars. At one point I was convinced there were half a dozen garbage bags in the ditch that a cleanup crew had left behind. Imagine my surprise when the bags suddenly got up and started running away! I had disturbed a herd of boars. The experience sure freaked me out for a moment. Suddenly I was wide-awake.

Eventually I actually reached the flashing light at a major intersection. I was hungry now and had hoped to grab a snack and a coffee, but there was no store. The only thing I noticed was some kind of industrial plant to my left. The next little town on my map was Chiefland. It had to be within a half-hour-ride.

The road continued straight as an arrow. Once again there was a flashing light some distance ahead of me. I figured this had to be Chiefland and that there would probably be a place to buy a snack once I got there. After cycling for what seemed like a small eternity, on a completely deserted road, I finally reached a gas station with a small convenience store that was lit up. The door was locked at first, but someone else was already waiting for the store to open. A lady opened up a few minutes later. Both the lady behind the counter and the other customer took a keen interest in me, and my bicycle.

"Where do you sleep?" the lady wanted to know. I had to laugh and tell her about my night. That broke the ice between us. As it turned out, both the store clerk and her customer a man who stopped here regularly on his way to work, wanted to know more about what had brought me to their little corner of the world, equipped only with a bicycle that had a pile of stuff strapped to it. We ended up having a conversation about fulfilling our dreams, Mexico and a number of weird things people do on full moon nights.

"You know Mexico is dangerous?" the stranger next to me tried to imply. I just shook my head as if I had never heard of that before. "You be careful out there, " the lady smiled "coffee is on the house."

The real daylight was coming up fast now and I decided to push the bike through Chiefland, a tiny village. Just down a block or two was another store that was advertising ice cream in the window. Why not celebrate the sunrise with ice cream? I went in and got some. Once again a curious clerk was asking me where I was from and where I was going. People seemed to like my idea of cycling all along the gulf coast, but could not imagine actually reaching the Mexican border that way, let alone going beyond it. In a strange way this boosted my confidence. I was high on cycling and ready to conquer the world, never mind Mexico!

With plenty of energy from coffee and ice cream I finally hopped back on my bike. At this point I did not feel any exhaustion from cycling all night, but it caught up to me later in the day. Besides a little detour to Steinhatchee, a place by the coast with some big houses and a nice marina, the ride was mostly on a straight and very flat highway. The weather was dry and hot with beautiful sunshine. I stopped two more times that day for meals, one of which was a portion of boiled peanuts at a convenience store, the other was a greasy burger with fries. I needed plenty of energy to keep going. Eventually I ended up in Perry, over 100 miles from where I had started at 1:30 in the morning. I gladly paid $ 28 for a campsite at the local KOA.

Being in a commercial campground not only gave me peace of mind, which lead to a very good night sleep, but also allowed me to connect to the Internet. Besides catching up with Facebook and trying to write my travel blog, I was checking out Couchsurfing, a hospitality exchange website where I had created a profile some time before my trip. After searching profiles in Panama City and further along my way, I sent out a few requests. A young lady in Panama City, I'll call her Maria here, replied almost instantly. Panama City was still too far away to get to the next day, but seemed within reach for the day after. I made plans to get there and spend an extra day to take a break and check out the city.

The next morning I was off to a slow start. First I took a walk to the store to get breakfast and coffee. Next it was time to take down the tent, which had a lot of condensation on the inside. Before seriously hitting the road, I stopped by the local Walmart to stock up on groceries. When I saw that some employees were sitting around a picnic table on their break, I decided to join them just as if I worked there. Nobody seemed to mind and I had a comfortable place to enjoy my sandwiches for lunch.

I did not get very far that day. The sun set around 5:30 in the afternoon and once again I had no idea where I could spend the night. I made inquiries at a gas station along the road where someone told me about the Florida Trail. I would be able to get off the road 100 yards or so, and find a spot to pitch my tent. Nobody was going to know or even care if I camped there. For lack of other options I followed the advice. To this day I'm not sure if the spot I found was actually part of the trail, but it couldn't have been too far off. The ground was rough and there was barely enough space for my tent. I liked that it was well hidden. It was not easy to pitch the tent in the dark. This time I had no problem falling asleep.

Reaching Panama City proved to a very ambitious goal for the next day. Was I crazy? Still early in the morning, I passed a sign: "Panama City 106 miles". Once again the weather was beautiful. The highway took me along the shore, offering glimpses of sandy beach and waves here and there, which seemed to have some kind of magic influence on my general mood. The morning passed quickly. I stopped in Carabelle, a small port, for lunch. There was a little park directly at the shore that had picnic tables under a roof. It was the ideal place to sit down and make sandwiches. There were some other people around, but it wasn't exactly busy. After lunch the ride continued along a beautiful shoreline that seemed almost deserted in places. I was getting a fist hand impression of what Hurricane Katrina had done four years earlier. A slightly run down motel was abandoned and sporting a "for sale" sign, a gas station looked like a complete mess and was also abandoned. Soon the sun went down and I was riding in the dark again, which was something I had really wanted to avoid at first. Almost as if caused by the lack of daylight, there was now a clicking sound coming from my front hub every so often. The wheel was almost brand new and supposedly of a high-end quality. How was this possible? I kept riding, focusing my attention on the road and on the cars that passed me every so often, but all the while wondering if I was even going to make it to Panama City. You're crazy! I could still hear the voice of the bike storeowner in my mind. Had I pushed my bike beyond its limits?

  I eventually arrived on the outskirts of the city. The road took me past a huge military installation, then across a high-rise-bridge. Panama City was the biggest city on my route so far. I had not realized that it would be quite a challenge to find my host. First I tried calling Maria from a phone booth, but the line was busy. After buying a candy bar and soda pop at a gas station I launched my second attempt. This time a friendly voice answered: "Hi, Maria here"! It turned out that I was only a few blocks away from her place.

  Maria and her roommates lived in a small, older home. There were about eight young people sharing it. They all worked at the army base I had passed on my way into town, only at different shifts. Maria was off tonight. I was about to discover the finest of couch surfing spirit.

  "Are you tired or would you like to go for a spin around town?" Maria asked me after a late supper of cheesy potatoes and chicken. I was exhausted from over 100 miles of cycling and my front hub was probably shot, which had me a bit worried, but this is what adventures are about. I simply couldn't turn down the invitation. We ended up at a run down little pub on karaoke-night, where I was introduced to some of Maria's friends and felt right at home. Singing is not really my strength, so I just took in the atmosphere and had a beer. By the time we left the pub it was quite late, but there was still something special Maria wanted to show me. Panama City had a four-headed palm-tree in a park downtown, which seemed to be a major tourist attraction. Indeed, it was unlike any tree I had ever seen before. We took a little walk around the park. Nightlife was busy downtown. I truly enjoyed the atmosphere and Maria's company.

Couch surfing turned out to be so much more than a free place to sleep. I stayed one more night in Panama City, had my front hub repaired by a local bike shop for a few bucks, and explored more of the city on my own. The last day ended with movie night at Maria's place. The house was full of friends and there was fresh popcorn. The experience was unforgettable and made me realize that I had been lonely for most of my trip up to this point. Suddenly I felt like part of a big family.

Chapter 7

The dark Side

Nights

Whenever I talked to people I met while on tour, one of the questions that came up frequently was: "Where do you sleep?" As you've noticed by now, finding accommodation for the night can be a challenge. For one, it is not always possible to plan an exact destination for each day, unless you are familiar with the road conditions along your route and can predict factors such as weather quite accurately. An educated guess is probably the best anyone could come up with. If you're like me, you probably don't even like to plan your trip to the smallest detail. The best adventures happen only if your mind is open to them. I believe that rigid planning is counterproductive to that. Often things don't go as planned anyways. A minor breakdown, like a flat tire, or bad weather is all it takes to throw your plan out the window.

Each day has a limited number of daylight hours. Riding after dark in an unfamiliar environment is never a good option, but can sometimes be the only one. Even if you don't intend to ride at night ever, it is important to be equipped for it just in case. A set of LED-lights can cost as little as ten or fifteen dollars and they are effective at making you visible to other traffic. Most of those lights have two settings; one constant, the other flashing on and off. It seems that the flashing mode is best for getting you noticed. You might have to get creative about how to install the lights on your bike, as they are not designed for bicycle touring specifically. A loaded rear rack or a handlebar bag can obstruct them to the point of uselessness. That's why it is important to figure out where they should go, before starting your tour. To further increase visibility I would highly recommend wearing a reflective vest. They are light and inexpensive. Even with precautions and after having ridden in the dark on numerous occasions, I cannot recommend it in good conscience, except as a last resort.

Let me get back to the question of where to sleep! It is not unusual, and actually part of the perks of bicycle touring, not to know where they day's ride will end. The downside is that you could end up in the middle of nowhere, after dark, exhausted, with no place to sleep. Sometimes trying to find a place can take hours or you can end up sleeping on a park-bench, literally.

As you have read in previous chapters, I've had some experience with stealth camping. For those of you who are unfamiliar with this term, it means setting up camp outside of official campgrounds, wherever possible. It is by far the cheapest way to spend a night and since you are already carrying a tent on your bike, you'll want to make use of it. Quite obviously, there are risks involved. As a cyclist you have a huge disadvantage compared to someone traveling in a camper or even a car. While motorists could just park somewhere and sleep in their vehicle, you have to set up a tent and lock up your bike nearby. There are not many places where this is possible or even allowed. It may seem like a good idea to ask for permission to camp behind a convenience store or gas station, but often the personnel does not have authorization to grant such permission. Chances are they'll send you away to cover their butt. It can be a good idea however to ask for alternatives. Sometimes people will offer up their backyard as a campsite for a night. Other options are public places like parks, churches, fire stations and so on. Again it might be crucial to obtain permission. Laws regarding stealth camping vary; saving a few dollars is not worth ending up in jail. Another risk is that someone with a questionable motive will discover your campsite and bother you. This could range from a harmless annoyance to full blown robbery. As a stranger to an area, you might pick a perfect looking spot in the wrong neighborhood and end up as entertainment for a group of partying teenagers, to name just one example.

Even with the best intentions and planning, there might be situations when stealth camping is the only option and it is impossible to get permission. The perfect camping spot might be an abandoned field with no one around. There are some precautions you can take to lower the risks of camping in such a place:

- Check out your surroundings. Does it seem likely that somebody might show up during the night and bother you?

- Set up after dusk and pack up before dawn. If no one knows you are there, you'll likely be fine.

- Leave your campsite as you've found it. Even if someone discovers you in the morning while taking down your tent, they probably won't care, as long as you didn't make a mess.

How often you stealth camp almost always depends on your budget, the price of other types of accommodation along your route and, most certainly, your sense of adventure. Over time you will develop a kind of sixth sense for where you can camp safely.

- Enough about stealth camping! There are plenty of other options to spend your nights. With a little bit of planning, Couchsurfing is an excellent one. CS is a website that helps travellers find hosts wherever they'd like to travel. The idea is a hospitality exchange. To take part, you must first create a profile. It is not a requirement to host other travellers, but the idea is that everyone on the site contributes something. It could be as little as taking a foreign visitor out for coffee and a walk through your town, or as much as providing bed and breakfast for a period you both agree on. In many cities regular CS meetings are held which are also a great way to meet people. Once you have a CS-profile, you can go online and check for other members who might allow you to stay overnight, wherever your tour might take you (CS is worldwide). Sometimes the question of security comes up when people first hear about Couchsurfing. Not everybody is comfortable hooking up with strangers and sleeping in their house or apartment. Once you get over the initial skepticism however, there are plenty of ways to ensure your experience will be a positive one. Extensive online profiles of potential couch surfing hosts allow you to pick likeminded people to stay with. You can check references and find out quite a bit about their backgrounds. Some members are verified by the CS website itself, which then allows them to vouch for other members they know. You can play this in a very safe way, or a bit more adventurous. If it does not feel right, follow your intuition! For the most part, Couchsurfing is very safe.

- Another option that is similar to Couchsurfing is the website "Warm Showers.org". Like on CS, you can search for hosts along your route and request to stay for a night or so, except that this site is geared towards traveling cyclists exclusively. There are many members, especially in the US. The advantage is that they are usually cyclists themselves and know exactly what your needs are, often from personal experience. While a host on CS might want to take you bar hopping till three in the morning, with warm showers you are among likeminded people who will understand if you are too tired to do much at all.

- The next option on my list is public parks with camping facilities. Weather they are state, national or provincial, they usually have very basic camping facilities and are relatively inexpensive. Sometimes they are beautifully situated and an ideal place to spend an extra day of rest. Keep in mind that many of those parks do not have a store nearby, so it might be essential to bring your own food supplies.

- For just a few dollars more, commercial campgrounds often have a lot to offer. The KOA chain of campgrounds is an excellent example, but by far not the only one. Wireless Internet and power hookup are standard, as well as on site laundry and convenience store. However, I would also like to mention that some commercial campgrounds cater to RV's only, which can be frustrating to find out at the end of the day.

- In many small towns older hotels and motels operate at bargain rates. They may not always be up to the highest standards, but virtually all of them offer individual bath and shower, as well as a freshly made bed. Even just as an occasional break from sleeping on an air mattress, those places offer a valuable service for any traveling cyclist. In many countries outside the US and Canada, hotels are even more basic, but the rates are so cheap that you may not even want to bother with your tent.

- Hostels are very popular in tourist hotspots, especially outside the US and Canada. They generally offer dorm rooms with anywhere from 4 to 20 beds. It is common to have "mixed dorms" with men and women in the same room. In general those hostels are excellent places to meet other travelers and exchange stories. You might even bump into other cyclists here. Sleeping in a dorm with 10 or more other persons can be just fine, but there is potential for restless nights. Some hostels depend on their "party atmosphere" for business. Don't be surprised if half a dozen of drunken youngsters show up in the dorm at four in the morning, laughing and talking in a language you don't understand, with no consideration for your good night sleep.

What if your planning is completely off one day and you don't make it to your destination before dark? Perhaps you are in a foreign country where stealth camping does not seem like a good idea and the nearest place you can get to is a small village without any hotels and perhaps even without stores. Situations like that can be scary, but any extended bike tour is likely to include them on occasion. My daughter Jessica and I once started a tour together heading North from Panama City, Panama. Just after crossing the bridge that crosses the entrance to the canal, my rear tire popped. Not only was the tube completely blown out, the tire itself was irreparable as well. We ended up pushing our bikes for a few kilometers when a small pickup stopped on the shoulder just ahead of us. Two men who were on their way home from work had spotted us and offered their help. They seemed all right, so we accepted a ride to the next town and the nearest bike shop. Miguel, the driver told us about his country and how one of the first jobs he had ever had in his younger years, had been on the construction of the massive bridge we had crossed earlier in the day. At the bike shop, he waited for us to make sure we had a new tire and the means to change it. "Where will you sleep tonight?" he finally asked us. We had no idea. There had to be a hotel nearby was all I could think of. Finally Miguel offered to take us to his house and meet his wife and kids. We could change my tire in his driveway and he would help us find a place to stay for the night.

My first thoughts were about safety. Was this man we had just met sincere, or would we be taking a huge risk by accepting his offer. I followed my intuition and asked Jessica, who understood very little Spanish, how she felt about it. We ended up fixing the bike in Miguel's driveway and meeting his wife and adult son. The offer quickly turned into an invitation for a home cooked supper and a free stay in the family's spare bedroom. To this day I remember how welcome Miguel and his family made us feel. While it is important to use caution when meeting strangers on the road, it always pays to have an open mind. Contact with local people in the places you're visiting is much more interesting and rewarding than staying in hotels or resorts intended only for tourists. Unfortunately many people travel in ways that avoid genuine interaction with locals, rather than pursuing it.

The bike tour with Jessica was short lived as we had only a week together in Panama and my (locally bought) bike broke down again the next day. That time we got picked up by the Gonzalez family (name changed), who invited us not only for supper and a night in their house, but offered us free stay at their vacant beach condo that was less then ten kilometers away. The hospitality didn't end there. After two nights in the beach condo we were invited to the family's Christmas party, a big outdoor gathering with lots of good food and beer. We made many friends that night and the experience was simply unforgettable.

Invitations like the one's Jessica and I received in Panama are rare, but in most places even a seemingly bad situation can turn into an experience of a lifetime. After touring for a while you will develop a sense of where best to spend your nights. You will also find out that you are not alone. It is possible to meet the same travellers several times along your route, whether they are cyclists or not. On my most recent trip across Central America I met a cyclist from the Check Republic on five occasions over a two-month period. We managed to stay in contact via the Internet even while on slightly different routes and often ended up using the same hostels and hotels along the way, even sharing a room once for two nights in El Salvador. We remain friends to this day, long after our bike tours.

Another question people like to ask is about if and why I like to tour by myself. One of the best answers for that is that it is an awesome way to meet people.

Chapter 8

Alabama

A Hurricane and some southern hospitality

I have to make a confession at the beginning of this chapter: I did not enter Alabama riding my bike. I arrived by pickup truck, driven by a park ranger. It was raining so hard that traveling by bike would have been all but impossible.

For my last night in Florida, I had camped out at a state park, just west of Pensacola. The weather had been nice the day before. I had been surprised by the news of an incoming storm, at a visitor's center outside the city. A hurricane was brewing in the Gulf of Mexico. For lack of a better place to stay, and due to reassuring comments by park staff, I had made my way into a park, that was located right on the gulf shore. My idea had been that I would deal the approaching trouble the next morning. It had seemed that there was plenty of time.

When morning arrived, things still didn't look too bad at first. I actually made a fire and cooked breakfast as the sky turned darker. The sea looked choppy and the wind picked up. Soon a park ranger stopped by to inform me that the park was under an evacuation order. "Sorry guy, you'll have to pack up and get out of here!" he told me. I hastily finished my breakfast and packed up my belongings. On my way out of the park I stopped at the office in order to inform myself about the situation and what my next move should be. It turned out that storm shelters were set up in the surrounding area, several of which were in Pensacola. When I asked the ranger if there were any shelters in the direction of the Alabama state line, she told me to wait a few minutes. A few minutes made a huge difference in the weather. I sat on a bench under the porch, outside the ranger station, watching my bike get soaked by the rain and wondering if waiting wasn't a huge mistake, diminishing my options rather quickly. I was going to be in trouble unless I could find shelter nearby. Finally one of the park rangers told me that there was a storm-shelter in Robertsdale, Alabama. I must have looked a bit troubled. How was I going to get to Robertsdale? According to the map she showed me, Robertsdale was safely away from the shore, but would take hours to reach even on a good day. Once again I was told to hang tight for a few minutes. The storm was growing angrier. Not good!

    I was growing more restless by the minute. Outside, one RV after another was rolling by on the way out of the park. A park ranger was giving advice on where to find emergency shelter, or where to go to escape the worst of the storm. Everything felt sort of surreal, almost like I was suddenly in a movie. Finally the park ranger who had helped me find out about the shelter, I'll call Colleen here, put on her jacket and approached me: "Let's get you to Robertsdale!" She even helped me get the bike into the box of her pickup truck. During the half hour ride the rain got much heavier. Colleen told me all she had found out about the storm. It had already caused severe damage in the Caribbean and authorities had given it a name: Hurricane Ida. Landfall was expected some time later that afternoon, somewhere between Panama City and New Orleans; quite possibly west of Pensacola, or right at the park we had just left.

    A short time later we pulled up at the Robertsdale high school. A make shift sign at one of the doors revealed the entrance to the storm shelter which was normally a school gym. "Here we are" Colleen said, "best of luck for the rest of your trip and be careful out there!" I was extremely grateful for the lift and offered her a tip, but she declined and mentioned good karma. "Just help out someone in need the next time you have the opportunity!" was all she asked of me. I proceeded to the back of the pickup truck, quickly retrieved my bike and ran for the entrance to get out of the rain. A brief wave good bye, and I saw the truck pull away. I had never been in an emergency shelter before, but now I was here and grateful for it. I did not hesitate to push my bike through the double doors.

There was a lady at a desk that was set up at the entrance to the gym. She was wearing a tracksuit and looked like she might have just interrupted her daily jogging routine. A badge identified her as Gail, a volunteer. Gail asked for my personal information and put it all into some kind of registration form. Then she said that there was a safe place to lock up my bike while I was staying at the shelter. Moments later a man, also a volunteer, led me to a storage-room. I took two of my panniers off the bike that contained essentials for my stay. Next I was led into the gym and assigned a cot, a bed that somewhat resembled a beach recliner. I put my panniers down, thanked the man and decided to take a look around the shelter. So far there were just a few people gathered in one of the corners, where some benches had been arranged around a TV. It turned out that most of them were local volunteers. A middle-aged couple stuck out. They introduced themselves as Harry and Francine. They had also been evacuated from a park, the nearby Gulf State Park. A brief conversation revealed that they were from Toronto, Ontario. "We were staying in our RV at the park, but this morning they told us to leave" Harry told me. It turned out that both of them were also avid cyclists who had been exploring the area extensively on daily bicycle trips. Before we knew it we were swapping travel stories and pretty much forgot about the storm outside.

Little by little the shelter started filling up with people. Everybody had some storm experience to share, which made the stay anything but boring. The volunteers served a free lunch, consisting of hotdogs and coleslaw that was followed by cookies and chips for desert. Later in the afternoon a news crew visited the shelter, looking for people to interview. I was a prime candidate. My story of cycling the Gulf of Mexico and getting surprised by Hurricane Ida made the evening news. I was mentioned by name and interviewed about my experience.

After having spent a number of days by myself out on the road, I truly enjoyed my stay at the hurricane shelter. For the duration of the storm it took care of all my needs and responsibilities. I didn't have to worry about where to stay for the night, food was free, and there was lots of good company. Reminders of the dangerous conditions outside were few. The occasional peek outside through one of the glass doors only revealed more heavy rain. Television news coverage kept us informed about the whereabouts of the storm center.

The next morning after a free breakfast, the brunt of the storm had passed and the shelter was closed down. The weather outside had cleared up and the sun was coming through. Larry and Francine approached me to find out what my immediate plans were. I had not thought about it very much. It turned out I was going to have to take a ferry to get across the Mobil Bay, or ride across the city of Mobile. Due to occasional strong gusts that were remnant of the storm, the ferry would not resume operations for at least a couple of days. "Why don't you come down to the park with us?" Harry implied. "We can share our campsite; there is plenty of room for your tent!" The invitation was to good to pass off. Harry helped me load the bicycle into the RV and we were on our way to the Gulf State Park, a huge area of natural dunes, wildlife habitat and campsites. I set up my tent, but the wind that was coming off the gulf shore was still very strong. When it repeatedly flattened the tent I gladly accepted an invitation to spend the next couple of nights in a spare bed in Larry and Francine's camper. The state park had all the amenities and a beautiful natural beach to make the stay interesting enough. In the evening we went for a bike ride together, before we shared food and wine inside the camper, swapped more travel stories and played Scrabble. Both Harry and Francine loved traveling and their experience spanned decades.

To keep myself informed on the status of the ferry, I had to take a ride to the nearby public library the next day, where I could access the Internet. On that second evening, I finally caught news that the ferry was about to resume service the following day. I felt that this was reason to celebrate. I would be back on my bike, heading west by the next morning. On the way back to the campsite I bought six jumbo cans of beer to share with my new friends on our last evening together.

I must have been excited or simply distracted. Tying thin aluminum cans full of beer onto the rack of your bike with a bungee cord is not a great idea, but to make the same mistake twice in a row seems downright stupid in hindsight. However, that was exactly what I did, piercing holes through two cans with one of the hooks. To rescue the precious beer I drank the entire contents of both before making my way back to the campsite. I might ad that most of the way was via a trail through the park, away from public roads. By the time I arrived at the RV, I was lightheaded and probably smelled like a brewery. To top it off, I was laughing at my own stupidity. Harry and Francine both raised their eyebrows at first, but then laughed with me too. We spent the evening drinking beer and wine while playing a board game.

I finally left the Gulf State Park the next morning after a quick breakfast and saying good-bye to Harry and Francine. Finally I was back on the road and the weather was beautiful again, despite the occasional strong gusts that came off the ocean. The quiet route 180 took me past a lagoon, through the town of Fort Morgan and ended at the ferry terminal.

There was about an hour wait for the ferry. I sat by myself at first, watching the water and the birds, reflecting on my trip so far and contemplating on what might still be in store further down the road. Eventually a small line up of cars built up and people got out of their vehicles. Two women showed interest in my bike while enjoying a smoke break outside their car.

The trip across the bay was smooth and relaxing. There were about half a dozen cars on the ferry, besides my bike and I. We passed numerous oilrigs and small vessels along the way. I could not get enough of watching the pelicans.

The ferry stopped at Dauphin Island, an interesting place all by itself, with lots of history that is connected to the mainland only by a huge high-rise bridge. In hindsight I regret not having stuck around a bit longer to check it out. After loosing three days to a hurricane I wanted to cover some more distance before the end of the day. The long bridge turned out to be the most fun for the afternoon. After the grueling climb to the top I was rewarded with two-mile long descent at record speed with a fantastic view. There truly is no better feeling than having a road to yourself, high above the shoreline, moving as fast as the wind, completely silent, except for the sound of your bike tires on the pavement.

I made it to Bayou la Batre that evening, where I rented a room at the only motel in town. It was a bit more expensive than I had hoped, but I figured that I'd deserved the treat after not having spent a penny on accommodation in Alabama up to that point.

Chapter 9

The Weather

When the going gets tough

To start off this chapter I have to admit that I'm not the guy to consult if you're looking for tips on winter cycling. While I ride my bike year round, I've never attempted an extended tour in sub zero temperatures, nor would that appeal to me much. Don't get me wrong, winter cycling, even in very cold conditions can have its perks, but the need to dress warm tends to restrict your range of motion. When you remove some clothing it limits your time outside, as you get cold faster. My solution is shorter bike rides and ideally an escape into a warmer place. My advice on weather covers anything you might encounter during the warmer part of the year, as we know it in most of North America.

Riding a bike in the rain is fun, for about five minutes. Once you, your luggage and everything else get wet it becomes a drag. Rain though, is not the only weather-condition that can spoil a bike tour. Precipitation in other forms, such as hail, sleet or snow is usually worse. Extremely windy conditions can make it tough to ride, unless you're dealing with a strong tailwind. Even picture perfect sunshine and hot conditions come with challenges, especially when you're on the bike for the better part of each day. To run into a named storm and having to find a storm shelter, as I talked about in the previous chapter, is extremely rare. Changing weather conditions are a daily reality however. You can't control the weather, but it will have some control over you.

Many cyclists try to plan their tours by assuming they can cover a certain average distance, each day. While distance is only one factor that will determine how much time you'll spend on the bike, this approach can work just fine, as long as you don't expect too much. It might be a piece of cake to ride 100 km per day, until you hit that inevitable rainy day. Perfect time to take a rest day, you might think. You'd be right! But would you still think the same way if the rain continued for three days straight? Perhaps you'd only need to get out of a certain region to escape the rain. This happened to me several times during my two major tours. In Central America for example, some of the Caribbean shores are prone to rain. In Panama, just to mention one scenario, I had to make it across a mountain range to reach the much drier Pacific coast. Believe me; I got soaked right through! It was bearable thanks to tropical temperatures, but far from comfortable or fun.

What is the best way of dealing with bad weather systems while on tour? To be honest, I don't have a perfect answer. More often than not a rainy day will start off just fine. There will be some clouds and high humidity, but no rain at first. Then, perhaps 20 kilometers down the road and in the middle of nowhere, you realize that you're about to get soaked! You keep riding simply because it's the only thing you can do. A few more kilometers and you are thoroughly drenched. The wind now saps your body of heat faster than you can think of something to do about it. With a little luck you find some temporary shelter not too far down the road where you can dry off. The rain might even be gone by the time you're ready to resume your ride. I remember days like that from all of my tours. As a hopeful optimist I typically expect to escape the worst of the rain, but this way of thinking often puts me at risk, as the weather doesn't always comply. When you're out on the road anything can happen. You could end up riding in rain all day, while there seems to be sunshine and a rainbow just on the horizon, ever so close. On the other hand, we're all familiar with those grey, overcast days when the rain is constant and everything, including the road is soaking wet and the drains are overflowing. I have my sure fire way of dealing with that kind of day. Simply put; I get off the road at the first good opportunity.

Once you are completely wet your body will loose heat at a faster rate than normal. Even in moderate temperatures you can run into serious trouble, like hypothermia. What about the right clothing? You might ask. Sure, raingear is certainly an option, but in heavy rain its effectiveness is limited. Truly watertight clothing is not advisable because it traps the moisture your body is releasing, which happens naturally when you're cycling. Sometimes it seems like you get wet just about as fast as you would without rain gear. Other, more advanced clothing repels water, but still allows your skin to breathe. This type of gear can get you through a shower or two without too much discomfort. When it comes to heavy rain however, nothing is more inviting than a hotel room with a private bathroom and a hot shower. It may not seem like the most adventurous solution, but if a room is available and within my budget, I'll gladly check in and be grateful for the dry, warm place to recuperate, no matter how few kilometers I've ridden that day. I can always find something to do, even if it's just watching TV. Of course you don't always have that kind of luxury available. Often you may not find any hotels for miles and miles once you've already run into bad weather. In this situation, any type of temporary shelter will do. I remember spending the better part of a day under what was left of the roof of a strip mall that had been destroyed by Hurricane Katrina. That same day I had also used a church to change into dry clothing. Sometimes of course, there isn't any form of shelter at all. You may find yourself roughing it through heavy rain before you know it, no matter how well you planned your day.

If you must ride in heavy rain, your first priority should be safety. Visibility is typically poor in heavy rain, so make sure others can see you! Turn on your lights both in front and rear of the bike and wear something bright and reflective! Visibility also is something to think of when you're purchasing your rain gear. As an emergency measure, even a very thin, disposable plastic poncho can help you stay dry for a while. You might find these for a couple of dollars in a variety store and since they fold into a very small package and weigh next to nothing, you can't go wrong carrying one in an outside pocket of your panniers, easily accessible. On one occasion in Guatemala I purchased such a poncho. It surely did wonders to keep me relatively dry for an afternoon of riding in constant rain. Any time you can find this kind of rain protection for cheap I'd highly recommend you to get it. Aside from that I only ever had a light windbreaker, the type that that repels water while still allowing your skin to breathe, on any of my tours. Of course, it would have been a good idea to have pants, made from the same type of material, which I never did. What it taught me is that riding in wet jeans is not comfortable at all. In light drizzle, the right clothing can keep you completely dry as the water on the fabric evaporates fairly quickly. In heavy rain it doesn't work so well, but you'll still keep warm longer.

Rain is only one form of bad cycling weather. Others include fog, snow, heavy wind, thunderstorms and any kind of other storms. Strong wind can put you at risk for veering off the road, or into the path of a passing vehicle. I would not recommend riding in any of those conditions, but again, sometimes you just run into poor conditions unexpectedly. Prepare yourself by dressing in layers. For cold days, a hoody is perfect under your windbreaker. Gloves and a hat will also make a huge difference.

Hopefully the bad weather will be short lived, but if not; don't risk your life because you're following a rigid tour plan! If necessary, ask people for help! You might be surprised how many people are willing to give you valuable advice regarding local conditions and available shelter. You might even get invited for dinner and a free stay in someone's spare bedroom. Circumstances like those can result in some of the most memorable highlights of an extended bike tour.

Even if it may seem far off when you're wet, cold and tired; sunshine will return, perhaps sooner than you think. Often it will last longer than is comfortable. Spending upward of eight hours in the sunshine on a bike is not without problems. Chances are you will get sunburned, unless you protect your skin. I would not start a bike tour without some sunscreen, factor 15 or higher in my bag. Further, it will be a challenge to stay sufficiently hydrated. Besides drinking lots of water, you'll want to consume foods rich in minerals that help balance your electrolytes. Examples are bananas, salty trail mix and the occasional bottle of Gatorade or a similar, mineral rich drink. Avoid drinking a lot of coffee, soda pop and alcohol. Those will actually dehydrate your body as your kidneys try to flush out the caffeine or alcohol from your system.

Here is some good advice that might be hard to take if you're like me and like to sleep in: Leave early in the morning! Then take an extended break when the sun is highest (around the noon hour) and ride again until sunset! I have to admit that this is often not practical and never worked well for myself, but it can help minimize sun exposure.

Is there such a thing as perfect cycling weather? Mine would look something like this: 20 degrees Celsius, sunny with cloudy periods, strong wind from behind. Some prefer slightly cooler temperatures with no wind, while again some others will tell you that cycling in cold weather, with studded tires for traction on ice, is their idea of perfect conditions. You are not likely to find your perfect cycling weather for extended periods, but the more you cycle, the less this is going to matter. Once on tour, you'll find that the weather is nice more often than not, and that minor disturbances, such as light rain, a chilly morning or some wind are not really a big deal once you get going. You will likely even begin to enjoy the changes. Getting soaked on occasion can be a memorable experience, especially when you end up in a warm place at the end of the day. I remember some rides when I got drenched, wearing only a light shirt and shorts, and dried off completely an hour later due to quickly changing conditions. It was fun.

What you have to keep on top of are extreme conditions, such as major storms, extreme cold or heat, or prolonged heavy rain. Usually the local weather forecast will cover those. If you do get caught in adverse weather, it's always a good idea to get off the road before it spoils your fun and puts you at harms way. Warming up under a hot shower, or with a hot cup of something under a blanket, can be the highlight of your day. You may even find good company.

Chapter 10

Mississippi and New Orleans

Crossing state lines

Mississippi is a beautiful state, but almost immediately after crossing from Alabama, I started to notice that the coastal region did not look well off. Gone were the freshly paved highways with bicycle perfect shoulders to ride on and there were more and more abandoned places that had never been rebuilt after the hurricane of 2005. On a positive note, there was an old service road alongside the highway for much of the way, allowing me to ride completely separate from motorized traffic, which was preferable despite the very rough road surface. Unfortunately this luxury didn't continue very far once I reached the first town on my route, Pascagoula. I took a side road with less traffic to enter the town, a place that had most certainly seen better days. There was plenty of evidence that major destruction had ravaged the town, some time not too long ago. After some searching I found a Walmart store, stocked up on groceries and moved on.

Back on the highway I could not stop thinking about the summer of 2005, when I had been a truck driver, hearing about hurricane Katrina on the news. It dawned on me, that I was now passing through the areas that had been most affected. Even now, four years later, there were many traces of hurricane damage.

Through a search on the Internet I knew of a campground in Biloxi and had made plans to spend the night there. My route took me through Ocean Springs and then across a huge high-rise bridge into the city of Biloxi. There was a "no bicycles" sign at the foot of the bridge, which made me a wee bit nervous. How else was I going to get to Biloxi before dark? Unaware of any alternative I decided to ignore the sign and cross the bridge as quickly as possible. At least there was still a narrow shoulder to ride on that separated me from motorized traffic. High-rise bridges are common in the gulf coast region and they're kind of fun to tackle with a loaded touring bike. You first have to work really hard to get up to the peak, but then you get rewarded by what I like to call a couple of free miles or kilometers. The bike picks up speed all by itself, especially when it is heavy with luggage. I went up and over in minutes, undiscovered by law enforcement, but not invisible to motorists. I can swear that some of them were staring at me with displeasure. Had I made a mistake by taking this route?

On the other side of the bridge, road conditions were not bicycle friendly at all. There seemed to be a disproportionate number of elderly couples in their big old style sedans, probably on the way to some casino. Biloxi is the gambling capitol of Mississippi. The huge casino hotel complexes, with their shiny neon lights, stood in stark contrast to the rest of what I had seen of this state. With increasing traffic, fast disappearing sunlight and lack of a shoulder or bike lane, my ride became increasingly dangerous. I got more worried when the city seemed to stretch on forever. *Where the hell was this campground? Had I missed the place already?* I started wondering if there even was a campground, or if it might have been paved over to make a parking lot for the newest casino. The area simply didn't look right for camping. At one point I got off the road to push the bike on the sidewalk and take a break from riding in traffic. I remember passing a park on my right, but still no camping facilities. Finally I came across someone I could ask. "Yes, there is a campground" the stranger replied. "Just keep on going for about a mile! It's on this side and you can't miss it."

At last, a faded sign "Southern Comfort Campground" let me know that I had arrived. I pushed the bike through the entrance way and across a small yard to stop at the office. An elderly man greeted me and took a keen interest in my bike adventure. "Yes of course we have tent sites!" he replied to my first question. I paid for one night and few minutes later I was setting up my tent, just in time to finish before complete darkness. The campground had Internet, showers and laundry facilities and was surprisingly well maintained by their owners, a very friendly family. I was the only person camping in a tent though. Most of the RV spots were occupied by older trailers, which looked like they had been there for a long time. Perhaps the people living here had lost their homes due to the hurricane. I spent the rest of the evening doing my laundry, chatting with other people at the campground and finally surfing the Internet.

Almost a week earlier, while still in Florida, I had sent a couch surfing request to a fellow in New Orleans, which would be my next major stop. Hurricane Ida had delayed me in Alabama for about three days, but I was hopeful that Chuck would still host me for a couple of nights in New Orleans, so I sent out a renewed request.

I left Biloxi late the next morning, hoping to reach New Orleans the same day. The highway west of Biloxi continued on through an extended urban area blending into Gulfport and finally across Bay St. Louis. I was glad when I finally left the urban area behind and the road was quiet again. The weather was excellent for riding and I truly enjoyed the flat, but somewhat wild landscape.

I could only guess my location, and at what point I was leaving Mississippi from following the map. There was no indication of a state border, except for the old iron bridge west of Pearlington; not even a rusty old sign. None of his really surprised me, as the whole area looked somewhat weathered and neglected. Once again, Hurricane Katrina was still showing its face. Even four years after the actual event it was still very much present, reminding me of how powerful nature truly is and how we are at its mercy in an ever-changing environment that is ultimately unpredictable.

    Louisiana started off with lonely patches of swampland and plenty of water. As it turned out, time was not on my side, but I witnessed and captured an amazing sunset from a high-rise bridge over Lake Pontchartrain. The trade off was yet another ride in the dark, into the spooky eastern outskirts of New Orleans. The area did not feel secure at night, but I found a convenience store with a clerk who helped me reorient myself by pointing out a nearby hotel that had just reopened for the first time since 2005. I decided to rent a room for the night and worry about finding my way into the city the next morning. The hotel was very basic and looked somewhat run down. It was hard to tell if it had actually been renovated, with the exception of some obvious repairs. Overall the place felt just as spooky as the area it was located in, which made it hard to feel comfortable. There was no window and the walls, that looked rough, were all painted over in a dirty shade of yellow, showing some stains and graffiti through the thin coat. In spite all this I was grateful to have found a place that rented rooms for the bargain price of $ 40 per night. There was no Internet connection, so I had no way of checking if Chuck had replied to my couch surfing request. The bed looked old, but with new sheets and a good mattress. I was tired and passed out quickly.

    The next morning was a Saturday. I got out of the hotel fairly early and started my trek towards the center of New Orleans. Wherever I looked there were reminders of the catastrophe that had happened here four years prior; abandoned houses, overgrown foundations, fenced in properties with warning signs, buildings in ruins. This city was a long way from recovery. I was actually surprised when I found a functional payphone and managed to call Chuck.

    The conversation went somewhat like this:
Chuck: "Hello!"
Me: "Hi, my name is George, I'm the guy who sent you a couch surfing request, the one doing the bike tour to Mexico."

Chuck: "Yeah right, how're you doing George?"

Me: "Oh, not bad. I'm a week late due to a hurricane in Alabama, but do you think you could still host me for a night or two?"

Chuck: "Sure, not a problem! Where are you now?"

Me: "Not sure, somewhere in New Orleans."

Chuck: "Ha-ha, well here is the deal: I won't be home until about five or six o'clock, but you can make yourself at home. There is a combination lock at my door. Line up the digits A B C and D (they were actually numbers). My house key will pop out. Just walk in and make yourself at home!"

Me: "Oh really, wow that's nice of you Chuck. I think all I'll do is unload some of my stuff and then go explore the city. So I'll see you around five or six?"

Chuck: "Yeah, something like that. I'm just hanging out at my girlfriend's place, no worries man."

Me: "Ok, well thanks so much! See you when you get there!"

Chuck: "Sure, enjoy the city, see you tonight!"

I could barely believe it! A complete stranger whom I had never even met was willing to trust me with his house key. From reading Chuck's profile on the CS website I knew that he had guests frequently, who generally rated him very highly. He too, had obviously had mostly positive experiences. Just the fact that he trusted me made me respect him so much more. After I found his house and managed to follow his instructions to enter it, I unloaded my panniers and did exactly as I had told him over the phone and went exploring New Orleans. There surely was a lot to see in this city.

New Orleans is world famous for it's French Quarter that includes many bars and restaurants. By the fall of 2009 many old buildings in this part of town were beautifully restored. There were street performers, an art market and more tourist attractions. Of course I spent considerable time checking out this area. It was magic in its own way. There were so many interesting people, both tourists and performers, seemingly from all over. The perfect weather was adding to the atmosphere, making that afternoon unforgettable in my mind.

However, this wasn't the only lasting impression the Big Easy left me with that day. There was another part of New Orleans that attracted my curiosity even more: Not far from all the glamour of the French Quarter were parts of the city still in complete disarray. Boarded up homes, stores, churches and apartment buildings were everywhere. Several blocks had no buildings left at all. There were roads and sidewalks, but only partial foundations, overgrown by weeds, where the houses had once been. This was eerie! Four years had already passed since the hurricane and the situation still looked hopeless. I simply couldn't get my head around the scope of the destruction.

Later during my stay Chuck, my host explained that even his house had been severely damaged and flooded during Katrina. As a building engineer he had seized the opportunity and bought the home at a bargain price before renovating it. I was impressed with the beautiful, original wood flooring and the atmosphere of the century old home in general.

I got to stay an extra day at Chucks place in New Orleans. Besides taking a break from cycling I visited a bike shop to get my rear wheel trued while I explored more of New Orleans on foot. I only got to meet Chuck on my second evening in New Orleans. He treated me, and one of his local friends to a delicious seafood gumbo and some drinks, while we watched a movie. Chuck made no secret of his enthusiasm for Couchsurfing.

"I happen to live in a pretty cool place. People come from all over and I just like to meet them." He told me.

As it turned out, some other guests from Australia had just left his house earlier on the day of my arrival.

My tour almost came to an abrupt end the next day when I left New Orleans. I was trying to find my way out of the city and back onto route 90, westbound. It was the same highway that had brought me across most of three other states and into the city. Right from the start I noticed that there wasn't any bike friendly route. However, I found route 90 and knew that I wasn't lost. Any deviation from it might have had me disoriented. At one point the sign for US-90 pointed me toward a left turn. Car traffic was busy, but I managed to go with the flow at the traffic light on a flashing green arrow. Next I was coming up on a tall bridge; the Mississippi River! All I had to accomplish was to cross this bridge and I'd likely be out of the busiest part of town. To my displeasure I now noticed that the bridge was under construction and down to one narrow lane. The speed limit was 45 miles/hour, which is a lot faster than I could do, climbing a hill with my loaded bike. I knew that I was going to piss of some of the people who were in a hurry to get across the bridge in their cars, but was at a loss at what to do about it. *I had to cross that bridge!* Slowing down traffic simply couldn't be helped. It never dawned on me to seek an alternate route, but according to my map there wasn't one anyways. I knew for sure that there was no other bridge within close reach and was simply focused on my mission.

Giving it my best shot, I started climbing up the hill, trying not to worry too much about the traffic behind me. The passage would be over in five minutes and everybody would be happily on the way to wherever. Suddenly I heard a voice over a loudspeaker: "Get off that bike right now!" A look behind me revealed a cop car with its lights flashing. Behind the wheel was an angry looking officer. "Put your bike in the trunk and get in the back!" he ordered. This was easier said than done; my bike was loaded with luggage and it took considerable effort to get it into the trunk of a cruiser. Once I was in the backseat the officer started driving across the bridge to the delight of the traffic that had started building up behind us.

"You're going to jail for that!" was the first thing he told me. I was in shock. Minutes earlier I was simply looking ahead to a perfect day of cycling across Louisiana. *What a bloody change!* Even though I consider myself adventurous, going to jail wasn't exactly my cup of tea. I was devastated and wanted to protest, but knew better than to say anything. Was this going to be the end of my trip? I had never seen the inside of a prison in my entire life and it sure didn't fit my plans now. Visions of a tiny room with concrete walls and steel bars shot through my head. What were they going to do with my bicycle?

Next, the officer asked questions: "What are you doing crossing this bridge with your bicycle anyways? Where are you from? Where are you going?" Hesitant I started telling him about my trip. Despite some lingering anger, he seemed to like the idea. After a moment of silence he regained his focus and barked: "Well, this bridge is for motorized vehicles only! Don't tell me you didn't know; there are signs on the approach!"

I was genuinely puzzled because I had not seen any "no bikes" sign. Perhaps I had come from the wrong direction. While I was quietly wondering about my route leading up to the bridge and where I might have missed a crucial road sign, the officer started talking to me more calmly: "You're lucky you're from Canada. I will give you a citation; no point putting you in jail." I was instantly relieved, despite the prospect of a hefty fine. The cop was now talking about me to someone else over the police radio. I heard a voice laughing in response, which made me breathe a little easier. Perhaps I wasn't in such deep trouble after all.

As we arrived on the other side of the bridge, we turned into a gas station. The officer told me to get out of the car and unload my bike. "Don't go anywhere!" he snarled. There was another cop car at the gas station and he started walking toward it. I pulled my bike out of the trunk and put the panniers back in order. To help the bike stand up I leaned it against the back of the cruiser. For a few long minutes I just stood there, still shivering from nervousness with hands in my pockets. What kind of punishment would be coming my way? A citation could be expensive, but it was not going to stop me from continuing my journey, so I calmed down a lot before both the two officers approached me together. As it appeared, they had some questions.

"So you've cycled here all the way from Orlando?" the second, younger cop wanted to know. "Yes sir, it has been an awesome trip so far." Next I got a two-minute lecture by both officers about how reckless drivers were in New Orleans and how I should be thankful about getting rescued off the bridge. "We're glad we didn't have to wipe you off the pavement!" the older one proclaimed.

I admitted to poor judgment and how I was unaware of any alternate route across the Mississippi River. "The only way for bikes is the ferry. You have to inform yourself about those things!" I got lectured and this concluded the criticism I had to endure.

Next we were engaged in a lively conversation about adventure travels of any kind. "Where do you sleep at night" the officer who had chauffeured me across the bridge wanted to know. I mentioned Couchsurfing, talked about camping both on and off campgrounds and how there were many cheap hotels along the way. I went on about how the thing I loved most was, that on most days I didn't know what to expect, but somehow it always tended to fall into place. They both nodded. I had captured their imagination.

Still not knowing what to expect next, I heard the first officer say: "Well, good luck with the rest of your trip, but be careful!"

"The highway down this way (pointing away from the Big Easy) is not well patrolled. And don't get yourself in trouble down in Mexico!" the other cop added with a chuckle. "There is great breakfast at the Waffle House half a mile on the left by the way." They both nodded and spoke the magic words: "Have a nice trip!" We shook hands and they both took off.

I could hardly believe it; I was by myself again, free, perplexed and relieved, all at the same time. My punishment for disobeying traffic rules had gone from arrest and jail to "Have a nice trip". It was reason enough to celebrate with a huge breakfast and half a gallon of coffee at the recommended Waffle House.

Chapter 11

Sharing the Road

It's about survival

In the previous chapter I got sloppy about respecting the rules of the road. I almost ended up in a New Orleans jail, if not as someone's hood ornament, which might sound funny, but would have meant a visit to the hospital or worse. So let me use the occasion to mention some of the risks involved with cycling in general and bicycle touring in particular.

Unfortunately cycling is dangerous for one reason: Cars are everywhere. Cars are big, heavy and powerful. In a collision, bicycles are no match for anything with a motor. What motorists call a fender bender can cost your life as a cyclist. It isn't helping that many drivers believe they are entitled to the road for any number of reasons, ranging from paying taxes and insurance to having a nice car. As a cyclist you often don't have a choice but to share the road with cars. You don't know who is driving them and obviously, there are all kinds. It takes just one person in a poor mental state, operating any type of motorized vehicle near you to destroy your tour and quite possibly your life.

One of the biggest problems is the lack of safe infrastructure that was built specifically for bicycles. While many highways in North America have at least paved shoulders that are suitable for riding a bicycle, most cities are not bike friendly at all. You generally have two equally poor options: Ride on the road and be an obstacle to motorized vehicles at a great danger to yourself; or use the sidewalks and be a danger to pedestrians while completing an endless obstacle course. Depending on where you are, either option may be illegal.

In any city I generally use the road. This can be nerve wrecking when maneuvering older urban areas, but the sidewalks are rarely well suited for riding. Constant interruptions are the norm and will wear down on your patience. Of course there are some exceptions. Roads on the other hand, usually mean a steady pace through the city and in most jurisdictions they are legal to ride on. Here are some of the main problems for cyclists on roads they have to share with cars:

- Bikes are slower than cars. The difference in speed translates into many dangerous situations that can ultimately lead to collisions.

- In case of a collision the cyclist has no protection. What is a minor fender bender to a motorist can mean serious injury or death to a cyclist.

- Roads are seldom designed with bicycles in mind. In many areas there just isn't any suitable space for riding a bike safely.

- Car traffic gets heavy in many areas. It only takes one driver error to cause a life changing collision.

In big cities the above can be enough to discourage cycling all together. Unfortunately bicycles, especially in North America, are not generally considered a serious mode of transportation. Too many motorists will get upset when a bike in their lane slows them down, even for a few seconds. Unsafe passing maneuvers and road rage are not uncommon. For now, cars with impatient drivers are in the majority. There seems to be a prevailing attitude that being in control of a big expensive car somehow gives drivers special rights to the road. Split second decisions in traffic are often based on that kind of thinking, without any consideration for safety. Of course this doesn't seem fair from a cyclist's perspective. However, in order to survive and consistently complete your daily travels unharmed, it is essential to be aware of this double standard.

There is hope that things will change over time. More and more places are adding bike lanes to their infrastructure. They are a huge step in the right direction. Even better options are bike trails that are entirely separate from roads. Cycling in and of itself is a very safe activity. It becomes risky only because of the need to share the road with other traffic, more specifically cars and trucks. Some readers might raise their eyebrows over my next statements, but it cannot be denied: Cars are the least safe mode of transportation. What were we all thinking when, in the previous century cars slowly but steadily took over as the main transportation for everyone? I'm pretty sure even people like Henry Ford never intended to disfigure our urban environment in the way that has become our reality today. In major cities rush hour traffic is so bad that it definitely makes no sense to participate in it. Still, too many people do exactly that because they see it as their only option, without giving it a second thought. Our society is built around the assumption that every adult, regardless of their mental or physical fitness, has a drivers-license and a motorized vehicle to get around. Many would even argue that motorized individual transportation is essential. This means there are millions of cars out on the roads that take up more of our public space than any other mode of transportation. To add to the problem, some normally sane individuals get caught up in a "me first" mentality when they are behind a steering wheel. There are soccer moms on a mission, insecure teenagers with beefed up old cars, alcoholics, senior citizens and their dogs; the list goes on. As if that wasn't enough in itself, everyone now has a "smartphone" that many can't resist playing with despite legislation. Those are just a few examples of who is out on the road, controlling machines that are capable of reaching 100 miles/hour within a few seconds, just by stepping on the gas pedal. The training required to obtain a driver's license is minimal and this license is good forever, with just a few minor conditions that usually mean nothing more than paying a fee every so often. The result is a disaster that kills people every single day in traffic. We have become desensitized to it, so not only do we no longer get appalled, we also don't think twice about adding even more cars and new roads to our landscape. Put into proper perspective, all this fits the definition of insanity.

As a cyclist you are not the one with the dangerous toy, yet your life is at stake when you choose to participate in traffic. Your bones are out on the road between big heavy objects that are hard and move fast, in unpredictable ways. You cannot afford to be ignorant. Many cyclists have died in traffic, so we can hardly lay claim to sanity. When I first became interested in bicycle touring I came across a blog by Ken Kifer that inspired me hugely. I literally spent hours reading everything Ken had written. It came as a shock to me, when I eventually found out that Ken had been killed by a drunk driver while riding his bike, long before I had ever come across his blog.

If you still want to cycle after reading this: great! The only way cycling will get safer is through more demand for safe cycling routes. In the meantime we can do a lot of things to improve our odds as cyclists. It would be counterproductive to my personal vision to advise people not to ride bicycles, but to recommend it without mentioning the risks would be irresponsible. Bicycle touring can be a dangerous activity. You must take precautions to protect yourself. On occasion this can even mean breaking rules. Here are some ways to cut your risk:

- When cycling in city traffic use the right lane, but do not stick close to the curb. It is generally safer to take up an entire lane, simply to discourage motorists from passing you too closely. Additionally, this will give you extra space in case an unforeseen obstacle, such as an opening door on a parked car that could appear suddenly in front of you. Some drivers will not be pleased with you taking up their space, but most will change lanes to pass you, or wait until traffic allows them to pass safely. In case someone gets very impatient or has to follow your bike for an extended period; pull over somewhere and let them pass!

- Do everything you can to be visible! Motorists tend to be in a hurry. As a result they may not be focused on their immediate environment on the road. If they can see you from far away however, they will generally pay more attention and be careful around you.

- Use extra care or stay off the road in bad weather! Reduced visibility, poor traction, strong side-wind; those are just a few conditions that considerably increase your risk of collision.

- Keep your eyes on the road ahead of you! Cities have plenty of distractions. It is never safe to give in to them.

- Inspect your bike daily! Are there any loose parts? Are the brakes functional? Any frayed cables? Do the wheels look okay? A surprise-malfunction can have consequences in traffic.

- Wearing a helmet is a good idea, but they aren't the solution to bike safety. Keep in mind that a Styrofoam helmet does nothing to protect your limbs, nor is it designed to protect you in a collision with an automobile. Still, there are plenty of situations when a helmet can prevent serious injury. A fall would be a good example.

- Respect the rules of the road, except where it puts you at greater risk. Let me give an example: Some highways with wide paved shoulders may be off limits to bicycles, while the alternate route is a heavily travelled highway with no shoulders at all. This is especially common with toll roads, as I have experienced in Mexico. I'd rather risk getting a ticket than becoming involved in a collision. Many cops will understand. Use your intuition and don't be afraid to ask for advice!

In an ideal (cyclists) world, there would be a network of bicycle trails and separated bike lanes spanning the globe. It would be perfectly safe to go anywhere by bicycle, without having to worry about motorized traffic. Does this seem idealistic and impossible? Just think about what was done for motorized traffic over the past 100 years or so! The cost of our system of highways and roads designed for cars was far greater than it would cost to build bike trails everywhere. Today we are facing congested cities, air pollution and many more problems as a result. Yet, infrastructure projects still tend to be all about cars. What kind of a world have we created? There are better ways! Bicycles have tremendous potential. More and more people are starting to recognize this. My vision for the future is a network of bicycle specific infrastructure that can take you anywhere you want to go in the world, safely!

As much as I've criticized the infrastructure in North America, when you decide to go on tour in so called developing countries, you will be faced with worse conditions. Good roads are often not a priority for governments to spend their limited funds on. As a result you will be sharing poorly maintained ones with an ever-increasing number of cars, few of which are in great shape. As a matter of fact, a lot of cars that are discarded in North America are given a second life in other countries where fewer people can afford new vehicles. In most of these countries the rules of the road are not actually enforced. People don't think twice about having a beer or two at lunchtime and hopping into their car to drive somewhere, right after. Generally, the biggest vehicles with the loudest horns have priority. You don't want to get in their way with your bicycle.

Now I've probably scared away a good number of people from ever touring in a developing country or perhaps from touring at all. Why would anyone put his or her life at risk on roads that were never meant for bicycles in the first place? To me the answer is simple: My life would not be worth as much without the experience of touring foreign places by bicycle. It is the best way of travel that allows you to experience your environment at a pace that actually puts the journey ahead of the destination. Destinations are fake, or at least determined by outside influences.

There are reasons why bicycle touring has not caught on in the mainstream and safety is one of them. That is unfortunate, but there is hope that it can change. There surely is no better way to truly explore foreign places while building a healthy body with the ease that most of us are missing in typical exercise programs. You can have your cake and eat it too, literally.

Even if you don't plan on doing any bicycle touring, please help the cyclists in your area! They don't do any harm and deserve a safe environment to enjoy their activity. Talk to your elected officials, wherever you are. Let them know that bicycle trails and, or safe lanes are important to you! A collision between a cyclist and a car may not physically injure the motorist, but it is still life changing in a very ugly way. It will probably take a while to get safe infrastructure for cyclists in place everywhere, but the trend is already underway. Ultimately separate bike trails are exactly what is needed, so that more of us can enjoy bicycle touring. With motorized traffic taken out of the equation, cycling becomes an ideal way of travel, even for the whole family. At present you could almost consider long distance cycling an extreme sport, but it is for the wrong reasons.

Hopefully I haven't spoiled all your enthusiasm, especially since I'm aiming to turn bicycle touring into a mainstream activity. We do plenty of things each day that aren't necessarily safe. As with everything, you can develop good habits and skills that go a long way at protecting you, even in today's conditions. Enjoy your bike tour and the freak status that comes with it, but please don't say I didn't warn you about the risks in case you do get hurt!

Did I learn my lesson after the adventure on the way out of New Orleans? Read on and judge for yourself!

Chapter 12

Louisiana

Cycling the "ghost coast"

After my adventure of leaving New Orleans in a police cruiser across the Mississippi River, and a fantastic late breakfast at a Waffle House just outside of town, I enjoyed a quiet and fairly uneventful journey for the rest of that day. The route took me through sugar cane country and a sleepy little town called Raceland, quite the contrast from the hustle and bustle of New Orleans. I remember passing the sugar plant and its sweet smelling exhaust, just before entering the town. Raceland looked very picturesque. I resisted the temptation to spend more time here and stuck to my plan, which was to take a short break to grab a drink at one of the convenience stores.

My destination for the day was Houma. I had found a place to stay via the "warm showers" website, which is a great resource for cycling tourists. A couple, who were both avid cyclists and curious about my bike tour, were willing to host me for the night. Due to Amy's busy work schedule, I only got to meet the man of the house, Phil. He was in surprisingly good shape for a guy 60 years of age and made no secret of the fact that he believed cycling had saved him from cardiac disease (I could not believe it when he told me about the stent in his heart). I was also impressed by the house they had. Phil and Amy had built it themselves. We had an engaging conversation and it became quite apparent that both of them were dreaming of a long bike tour just like mine. They had joined the warm showers site for that reason. Up to this point, both their work schedules had not allowed a long enough absence from home. Phil was an expert when it came to bicycles. He noticed right away that my bike was not high end touring material, but completely understood that it was sufficient for what I was doing. I got to sleep in the spare bedroom and had to get up early the next morning, to join Phil for breakfast before he had to leave for work, while I was off to an early start. It suited me fine, as it would allow for a big day on the road.

From Houma I had to backtrack just a little to rejoin US route 90, the road that I had followed, more or less, all the way from Florida. Once again the weather was picture perfect and sunny, ideal for cycling. Aside from Hurricane Ida in Alabama the weather had treated me extremely well up to this point.

It was in Louisiana, first New Orleans, that I discovered a new favorite high-energy lunch. Burger King had a special for the month of November. It consisted of two huge fatty burgers and a soda with free refills. In hindsight I believe that I literally became addicted to the high calorie burgers and the sweet cold drink. My body had burned through all its fat reserves and needed more to fuel the ride. I had always liked burgers, so I was happy to find a Burger King restaurant, just in time for lunch, in Morgan City that day. After the meal I resumed my ride to Franklin, a little town I had chosen off the map as my destination for the day. I was riding through a beautiful region of Louisiana on a relatively quiet highway. At times I hardly observed the landscape because Mexico was already on my mind. I was getting closer. What would it be like?

It was still early in the afternoon when I arrived at the Belmar Motel in Franklin. The place had inexpensive rooms to crash and was probably over 50 years old. It was still daylight outside when I fell asleep while watching TV.

I woke up to a little surprise the next morning. Still half asleep I glanced at my bike, which was leaning on the wall next to my bed. The rear tire looked flat! My first reaction was not exactly positive. I dreaded the thought of getting up to patch a tire. I would get my hands dirty before breakfast, so I rolled over instead. Minutes later I changed my mind and got up, feeling thankful for having the first flat of my tour in a cozy motel room, rather than out on a busy highway. The tire was patched in under twenty minutes. A piece of wire that had penetrated the inner tube appeared to be the cause.

The weather was nice, but the temperature outside had dropped considerably. I took advantage of the 12 pm checkout time, as accumulated fatigue had caught up to me. My ride for the day wasn't going to be a very long. Abbeville was the last town on my route before I would end up on a very lonely coastal road. I took my time getting there and captured many photos along the way. Upon entering Abbeville I stopped at the local Walmart to replenish my food reserves, the usual; trail mix, fruits and everything it would take to make sandwiches. A good part of it ended up in my stomach before I even left the premises. While I was outside the store, chewing on my hastily prepared sandwich, a freckle faced young guy in a Walmart vest approached me and asked about my trip: "Where you headed and, (pause) where you from?"

I told him I was from Canada and that I was going to Mexico.

"Oh man!" His expression had changed from curiosity to disgust and he spit out some of the tobacco he was chewing. "Mexico is crazy! I wouldn't go there on a bike." He went on to tell me about a trip he and some of his friends had taken a while back. Supposedly, they had ended up getting robbed by gangsters after their car had broken down in a mountainous area.

"I'm never setting foot into that country again!" he proclaimed. "Oh and by the way, the coastal region of Louisiana is pretty scary too, you'll see!" He indicated with a frown. I wasn't really sure how to respond. No scary story in the world was going to keep me from following my dream, but I pretended to be concerned just to play along. It got him going even more. Now he was right in his element, going on about drug cartels, telling horror stories about their gruesome smuggling practices.

"So you think I'm crazy?" I finally decided to interrupt him. He paused briefly before grinning and saying: "You're going to get your head chopped off!"

Now I was laughing and he realized that I had not taken him seriously all along. "Good luck buddy" he mumbled while retreating toward the store entrance.

There was supposed to be a commercial campground in Abbeville. I had trouble finding it at first. With the help of some locals I eventually ended up at an RV campground a couple of miles outside of town. When I looked around to find the office, a lady in a robe came out of her trailer asking me if she could help me.

"I hope you can." I replied, "Do you have any tent sites?" Her answer was short and firm: "no!"

The disappointment must have shown on my face, so she explained: "Sir, we don't have bathrooms here or anything. Before commenting: "By the way, it is going to rain, why would you want to sleep in a tent?"

I thanked her for the information while shaking my head and jumped back on my bike. It was almost dark now and I was facing the task of finding alternate accommodation. After some running back and forth I discovered a relatively cheap motel. It was already dark and there wasn't really much choice at this point, so I checked in. Next door, was a liquor store; reason enough to celebrate with a couple of beers.

By the time I left Abbeville the next morning the weather had changed. The sky was gray and the air felt thick and humid. So far there was no rain, but it seemed only like a matter of time. My plan was to take state route 82, also called Grand Chenier Highway. It was going to take me through swampland and seemingly untouched wilderness. There were no towns or places to stop on my route for a very long way. I had no idea where the day might end, but was hoping to find accommodation at the Rockefeller Wildlife and Game Reserve that was definitely within reach. The prospect of rain bothered me quite a bit, but I had seen overcast days before, without ever catching a drop of rain. It seemed reasonable to take a chance. I stayed completely dry for about 20 kilometers, when it finally began to drizzle in the middle of nowhere. The area was extremely quiet and I understood completely why some would consider it scary. At one point I encountered the remains of a dead crocodile on the road and prayed that there were no live ones lurking in the ditches, looking for a protein rich meal. Was this what my friend at Walmart had been talking about? The rain was still light enough to carry on without getting completely soaked, which actually made for a pretty good ride. It stayed that way through most of the afternoon.

Later in the day I finally reached a small general store someone had told me about. I decided to stop for some coffee and a snack. When I entered the store, there was an old lady behind the counter by herself. "Coffee is on the house young man!" she proclaimed with a smile. Then her face turned serious. After a brief pause she asked: "Where are you going to spend the night?" She had obviously seen my loaded bicycle outside where it was still raining. "It will be pitch dark here in an hour." She added.

I admitted that I didn't know, but was hoping to find a place to sleep near the entrance of the wildlife reserve, which I thought couldn't be too far away.

"Tell you what," the lady went on, "if you go on for about two more miles, you will see an antenna tower on your left. It is sitting on top of solid wooden columns. Sometimes the rangers let people pitch their tents under there for protection from the rain. It is going to get nasty out there, you know!"

Any sleeping place with protection was going to be a bonus, so I thanked her and asked a few questions to make sure I couldn't miss the place. "It's a huge tower, you'll see it!" she said, indicating it was impossible to miss. "But you should ask the ranger first, the office is just a few hundred yards further down on the same side." She smiled and added:" You can come back here for coffee in the morning."

I thanked her again. Another customer threw in a comment about how you could always count on the local people of the area. I responded with a nod and a smile. What followed was a conversation about the store. I found out that it had been at this exact location for many years, but Hurricane Rita had destroyed the original building in 2005. The newly rebuilt store had only opened recently.

"Not to worry young man," the old lady finally said, "we're not in the hurricane season now. All we're getting tonight is a little front from the gulf!" Somehow that comment didn't do a lot to put me at ease. Didn't she say it was going to get nasty? I had to get out there before it was too dark and wet to go anywhere.

I found the tower right away, but it took a while to find the ranger's office. When I finally did, no one was there. I was unable to locate anyone at all, so I decided to take a chance and set up camp before it got too dark. There were a few other buildings around the ranger-station, but all of them had suffered various degrees of damage. It appeared they had been residences before Hurricane Rita had wrecked them. The inhabitants had apparently never returned. All were built on ten-foot pillars, creating a relatively large protected area underneath. For a few minutes I considered setting up my tent under one of the houses, but the ground was concrete and this meant my tent wasn't suited for it. My only good option was the antenna tower. It was hard to set up the tent because of strong gusts. When it finally stood, it didn't look so great, but looks were not on my priority list; at least I had shelter! I set up my bed, crawled inside and made myself comfortable.

The tour had changed me a great deal already. Stealth camping in the middle of nowhere didn't stress me out any more in the least. Despite the wind howling outside and the tent nearly caving in, I was asleep within minutes.

When I woke up it was daylight. My tent had collapsed, but I was dry and had slept through the entire night. There was no point trying to fix the tent; it was just too windy outside and I was practically ready to hit the road anyways. I crawled out of the mess and looked around to see what the weather situation was like. It was raining sideways, but actually not too heavily. The wind was the main problem and it was blowing from the south, the direction of the gulf shore. My tent was a bit wet on the outside, but all my gear inside had stayed dry. One by one I started pulling out the pieces, to load them back into the panniers. Amazingly I managed to pack it all in without getting any of it dirty on the muddy ground. The last thing to wrap up was the tent itself. After pulling out all the anchors I had to hold onto it tightly, so it wouldn't get blown away. It formed a huge green bag full of air that was flapping around like a windsock. Despite the rain, the wind was strong enough to dry it off in minutes. The big challenge was to try folding and packing it away without getting it wet and muddy again. I managed to complete the whole ordeal of loading everything back onto the bike relatively quickly, considering the circumstances. The weather wasn't cold, but the strong wind made it quite uncomfortable.

I decided to backtrack a couple of miles for my free coffee and whatever breakfast I could get at the same store I had stopped at the night before. To my knowledge it was the only place within close reach. I was quite curious to find out if the old lady from the previous evening would be behind the counter again. Sure enough, when I entered the store a familiar face greeted me. She wasn't alone this time; another lady who turned out to be her daughter was keeping her company. Both ladies were quite busy serving customers. I picked a ready-made sandwich and a cup of coffee for breakfast. When it was my turn to pay, the ladies wanted to know more about my trip, so I told them about my plans to travel to Mexico.

"You started in Orlando three weeks ago?" the younger one wanted to know. "You're already more than half way to the border!" the older one threw in. "What do you do in the rain?" she asked. I had no good answer and shrugged my shoulders. Both looked concerned for a split second or so, before the younger one said: "It is actually letting up a bit right now. I'd finish that sandwich and get some riding in before it gets worse again!" Her mom nodded and added: "Cameron is around 30 miles from here, you'll find a hotel there".

"Wow, all the way to Cameron on a bike in the rain?" a customer appeared from behind me. He had overheard the conversation and was shaking his head. "You're crazy!" the old lady laughed and offered me a cookie. Then she went on: "There are also some places to seek shelter in Grand Chenier, just a few miles from here, but no services and no hotel. Everything there got destroyed by Hurricane Rita four years ago."

Now I was baffled. The women picked up on my surprise. "This entire region is like a 'ghost coast' now, it is way too expensive for people to rebuild." the younger one explained. I had heard about Hurricane Rita, but to me it had always been a blur, stories in the news, that had been overshadowed by the huge disaster of Hurricane Katrina. The Gulf coast of Louisiana had been hit twice in the same year. Hurricane Rita, the second blast, had actually been the stronger one of the storms at landfall. The difference was that it had hit a much less populated area.

"You will probably see a lot of damage along your way, because it has been left untouched. People have just given up! We almost couldn't reopen our store." The younger one of the two store clerks explained.

As much as I enjoyed the conversation, coffee and cookies, it was time to get back on my bike and cover some distance. The weather could not be trusted. Sure enough, after riding for a while in a windy drizzle, the rain got heavier and heavier. By the time I realized it I was already soaked to the bone. There was nothing I could do, except to keep going. Eventually I reached what had to be Grand Chenier. There really wasn't much worth mentioning, except for some homes, many of which had been destroyed. I found a church that was operational and first took shelter in the entranceway. After a few minutes I decided to sneak inside. To my amazement the door was unlocked, but no one was inside. I was confident nobody was going to sue me for trespassing, so I used the church bathroom to put on some dry clothes while the rain outside got even heavier. I was stranded! There was nothing more to do than wait for the rain to subside. I spent a small eternity sitting by the church entrance, doing nothing but observing the water that was pouring down the drains.

Eventually I gathered all my courage. It seemed like the rain was beginning to taper off. When it appeared to rain only lightly, I hopped back on the bike and went on. It was the wrong decision. Within a few minutes my previously dry clothes were drenched. I was uncomfortably wet again and shivering. What were my options? I either had to turn back, or find another shelter. Then I saw a huge angle shaped foundation with a metal roof above it, supported by steel columns. I would surely be able to hang out under the roof for a while!

The little while turned into a longer period that stretched into the better part of the afternoon. I simply could not believe the amount of water that was gushing down the side of the roof where the downspout had once been. I had found a column in the center of the structure to lean my bike on and set up my homemade stove. While it was barely helping to warm me up, I was able to cook a meal with supplies I had been carrying for weeks, mainly rice and lentils. A small bottle of gas line antifreeze I had bought in Florida, served as fuel. The meal was exactly what I needed; I felt warmer right away.

Still a good while later the rain finally let up. I had spent enough time under the big roof, which I figured was the remains of a strip mall. Finally I was able to leave it behind with some relief. The place wasn't exactly what I had envisioned to spend my next night in. I was overdue for some real comfort.

Back on the road here were huge puddles everywhere and the ditches looked more like rivers, but the sun was breaking through the clouds, making it all look pretty good. I even managed to reach Cameron before dark. There was exactly one Motel in town and it was pretty busy with weekend travelers, but a room was available. The entrance was via a second floor balcony, which meant I had to carry my rain soaked gear upstairs one piece at a time. When I unpacked my panniers, I found that nearly everything was wet. Luckily there was a coin laundry at the motel, which truly saved the day. While my clothes were in the dryer I took a walk to the nearest store to buy something for supper. I returned with a big can of chili, some bread and two tall cans of beer. The highlight of my evening was a long, hot shower, followed by watching TV in bed while gobbling down my beer. I finally passed out with the TV still on.

Chapter 13

Camping

A few things I've learned from experience

One of the problems of touring by bicycle, compared to a traveling by car, is that you cannot sleep in your vehicle. If your budget is limited, this can offset the savings in fuel. In my opinion, the best way of dealing with this challenge is to take a small tent along and camp wherever it is convenient or possible. As a cyclist you are already engaging in an outdoor activity. Sleeping outdoors in a tent takes this to yet another level that most outdoor enthusiasts can appreciate.

There are options other than a simple tent. Camping trailers for bicycles are available and some cyclists have built them to their own designs. If you decide to give this option a try I would recommend searching the Internet for inspiration and information. You will come across all kinds of trailers you can pull with your bike. While some serve merely as a way to haul your luggage, others allow you to sleep in them too. I have no experience with trailers and will therefore limit my comments about them. Personally, I would not choose a trailer for touring. What seems like a fantastic idea at first glance will most certainly make your bicycle harder to maneuver. Besides campgrounds you may not find many places where you could park your combination and crawl into the trailer to sleep. More often than not, the trailer would be rather awkward to deal with while on tour. In my opinion, one of the greatest advantages of a bicycle is the almost unlimited maneuverability it gives you. Pulling a trailer that is big enough to accommodate a bed would most certainly take away from that. Further, even the most hardcore camper might want to sleep in a real bed on occasion. Cheap hotels are often available and your bicycle usually fits even into a very tiny room. Keeping the bike in your room is secure and practical and most hotels won't object to it. Even the ones that do usually have some place you can store the bike securely. It would be more of a problem to find a secure place to park a bike/ trailer combination, as it would take up considerably more space. Of course in certain localities the advantages to having your bed already set up in a little trailer behind your bike could outweigh the drawbacks, so if you're intrigued by the idea, why not give it a try?

Having mentioned trailers, my personal choice remains a small tent, along with your air mattress, sleeping bag and even a small pillow. All this will fit quite easily into one of your panniers. You will be able to use it whenever the occasion allows and other times it will remain in your luggage as a neat little package that won't bother you.

There are a few things to consider when shopping for a tent. In the previous chapters you may have noticed that mine had some shortcomings. When I originally bought all my gear, low cost was a priority. I ended up buying one of the cheapest tents available; the price was somewhere around $ 35. Looking back, it was money well spent. Over the course of several bike tours the tent saved me hundreds of dollars in accommodation. It could have been more cost effective however, had I spent just a little more money initially. My first tent had no frame, which was big drawback. It relied entirely on one pole and several pegs to hold it up. You can't use those kinds of pegs on pavement or a concrete floor, even a hard dirt floor sometimes won't work very well. The problem became very limiting at times, whenever I had found a place that was relatively well protected from the elements, but where I couldn't pitch my tent because there was no way to get the pegs into the ground. One example of this was the roof I used for shelter from the rain in Grand Chenier (see the previous chapter). The roof was actually part of the remains of a strip mall and the entire structure had a concrete floor, which would have been fine for any type of dome tent, some of which cost just a few dollars more than the one I had. Thankfully I didn't have to spend a night under that roof in, but there were a few hours when it seemed like exactly this was going to be my only option and I was wrecking my head about how I was going to pitch my tent.

I highly recommend buying a good quality dome tent. Unfortunately, the good ones that compress into a very small bundle don't come cheap. Still, there are suitable options in all price ranges. I no longer have the tent I used on my first tour, but have used a small dome tent on several occasions that didn't cost much more. When shopping for a tent, two of the main considerations are size and weight. Simply put, the more money you spend, the smaller and lighter your tent will be. It is especially important to have a compact package when the tent is folded up, so your luggage is less bulky. The same considerations are relevant to sleeping bags and pads as well.

I would always recommend a two-person tent, even if you're planning on touring by yourself. The extra space will allow you to keep your panniers inside the tent with you while you sleep, for security and protection from the elements. Aside from that, you'd want the smallest and lightest package you can afford. That does not mean you should postpone your tour until you have enough money to buy the perfect tent. Some tents can cost a thousand dollars ore more. What a nice budget for a tour that would make! My own trips are proof that you can make even the cheapest tent work for you. That's why, any time your budget is limited, I would suggest spending more money on the tour and less on equipment. Definitely shop around! A well-designed tent gives you more options and it will be easier to set up and take down. In the long run this will save you money and time.

Some higher end tents I've seen even have you supported off the ground while sleeping, virtually eliminating the need for a sleeping pad or air mattress. The tent floor doubles as a bed and is similar to a hammock. This feature could give you exceptional flexibility, but of course it comes at a price. I have not been able to test this kind of set up myself and therefore can't give you any information that is based on first hand experience. However, I've had the privilege of sleeping in a hammock and it sure beats sleeping on the ground or on a pad.

Carrying a quality tent is almost like having your own hotel room with you at all times. You can set it up quickly and instantly have a place to sleep. In many countries hostels offer camping in their yard for about half the price of a bed in a dorm room. You have the advantage of having your own private space, while being allowed access to the kitchen and bathroom-facilities. Unless the weather is wet or extremely cold, this is an excellent option that will help stretch your budget.

This chapter would not be complete without mentioning stealth camping. As previously described, it means that you pick your own campsite regardless of whether it is designated as such. As far as I know, stealth camping is the only truly free way to spend a night, short of sleeping on a park bench. To really take advantage you need a tent that is quick and easy to pitch, as well as take down and pack. I have met people who chose to stealth camp for the their entire multi months trip, surely saving them hundreds of dollars in accommodation costs. For myself, it seemed to be the perfect option only on occasion. With stealth camping you generally have no access to showers or bathrooms. Your food choices are limited to what you carry with you, unless you stop and eat somewhere before you set up camp, which is not always practical. Then there is a very real risk of picking the wrong place. Imagine falling asleep in your tent after a long day of cycling, only to be woken up by some angry landowner in the middle of the night! You never really know what kind of person you're dealing with once this happens, so that kind of scenario is never desirable. Someone might tell you to pack up and get lost, or worse, call the cops. Others may even stick a gun in your face. The key to stealth camping is to use your intuition, which takes a while to develop. In the meantime you pretty much rely on good luck. It is always a good idea to ask around.

There are still plenty of opportunities to camp for next to nothing. Asking people is often the key to a free campsite. Quite often, someone will agree to let you camp on their property, but you'll never know unless you talk to them first. Many people may be intrigued with the kind of adventure you're undertaking and a good conversation can easily land you an invitation.

On my journey through Mexico I met a young lady from Sweden who was camping quite regularly at roadside restaurants after eating her supper there. In Mexico those places are usually family businesses that are quite flexible and accommodating. More often than not they'll have a spot for your tent and even some kind of shower (even is it's just a garden hose). It is very common for restaurant staff to take interest in your tour. When you order a meal, tell them about your adventures and ask politely where you could camp for the night, chances are you will get some valuable advice or even a free camping spot right on site. It works in their favor as well, as you are likely to have breakfast at the same place the next morning.

Even if you decide to camp on commercial campgrounds, state or provincial parks, camping is always more economical than most other means of accommodation. The differences with actual campgrounds are that you have at least basic facilities and you will usually meet other campers, especially on weekends. Sometimes this can be a good thing, but not always. On long weekends campgrounds can be full of youngsters trying to party hard. Imagine camping next to a bunch of rowdy teenagers fueled on cheap beer! Perhaps you're the kind who couldn't be bothered by anything, but otherwise you might want to choose a different option for long weekends and holidays. Occasionally you will even meet other cyclists in campgrounds, which can make for memorable get-togethers. Shared rides and long-term friendships can result.

For an extended bike tour, basic camping equipment is simply essential. Even if camping is your least favorite form of accommodation, it is always an option you can fall back on if all else fails. You may not always reach your planned destination for the day, or there might not be any hostel or hotel where you had expected to find one. When it comes to bicycle touring your trip is never about any destination anyways. With a tent and some basic gear you are at least prepared. An unexpected night of camping in an odd location is sure to become one of the most memorable ones of your tour and perhaps your life.

Chapter 14

Texas

The big one

My day started with a ferry crossing west of Cameron and continued with a very long and straight ride against the wind along the Gulf Beach Highway, route 82. The flat terrain and harsh wind made the ride to the Texas State line seem much longer than it actually was. It was early afternoon when I finally crossed the bridge to Port Arthur. On the other side was a big old style general store called SGS Causeway Bait & Tackle. It was more than just a store and also incorporated a cozy restaurant. I was late for my lunch, so I ordered the biggest burger on the menu. Burgers are bigger in Texas. This one was not just big but also very delicious. The staff at the restaurant took interest in my tour and informed me, that I would not have been able to use the bridge across the state line, just a few weeks prior. "They just opened up the bridge again!" my waitress hummed as she topped up my coffee. "There was no way to get across here for a while after Hurricane Rita."

The restaurant was not busy this Sunday afternoon so the waitress came around to ask me about the highlights of my tour. By now I had quite a bit to talk about, like my moonlight ride in Florida, the hurricane in Alabama and the bridge crossing in New Orleans that almost had me arrested. The young lady took a keen interest and I probably made her day, even if just by providing entertainment on a really slow Sunday at work.

An hour and a half or so later I was finally back outside and ready to continue on to Beaumont, where I had a couch surfing invitation by a friend I had met via a photo sharing site. The landscape of Port Arthur was quite different from anything I had experienced so far. For the first time since the beginning of my trip, the terrain was what can be described only as ugly. Huge refineries and other industrial installations were dominating. The road was perfectly straight, but I still managed to get disoriented at a four-way intersection with a set of lights. Why wasn't there a sign indicating which way would lead to Beaumont? My poor sense of direction along with a not so perfect map of Texas had me waste a good half hour exploring the wrong way; more refineries and employee parking lots. When I realized I had to turn around, the sun was setting and lighting up the sky with shades of blue and orange that made the area look surreal. I felt that I was in a bit of trouble. The way to Beaumont was longer than anticipated. I wasn't going to get there before dark. There was no shoulder on the two-lane highway, so I was riding in the same lane as the cars and trucks, putting me at greater and greater risk the darker it got. Thankfully traffic was light, but the ride in the fading light did not feel safe. By the time I finally entered the city of Beaumont it was pitch black. Now I had to find a phone booth and try to get a hold of Kelly, my couch surfing host.

It took a few tries before Kelly answered the phone. She told me that she tended to be careful about how to meet the people she was hosting. Instead of giving me directions straight to her house, we first had to meet up in a public place. It seemed like everything in this part of Beaumont was shut down for the night, even though it was just around eight o'clock. Kelly gave me directions to an ice cream parlor. When I arrived there it was open, but dead quiet. I ended up waiting in the empty parking lot, wondering if I had found the right place. Finally a car pulled in. I noticed a couple inside and figured they had to be someone else, but the driver pulled right up to me, lowered his window and introduced himself as Ben. My first impression was that Ben was Kelly's boyfriend. A brief chat revealed that he was also a couch surfer who was in Beaumont on business. He wasn't actually using CS to find accommodation, as his company was providing him with a hotel room and a rental car. He had used the CS site to hook up with some local friends. Kelly, who was in the passenger seat, was one of them. The two had already made plans to get together with another young lady, also a couch surfer, later that evening. Kelly said that I was welcome to join. After a few more moments of talking things over, I followed Ben's car through several blocks of a dark neighborhood until we reached Kelly's house, an older duplex. Once inside, Kelly wasted no time to show me her big old couch and a place to put my stuff.

"Do you need to grab a shower before we go out?" she asked. "Yes that would be great" was my reply, "I just spent the better part of the day riding my bike here from Louisiana". She smiled and asked if I was too tired to go back out. My answer was no. A short while later Ben drove us to a 24-hour supermarket. "We need ice cream!" Kelly filled me in, "then we're going to visit my friend Liz who is also a couch surfer. Liz has some wicked beer at her place and she'll share it with us."

Here I was; just in from a lonely ride on a dark highway, over 100 kilometers in my aching bones, but I had already forgotten about being tired. Once again couch surfing had brought me together with some great people. After my lonely ride across Louisiana, with all its challenges, it was a welcome change. We talked about our adventures with travel and more specifically couch surfing till the wee hours. Kelly was the only Beaumont local in the group. Ben was from Nevada, but had traveled the world as an engineer. His stay in Beaumont was only a few days long. He would be on his way to Korea by the same time the following day. Liz was a reporter with a local newspaper who had moved here from Ohio after spending some time unemployed and eventually becoming homeless. Couch surfing had been her way back from rough times and Kelly had hosted her for her first few weeks in Texas. For a change I wasn't the only one with a good travel story. By the end of the night we parted as good friends, even though we had just met.

I spent the entire next day in Beaumont, checking out a few tourist attractions, including the museum Kelly worked at and the world's second biggest fire hydrant. In the evening I took Kelly to her favorite Mexican restaurant for supper.

The next stage of my trip was once again over 100 kilometers long and took me to Houston, Texas's biggest city. The ride on US 90 was somewhat straight and boring. It was made tougher by occasionally strong headwinds. On the previous evening in Beaumont, I had searched the Internet for possible accommodations. I had found a host on warm showers.org. By the time I finally reached the outskirts of Houston it was almost dark again. I had picked up a map of the city and highlighted a route to Carol's house on it, but that didn't prevent me from getting lost in a maze of old industrial parks. Eventually I found a run down convenience store, so I stopped to buy some soda and ask the clerk for directions. This was how I found out that I had landed in a Spanish speaking part of town. "No hablo Ingles" was all the man was willing to respond to my questions. He gave me a chuckle though, when I told him in broken Spanish that I was headed to Mexico on my bicycle. At least this reaction broke the ice and I managed to get some information on my whereabouts out of him. We ended up communicating quite well in "Spanglish", a mixture of English and Spanish. The guy turned out to be quite friendly in the end. On my way out he actually gave me the thumbs up and yelled "viva Mexico".

My adventures of the day weren't over yet. I rode through block after block in the dark, much of it on sidewalks due to traffic. All the while I was just guessing that it had to be the right way. Eventually I decided to stop and make sure, only to realize that I had lost my map somewhere. Now I had to dig out my notebook, where I had originally written down the directions to Carol's place. Once I was reoriented, I found a payphone and called call my host. She confirmed that I had almost made it.

Carol was also cycling enthusiast who had her perfectly clean high end touring bike on display in her living room. She told me that for her, bicycle touring was a way of life, and that she would tour whenever time allowed it. She had been to many parts of the US, most notably the Colorado Rockies. Mostly her tours had been group adventures, but she wasn't afraid of riding by herself. Unfortunately I only got to spend one short evening with Carol. We went out for supper and had a good conversation, but went to sleep not too long after. Carol had to get up early for work and I was tired from a long ride.

Getting out of Houston the next day was not nearly the ordeal it had been to get into the city. It seemed like I had already passed through the most challenging parts. All that was left to do was to follow a main road that eventually turned into state route 35. Before I knew it I was on a quiet country road again, actually heading south for the first time since leaving Orlando. A look on my Texas map revealed that I was likely to reach the Mexican border within just a few days.

The journey through the rest of Texas was uneventful. One of the highlights was an overnight stay at the Goose Island State Park near Aransas. The camping actually cost significantly less there than at comparable parks in other states, like Florida for example. The park had a beach area and a wooden boardwalk with a long pier. There was a truly stunning sunset that evening. This turned out to be was one of the few truly beautiful places along my way through Texas.

I also spent a grueling day finding my way through the industrial areas of Corpus Christi. Instead of heading for famous Padre Island, I chose to go west to Robstown, then south on route 77, through Kingsville and finally to Robertsville on a perfectly straight and flat highway, where the strong headwind slowed me down to a crawl. Once I arrived there, again in the dark, I spent another night in a cheap Motel.

It was at a convenience store in Robertsville that I almost changed my mind about going to Mexico. I had searched the recent news-reports about the area immediately south of the border, like Matamoros and San Fernando in the state of Tamaulipas. Several crime scene pictures were still fresh on my mind when I got into chatting with two guys outside the store who said they had both grown up in Mexico. They went on to tell me that neither of them would ever go back, because of "excessive gang violence". One of them put it this way: "There are shootouts every day down there man! Why would you go to Mexico on your bicycle, by yourself? I grew up there and speak the language, but won't even go down there any more. It's just not worth it!" The other guy was just nodding the whole time.

After returning to my motel I couldn't sleep. Mexico was the country I had come so far to discover. Nothing was going to make me turn around. I found that I was quite determined, or perhaps stubborn, but part of me was also very afraid. After some debating inside my own head, I finally passed out in the wee hours of the morning. When I woke up again, my concerns were of a totally different nature; more rain was on the way and my rear tire was flat again. Once more I had to start my day by patching a tire in the comfort of a motel room.

That day would have been my last in Texas, but the weather was lousy, so I decided to search for a couch surfer in Brownsville, which was only a short ride away. At one point the rain actually got so heavy, that I had considered staying in Robertsville, but there was nothing to do in the motel. Getting rained on seemed like a better option than just waiting. Once on the road, my ride was pretty steady. The rain was tolerable and always seemed to taper off. I made it to the outskirts of Brownsville when I noticed that my rear tire was flat once again.

I finally arrived at what had to be Simon's house pushing my bike. Simon was my couch surfing host in Brownsville. "Don't ring the doorbell!" he had told me over the Internet, so I knocked. After a few minutes a clean-cut man who appeared to be in his mid 30's opened the door. "Hey dude, you made it!" he greeted me. "Come bring your stuff in and then we'll put the bike in my garage!" I started taking off my panniers and he took them into the house. Next I was presented a list of rules for his couch surfing guests. It took up an entire page. Things like "always make sure the door is locked and the security chain is in place" were on it, even some rules about the lights in the hallway. I was not exactly impressed and had to wonder, but with the rain still coming down and a flat tire on my bike I could not afford to be picky. The uneasy feeling went away after talking to Simon a bit more. He turned out to be a really nice person and a retired soldier who had served in Iraq. Some of his behaviors seemed odd for a person his age. Perhaps his habit of secretly smoking marihuana on his patio quite regularly might explain some of his paranoia, especially since he was living in a kind of upscale neighborhood. I liked Simon as a person and wasn't going to judge a guy who had been through several tours of combat.

When I told Simon about my flat tire, he replied: "I have to go to the bike store tomorrow anyway, my tandem bike has a problem with the bottom bracket". It turned out he had three bicycles and loved riding them. Later in the day, when the rain had finally subsided, we took a ride through his neighborhood together. Simon let me try out his cruiser bike, which felt very different from my own.

Due to the amount of water on the roads and my flat tire, I ended up staying an extra night with Simon and also got to meet his son and his girlfriend. We went all over town for shopping. Besides a couple of spare tubes I also picked up a map of Mexico and some iodine tablets for water purification. Simon told me all he knew about Mexico. It wasn't nearly as scary as the two guys I had met the other night had led me to believe, but contaminated drinking water and corrupt police were keeping him north of the border as well, at least most of the time.

Chapter 15

Hospitality Exchanges

So much more than a place to crash

I already mentioned Couchsurfing, or CS, as a great way to find places to stay for a night or two. However, there is a lot more to CS. The website is set up in a way that allows you to find out a lot about your hosts and/or guests, before you ever meet them. My host in New Orleans, I called him Chuck, was a perfect example. Not only did he trust me with the keys to his house before we had ever met, but he also enjoyed hosting travelers from all over the world on a regular base. For him, CS was a way of life. Maria from Panama City, Kelly from Beaumont, Phil from Houma, Carol from Houston and finally Simon from Brownsville, were all actual people (their names have been changed) whom I had only met online, either through Couchsurfing or Warm Showers. All of them were extremely friendly and helpful. They hosted me at their home like a family member. After crossing the Mexican border it was a bit harder to find couch surfers along my route, as most were located in big cities that were quite far apart. However, I had a fantastic experience with couch surfers from all over the world during the Carnival of Veracruz, which I will tell you about in a later chapter. The point here is, hospitality exchange websites are a great way to enhance your travel experience, no matter what your mode of transportation may be. Most often a visit will lead to lasting friendship, but of course, any exchange is a two way street. The trade off is that you too are expected to host somebody at your home, or help in other ways, when the opportunity arises and you are not traveling. In case of Couchsurfing the rules are pretty relaxed. There is never any pressure to host people, especially not on short notice. Many cities have their own local groups and monthly meetings where it is easy for travelers and locals to meet and form friendships. If your home is not suitable to have somebody stay over, you can participate by showing a traveler around town or taking them out for coffee or a meal.

After completing my first bike trip it was my turn to give something back to Couchsurfing. I joined the local group in Edmonton and made the recliner chair in my bachelor's suite available as a "couch". Before long I met a lot of awesome people and even got to host someone I'll call Tony, who was on a bike tour from Alaska to Argentina.

Tony's stay at my place was not without problems. When he arrived at my place on a Thursday evening, his plan was to spend one night and move on to Red Deer, almost 100 miles to the south the next day. Since I was living in a very secure apartment and had few valuable possessions lying around, I told Tony he could sleep in as long as he wanted, even after I had to leave for work, as long as he would just shut the door behind him. It was a rainy Friday morning and I got up at the usual time, trying not to make too much noise. When I went outside to leave for work on my bike, I noticed that Tony's bike was no longer where he had locked it up the night before. In its place was a very old bike in poor condition. The cable lock Tony had used was on the floor; it had obviously been cut. I went back inside and woke up my guest. "Hey Tony, where is your bike?" is how it first came out. Knowing the bike had been stolen I still couldn't accept 100% that Tony was stuck in Edmonton without his ride. Out of all the places in the world, it was from behind my apartment building, in what I considered to be a secure neighborhood that my friend's first class touring bike had disappeared. I felt terrible, but had to leave for work, just telling Tony it was all right to use my computer and Internet and that I would do whatever I could to help out, as soon as I got back from work.

We never managed to recover the stolen bicycle, but through Tony's contacts with a news reporter in his hometown, Phoenix, Arizona, and my contact to a local couch surfing friend who also happened to be a news reporter, we were able to get the story out all over Edmonton, through TV and newspaper reports. Within days, United Cycle, a local bicycle retailer took the opportunity to contribute in a big way to Tony's adventure and donated a brand new touring bike. In the meantime Tony got to meet a number of other couch surfers from all over the world and ended up having a very memorable time in Edmonton. Before he continued his journey southward on the new bike, he appeared once again on the local television news reports. His story, as well as his easy-going way of coping, had made him somewhat of a local celebrity.

About a year and a half later Tony reached his goal, Ushaia, Patagonia, Argentina. At that point he had burned through his entire travel budget. He couldn't even come up with the money it would take to return to his home in Phoenix, Arizona. Eventually Tony found work at a hostel, which allowed him to save up for his plane ticket. Once again the Edmonton news channels ran a follow up on his story. I was able to follow Tony's adventures on the Internet the whole time, because of the connection we had made, even while I was unable to be out there travelling. At the time I had hosted Tony, my place had been only a bachelor's suite. The couch had been nothing more than a recliner chair, but none of those were big issues.

I would also like to mention that since my profile has been on CS, I had couch requests that I turned down all together. Sometimes people don't give proper notice, or their visit just doesn't fit into my schedule. With couch surfing or warm showers, you are never obliged to accommodate someone just because they happen to claim that their request is urgent. You can also turn people down for bad references, lack of references or any reason at all. If you do your homework by checking out people's profiles before taking them into your home, and you are not afraid to be somewhat selective, you're almost sure to have good experiences with hospitality exchanges, even as a host. Websites like Couchsurfing are a great idea. If used correctly they contribute to making the world a better place and give you the opportunity to make friends in many different locations. For your bike tour, no matter what the budget, they are sure to enhance the experience a great deal.

Chapter 16

Mexico

Cycling in a different world

It was a sunny morning in Brownsville, Texas, December 1st, 2009. It had taken me a whole month to reach the Mexican border, but here I was, still without a plan where in Mexico to go and what to do, besides exploring the country. Simon, my host in Brownsville accompanied me to the border. "Good luck dude!" he said once we got there. I thanked him and we said our good byes. I waited a few minutes while he turned around to go home. Finally I was ready to take the big step into the unknown. All kinds of questions raced through my head. Was it safe to cycle in Mexico? Was my Spanish sufficient? Was I going to be a prime target for muggings? I had come so far without changing my mind about where I wanted to travel. There was no way I'd give in to fear now. There are no guarantees in life no matter where you go. Mexico couldn't be that much different.

The border crossing from Brownsville into Matamoros, Tamaulipas was not very busy. It felt awkward to cross the bridge across the Rio Grande. Of course there was no designated lane for bicycles, so I ended up taking the same lane as the car traffic. It sure reminded me of my illegal bridge crossing to exit New Orleans. "Bienvenido a Mexico" a big green sign announced overhead. A guard at the booth pointed me in the direction of "la migra", the immigration office. I had to present my passport, fill out a lengthy form and, of course, pay money. Since I had very little American money left and absolutely no Pesos, I decided to pay with my credit card. Stories about corrupt border guards I had read on travel sites, briefly came to mind, but the guys who were serving me seemed professional, which put me at ease until I got called back for a second transaction on my card. I asked, in the best Spanish I could muster, what it was about. "Sir, we made a mistake, charged you too much." was the answer. Minutes later I was back outside with a tourist visa that was valid for the next six months, ample time to explore Mexico to my heart's content.

People outside had noticed my loaded bike. Some had already taken interest before I realized it. When I discovered a foreign money exchange wicket, I decided to convert my last American twenty-dollar bill into pesos. While I was leaning my bike against a nearby fence, a skinny older man in filthy clothes, armed with a rag, started wiping my rims. Obviously, he wasn't doing it just to welcome me to Mexico, but because he was hoping to get paid. By getting to work quickly, he made it almost impossible for me to turn down his services without getting aggressive. A dollar-bill solved that problem quite nicely and efficiently. I told him it was all I could afford. After changing my twenty, all I had left was one American dollar, which also wasn't going to last long.

The entire border zone was creepy. There were numerous desperate people hanging out like hungry birds outside a fast food restaurant. They were obviously hoping to make a dollar or a few pesos. I felt like a prime target because I had just come from the US, so there obviously had to be some money in my pockets. I hopped on the bike and started pedaling away, when I noticed a building with a sign "Buro de Tourismo" above the door. A uniformed man spotted me right away and was trying to get my attention. "Sir, can I help you? I'm a tourist information officer!" he proclaimed. "Yes" I replied, "do you have a map?" The answer was no, so I thanked him in Spanish and was about to move on. "Hey no problem", the man tried to hold me back.

"See over there, that's my car! I will lead the way and you follow!" I looked at the man and declined the offer. He was persistent: "Come on, you can see that I have a uniform and a badge, so you can trust me!" This raised a red flag in my mind and I declined again. Finally he got straight to the point: "Come on, you're a rich man. You can at least give me a couple of bucks!" Nothing surprised me at this point and out came my last dollar, just to get rid of my new friend.

  I climbed back on my bike and started pedaling into Matamoros, a completely foreign city to me. The key was to find a main road that would lead me out of town, direction south. I had to find highway 101 and then follow it for about 100 km, to San Fernando, a small town that would most certainly have a cheap hotel. First however, I had to find a place to eat. I was not picky. Once I had discovered the main highway, all kinds of businesses appeared alongside of it. Ironically, when I saw a Burger King restaurant I decided to go for it. It was the most familiar place in an environment that was foreign to me.

  The restaurant was busy. Now I had to find some kind of pole or railing to lean my bike up against and lock it. In the US or Canada I would have been content to have the bike within viewing distance, but this was Mexico. I was nervous and wanted to be extra careful. The weight of my luggage would have made the bike an awkward target to run off with, but I didn't quite trust the environment yet. It was just a little extra effort to lock the bike to a railing outside the restaurant window.

  The food was slightly cheaper than at Burger King in the US, but my meal ended up costing me more because of my big appetite. The familiarity of the restaurant and the variety of its patrons put me at ease. Soon the new reality started sinking in; I had actually made it to Mexico!

  The rest of the day would have been quite boring, if this hadn't been the first in a different country. The highway was long and straight and looked very similar to the roads in Texas. The terrain was completely flat. I eventually reached an intersection with some businesses, including a major gas station, convenience store and a motel. My original plan had been to reach San

Fernando, but only because I had assumed that there probably wasn't any safe place to sleep between Matamoros and there. I was tired enough to call it a day and checked into the motel. The place was modern and well equipped. It even had card keys for all the rooms. However, there were differences compared to motels in the US or Canada. The most notable were steel doors all around and iron bars covering the windows. The room had no carpet, but shiny marble tiles on the floor. It was sparingly decorated and the bed had an iron frame. Armed guards were walking around just outside the gate to the motel yard, which failed to make me feel secure.

After putting the bike into my room, I decided to scope out the immediate area while there was still daylight. Several food vendors had set up shop along the road, across from the hotel. They waved at me as soon as I stepped outside the gate, so I decided to take one up on the invitation and walked over. The place was set up with only the bare essentials; a table, some plastic chairs and a huge charcoal barbecue. All of it was under a tarp that was held up on a make shift timber frame. Using my basic Spanish, I managed to find out that they had a choice between chicken and beef, along with rice, beans and tortillas. It was their daily special, "comida del dia", which also included a cold drink. I decided on the chicken. The meal tasted great and was more than enough for my appetite. When I went through the entire stack of tortillas before finishing the rest of the food, the lady who seemed to run the place by herself brought more. When I eventually left the stand, I was so full that I could barely walk. The whole meal cost the equivalent of about three dollars.

Darkness was moving in quickly now. However, this was my first night in Mexico. My curiosity was going haywire, so I decided to walk around and explore the area. A bright and modern looking Pemex gas station was just across the street, not even 100 meters from my motel. I walked along the narrow shoulder of the highway, past a very old looking shed. In front was a hand painted sign: "llantas 24 horas". The door was wide open. When I took a peek inside I noticed that it contained nothing more than a bed. A man was asleep on it, snoring. Next to the shed were two guys changing a tire on a shiny SUV. Besides the impact wrench and a compressor, all they had were hand tools. The apparent owner of the vehicle, a well-dressed man, was standing around smoking a cigarette.

I finally reached the gas station, which incorporated a well-organized convenience store that also carried beer. I bought a large can of Tecate, some cookies and tortilla chips for a bedtime snack and returned to the motel to spend the rest of the night watching Mexican TV in my room, until I fell asleep.

I began the next morning without really knowing how far I would go, but the idea was to leave the border zone far behind and do so without having to ride in the dark at the end of the day. On my Mexico map it didn't look like there were a lot of populated places within my reach, besides San Fernando, which was less than an hour away. When I reached the outskirts of the town I had the choice between bypassing it on the highway, or going right through. Since I was low on cash and needed an ATM, I chose the latter. On the way through the streets I noticed a late model pickup truck pull over just ahead of me. As I caught up to it, the driver lowered his window and addressed me in English.

"You need some kind of mirror on your bike!" he warned me, "the roads here are narrow and full of heavy trucks." He seemed a bit concerned about seeing me travel this part of Mexico by bicycle, but told me that other cyclists were coming through, once in a while.

"I think you people are crazy, but it is kind of interesting too." He smiled and went on to warn me about traveling further south. "Guatemala is terrible, people won't leave you alone because they think you're rich!"

I managed to steer the conversation towards my more immediate needs and found out that there were three ATMs in town. "Effectivo", which is Spanish for cash, was the only way to pay at local restaurants, food stands and many hotels. I had to get at least a few days worth of Mexican currency. To my surprise the ATM worked the same way as the ones in the US, except the instructions on the screen were in Spanish and out came Pesos. I still had to get used to that currency. The 2,000 Pesos I took out were not even worth $ 200, but I was hopeful they might last a while.

The rest of the day went by pretty fast. I was truly thrilled about being in Mexico, but the ride was uneventful. Traffic was light, except for large trucks that were passing quite frequently. Due to the narrow shoulder they came much closer than I was used to. Around mid afternoon I finally reached a large highway travel center, with gas station, store and restaurant. I decided to check it all out, but first I had to figure out where would be a good place to sleep that night. As it turned out there was a small hotel about half a mile down the road, visible from the rest stop. It seemed like a good idea to go to there first and secure a room, so that was what I did.

The place was much smaller than the first one I had stayed at. There was only an unpaved yard for parking. The building looked old, but recently painted. All the rooms seemed to have names instead of numbers and there even was a laundry room. One door that had "officina" written above the door, so I knocked and opened it carefully. My jaw almost dropped to the floor when I saw a young woman, dressed only in underwear, sitting on a bed, brushing her hair. To complete the picture, a couple of toddlers were crawling around on the floor, playing. I just about shut the door, thinking it was the wrong one, when the woman smiled and reassured me that this was actually the office. After asking in the best Spanish I could muster, I was offered a room for 200 pesos a night. "Five minutes!" she told me in awkward English. Shortly after, I handed over the 200 pesos and asked her for the key, a request that obviously caught her off guard. She regained her composure quickly however and said "five minutes" again, disappearing to the back of the room, with a smile on her face. She came back shortly after and handed me a tiny brass key. There was no doubt in my mind that it would be the right one for my room, even though it lacked any kind of tag. Little by little I brought my panniers and the bike into the room. Once that was done, I locked the door by pushing the button on the inside doorknob and walked back to the highway service area.

The restaurant was fairly busy, but I had no problem finding a table. Here too, the food was basic and inexpensive. I ordered a plate with 3 enchiladas, rice, vegetables and beans, all for next to nothing. When looking around the restaurant I noticed a middle-aged couple at a nearby table, speaking French in a Quebec accent. They had noticed me too. "Where are you from?" the man asked me. I told him I was from Ontario and that I had also lived in Quebec for a number of years. We continued the conversation in French. After the meal the couple, I will call them Jaques and Celine, invited me to their van. We had some wine and a lively exchange of travel stories. I found out a lot about the road ahead and a few things about the Mexican mentality. It was already dark when we said our good buys and I started my walk back to the hotel.

The yard was barely lit, but I had no problem finding the door to my room. Opening it was a different matter. The key I had in my pocket didn't even fit the lock. I briefly recalled the moment when I had asked the receptionist for a key. The expression she had had on her face was all the explanation I needed. It all made sense now and I wasn't surprised at all. First I tried my luck knocking on the "officina" door, but it was locked now. The young lady had found a key for me, knowing that her shift was about to end, but it sure wasn't the key I needed to get into my room. Now I was standing outside in the dark, wondering what to do next.

Breaking into my own room was not an option, nor was sleeping outside, so I looked around the property to see if I could locate anyone. Next to the hotel was a bar with a patio. A light was on. As I came closer, I saw five men sitting at a table, playing cards. One of them noticed me and told the others. They interrupted the game and all five of them wound up staring at me.

"Hola, tengo un prroblema" I started explaining my situation. My Spanish wasn't fluent, but I knew just enough to explain my dilemma. "Llave no functionne", I stated. They started talking to each other in Spanish, then one of them turned toward me and said: "No problem, amigo!"

Next, three strangers escorted me back to my room. They were armed with knifes to help me do what I had hoped could be avoided; break into the room. So much for being careful at night in unfamiliar surroundings! After each of the men had several turns at trying out their burglary skills I definitely knew that neither of them had ever broken into any place before, which was probably a good thing, except that it didn't help my situation at the moment. I just stood there hoping my helpers would eventually get fed up and make room for me to try opening the door myself, or perhaps somebody would show up with the right key. Just when I thought this was going to turn into a very long night, I heard a click and the door opened.

"Wow, gracias" was all I could say. The guy who had opened my door turned around and smiled proudly. "No hay problema" he said. All three of them, who appeared to be brothers, now took turns to shake my hand. "Donde esta la llave correcta?" I couldn't resist asking. The guy who had opened my door started laughing and said something I didn't understand, before he turned around and walked back towards the bar. The other two stayed behind and asked me about who had given me the key that didn't work. I told them about the young lady in the office, and my suspicion that she given me a key she probably knew wasn't going to work. They both giggled for a moment, but then the older one got serious and told me that a new girl had worked the afternoon shift, but had now gone home. They explained that nobody knew where the key was. Why did I need one? I could just lock the door from the inside, right? I was way beyond tired and didn't care to question the simple suggestion. My bed was waiting and there was even a TV in the room to help me unwind before falling asleep. It only took me a few minutes to shower and get ready for bed. The ancient TV was a just decoration; it didn't work. I was tired, so it didn't really matter.

The weather had changed over night. It was a windy morning with slight drizzle and the temperature couldn't have been much over ten degrees. All my stuff was ready to go, and loaded onto the bike when I noticed a girl cleaning the room next to mine. I approached her and showed her the key, indicating I was leaving while also trying to express that it was the wrong key. She didn't seem concerned, but told me to leave the key in the room.

A few minutes later I was back on my bike, bundled up for the colder weather. My destination for the day was a town called Soto la Marina. It was not that far away, but I was in unfamiliar territory and the road was no longer perfectly flat. The wind was on my side this morning however and I wound up having a fantastic ride. I was in Soto la Marina less than three hours later.

For the first time I had the chance to finish my cycling early and truly explore a small Mexican town. The first thing on the agenda was to find a place to spend the night. On the main street was a fairly large hotel that looked old, but had a pool and cable TV. I wondered if it was too expensive for my budget, but a room without air conditioning was just 180 pesos. Quite contrary to what I now expected, the staff at this place was professional and friendly. The room was basic, but everything looked well maintained and worked perfectly. After a shower and a conversation with the clerk, who had taken interest in my bike tour, I was on my way to check out the town and grab a bite to eat, armed with a list of recommendations. It took me quite a while to pick a place to have dinner, simply because there was so much to see. Eventually I ended up at a sidewalk food-stand, run by two friendly women, presumably mother and daughter. They had two choices of "comida del dia": Beef or chicken, served with rice, beans, vegetables and tortillas. There were tree kinds of sauces: Red hot, green hot and red mild. The meal came with a flavored drink they called "agua naranja" which means orange water. It was much like Cool Aid. The meal was excellent and once again very inexpensive. I was happy and relaxed. Mexico was finally treating me well, or was I just getting used to it?

Even after the meal I couldn't help walking around to explore Soto la Marina. After dark I went into a store, bought a bag of tortilla chips and two cans of beer. Then it was time to head back to my room and enjoy some Mexican TV, a great way to practice listening to Spanish.

Chapter 17

Dangerous Places

There is a Devil

When I first crossed the border into Mexico I had no idea what to expect. Deep inside I knew that it could not possibly be as dangerous as the news and travel advisories were making it out to be, but much of my information came from these sources, as well as from people influenced by them. As a result I was scared of crossing the border. Once on the Mexican side I was paranoid for about a day. My first interactions with people in Matamoros even seemed to confirm this was justified because they were with people who had targeted me specifically to beg for money. Who hasn't heard horror stories of people getting robbed in foreign countries? Of course, those things were on my mind that day in Matamoros. I did not go sightseeing in the border-city. As a matter of fact I left it as quickly as I could. Word had it that it would be much safer a few hundred kilometers south, so south I went.

The truth is that even Matamoros is not much different from any city in almost any country. Wherever a lot of people are living in the same area, there are bound to be places where crime is concentrated. As foreigners we typically don't know where these are. Further, the border between two countries with very different standards of living is bound to attract some opportunists. In the case of the US/Mexico border, pretty much any foreigner crossing into Mexico is seen as potentially rich. Some will use any opportunity to approach them in the hope of squeezing out a buck or two. However, the real question is how dangerous those people really are. Even today I choose not to trust anyone who approaches me for the sole purpose of begging. This is not prejudice, but a good insurance policy. It is one thing to be polite and perhaps hand out a dollar or two, but following somebody to an unfamiliar place or letting them control any part of your agenda at all is quite another. A red flag goes up whenever someone calls me friend ten seconds after having met, because this is a distortion of matters, intended to gain trust in a hurry. Trust is always earned, no matter where you are in the world. You probably know places in, or near your hometown, where desperate people will use the exact same strategies. Those people are harmless when confronted in a polite, but firm and confident manner; they will simply move on to an easier target. On the contrary, give in to their rhetoric and they will cling to you; the more you give the more they want. The potential for violence exists and can escalate when disappointment sets in. The best policy is not to set the stage for such disappointment in the first place.

When people talk about the danger of becoming a crime victim in a foreign country, such as Mexico, they seldom refer to the poor people in the streets however. There seems to be a much deeper fear about being targeted by more sophisticated criminals. Professional kidnappers, gang members and robbers with weapons are some examples. The bad news is that all of those exist and their numbers vary according to factors such as poverty levels and government corruption, to name just a few. The good news is that as a traveling cyclist your odds of getting caught up with them are next to nil. Kidnappers are opportunists to some extent, but unless you are a worthy target (meaning rich), and they had some time to find out about your vulnerabilities, they're not going to pick on you. Kidnappings are planned some time in advance and involve several people at considerable expense to make them potentially successful. A cycling tourist who has fifty pounds of dirty laundry, a camera and an old laptop on his bike simply doesn't warrant those efforts.

Kidnappers just wouldn't bother with you. The same is also true for gangs, whose members are usually busy with their own, more profitable dealings. Unless you are extremely unlucky, like getting caught in the crossfire at the wrong place and wrong time you will not be plagued by gangs. You can minimize the chance of this sort of encounter even further by informing yourself locally about the area you're about to visit. This means talking to local people who seem trustworthy. Ask the waitress at the restaurant or the clerk at your hotel! Wherever you go in the world, the majority of people are not criminals and will gladly help out a foreigner.

There is one kind of criminal they might warn you about and rightly so. Robberies are quite common wherever poverty is a reality. With the help of locals you can find out where the risk is greatest, but it is always a good policy to use caution after dark. I would not recommend cycling at night and nor would I say it is safe to walk around a foreign city in the dark, unless it is in well-lit areas with a lot of pedestrian traffic. If you do get robbed, don't panic! Those criminals are not out to kill you; this would be way too much trouble! They are after your possessions; your money, your passport, the watch you are wearing, your camera and the list goes on. It is better to loose any of those than getting beaten up or killed.

It took me a few days to realize what the true danger of cycling in a foreign country, like Mexico, really was. While crime is stealing all the headlines and seems to get the most attention by far, the greatest threat to cyclists is of a very different nature. It is simply about road conditions and traffic. I already mentioned how dangerous cycling can be on roads that are designed primarily for cars. In less developed countries, roads are often neglected, or simply built to a different standard. Too often there are no shoulders. Potholes are a fact of life. Traffic is increasing all the time as cars become more affordable. The automobile is still a status symbol and many drivers have the attitude that nobody should get in their way, especially not somebody on a bicycle. If they do, they probably deserve to get run over. For you, the cyclist, this can mean dangerous situations without warning. To top things off, drinking and driving, vehicles in poor repair and inexperienced drivers are common. Pretty much all convenience stores and restaurants located along the highways sell beer and even hard liquor, and though you might see the occasional warning sign about driving under the influence, enforcement is lacking. I have personally met someone who is regularly driving an old pickup with expired Florida plates near his home in Mexico. His secret is to carry the equivalent of $ 20 cash with him at all times, just in case he needs to bribe a police officer. This is a pretty good example of how Mexican traffic enforcement works. Cops don't get paid well, so they accept tips. A good part of the driving public doesn't have enough money to afford safe vehicles, but have the means to acquire something that still moves quite well. As a cyclist you are sharing the road with any and all of them. You are also among the most vulnerable.

Have I scared you enough yet to change your cycle tour plans? There is more! In many rural and suburban areas people have dogs, many of which are not trained or tied up. I have experienced this many times: dog will run after cyclist and dog doesn't care about or even see traffic. The worst experience I've had on any bike tour so far, was the horrible death of a dog that got run over by a transport truck because it was part of a pack of five, that were all running after my bike. I was on my way towards Merida, Yucatan. While passing a small village with only a couple of houses, I noticed a woman hanging up her laundry outside. All of a sudden I noticed the dogs; all five of them! They were after me and they were fast! The woman, who seemed to be their owner, yelled out but could do nothing to stop them. I tried to ignore the pack as best as I could and carried on, trying to focus on the road. Those dogs were persistent though and kept going after me, barking and snapping. I was scared, but knew that the worst I could have done, would have been to get distracted and loose control of the bike, so I worked hard at maintaining my calm and focus just to keep going straight. It is needless to explain why the risk of getting involved in a crash is off the charts in such situations, but it is quite important not to dwell on that. I knew that after following me for a certain distance the dogs would turn around and go home, but sometimes that distance can be quite long. Those five beasts just wouldn't let up. Finally, after what seemed like an eternity, one of the dogs turned around. One by one the others followed. I was relieved when I noticed that my ordeal was going to be over, or so I thought.

What happened next was at least as bad as getting bitten. I noticed a big truck appear at the horizon, traveling in the opposite direction. The truck was going fast and getting closer. Within a few seconds it passed by me, still moving at a pretty good clip. Suddenly I was reminded of the dogs! Were they still on the road? I turned my head to see where they had gone, still moving forward. That was how I witnessed how the last dog got run over and squished into a bloody mess. The scene was horrific. I will never forget the sound of the truck wheels flattening the body of the dog. Of course I had to stop to calm myself down and digest what had just happened. I saw how the other dogs stopped and returned to the scene. For a moment it looked as if they were trying to rescue their friend. It became apparent quickly that they knew exactly what had happened. It was too late; their companion had died instantly. The truck was long gone. It had not only hit the animal with its front wheel, but had rolled over it again with the dual rear tires, albeit without even of a hint of slowing down. The four other dogs seemed devastated and were letting out the most desperate sounds I have ever heard. It was a very sad scene. Terrible thoughts went through my head. I was shaken! This could have been me getting run over. The experience pretty much spoiled the rest of the day.

Perhaps you think that this was a rare encounter, but you'd be wrong. As a matter of fact, dogs attack cyclists all the time. What I have learned is, that no matter how loud they bark or how much they snap, they don't usually succeeded in actually hunting you down or even landing a bite. As long as you can maintain focus on the road and there are not too many other things happening around you, I'd suggest you just ignore the dogs. Eventually they will be too far away from their territory and then they will let go. Another strategy is to stop, get off the bike and talk to the attackers in a calming way.

After doing this you may have to walk the bike for a kilometer or so. Chances are that they would just keep up their pursuit if you continued riding immediately.

Cycling seems a lot safer, wherever there isn't a lot of traffic, but even in places where the average citizen can't afford a car, traffic is on the increase. You may see small pickup trucks in rough condition passing you, overloaded not with goods, but with people. In agricultural areas you will see bigger trucks on the road that are loaded to the max with bales of hay, corn or sugar cane. To top it off, it is not uncommon to see people riding along with the freight. The emphasis in all that is just getting stuff moved, not safety. Ironically, it seems that freight is often treated much more carefully than passengers. Riding a bike where all this is happening means taking a risk.

Mexico has a lot of toll roads, which are very much like interstate highways, in the US. They feature two lanes in each direction, a wide paved shoulder and are also completely free of ground level intersections. The problem is that officially, they are off limits for cyclists. I previously mentioned that it is often safer to break the law and ride on the shoulder of a toll road anyways.

Ironically I also have a story about almost getting killed using the shoulder of such a divided highway. I was riding on an expressway that was pretty much empty, when a big semi approached from behind. I thought nothing of it because the extra wide shoulder felt very safe. The truck came closer and closer until it eventually passed me. I barely saw the rear bumper, when I suddenly heard a loud explosion and felt pieced of debris hitting my bike, just barely missing me. I was in shock but unhurt. Fragments of what had been a tire a split second earlier were now scattered all over the shoulder. The wave of pressure had felt so intense that it had to have been a small miracle that I hadn't been touched at all. The outside tire on the semi trailer had blown out into pieces, right after it had passed me. Had this happened even just a split second earlier it could have meant the end of my trip, or perhaps my life. The semi continued on as if nothing had happened. It made me wonder if the driver had even noticed the blowout.

I'm the last person who wants to scare people away from bicycle touring, but it is also important that everyone who is considering it, is aware of the inherent dangers. Contrary to popular belief, crime is not the main problem the average cyclist will encounter. Even in less developed countries with a reputation for unstable government and high crime levels, a cycling tourist is hardly a likely target for assault or even robbery. The overwhelming majority of people are well intended no matter how poor they might be. To meet and get to know people from other cultures and different backgrounds is one of the greatest perks of traveling. Fear can get in the way of this, which is why a lot of people won't even consider touring by bike. However, the most prevalent danger is traffic and many cyclists get on the road without any awareness of that (I was one of them). At the present time, awareness is the best defense we have against that reality. Some accidents are not preventable, but the vast majority of them can be avoided by paying attention to your surroundings and acting accordingly. The danger always increases near or in big cities. Patience is essential here. Sometimes pushing the bike through a particularly busy area may be your best option.

There is an upside to traffic in less developed countries. Many people are too poor to buy their own automobile, but use bicycles as a means of transportation. You are never completely alone on the road. It might be a long way off, but perhaps there is even hope for bicycle infrastructure to emerge. I was more than surprised to find a bike lane in a small town in El Salvador. While it was a far cry from being well designed, let alone ideal, it is a step in the right direction. As described in the chapter on sharing the road, ultimately it is because of because of motorized vehicles, that cycling can be unsafe. To build trails exclusively for bikes would be relatively inexpensive, but would solve a huge problem. Cyclists everywhere will have to get organized and start pushing for change. The possibilities are endless for all countries, regardless of how many people may have access to cars.

Chapter 18

Veracruz

The Journey takes a twist

On the east side of Mexico, the first state south of Texas is called Tamaulipas. I experienced culture shock in Tamaulipas, my first real Mexico experience. Besides an initial feeling of insecurity toward locals, there were a number of things radically different from what I was used to. Food choices were fewer. Instead of stocking up on packaged food I was now eating at small, family run eateries, right next to where momma cooked the dinner, usually outdoors under makeshift awnings. Accommodation was getting cheaper every time I looked, but it lacked the luxuries we take for granted in other parts of North America. Then there was a language barrier, which I was determined to overcome by fully immersing myself into situations where I had no choice but to apply what little Spanish I already knew.

By the time I reached the state of Veracruz, the next one down on the eastern coast, I was quite comfortable with the Mexican ways. Despite all the bad publicity I had been influenced by, I now felt very safe and actually enjoyed the simplicity of life here. Hotels without room keys, roadside restaurants that were run by people who couldn't cough up change for the equivalent of ten dollars, roosters waking me up at sunrise; it was all part of a mentality I had begun to fall in love with.

I entered the state of Veracruz via a huge elevated bridge with a great view of Tampico and the shoreline. My general route was Mexico's Highway 180, a road that pretty much spans the eastern side of the country from north to south and around to the Yucatan. On my first day after leaving Cuidad Madero, where I had spent a relaxing extra day that had even included a visit to the beach, I covered around 85 kilometers for the simple reason that there was no place to stop for the night anywhere closer. I eventually reached a place called Ozuluama de Mascareñas, just before dark.

Upon arrival I experienced a real taste of Mexican culture. A religious parade was going through town. Participating were kids of all ages, dressed in colorful costumes and carrying lanterns. It was a beautiful sight to watch. For a short while I felt like I had arrived in a fantasy world that made everything else fade into obscurity. The magic seemed to intensify as the sun disappeared from the horizon. There couldn't have been a place, or moment in time that would equal this atmosphere. The realization that I had stumbled upon it purely by accident almost brought me to tears. As it turned out, the occasion was a celebration for "La Guadeloupe", a uniquely Mexican festival, based on an appearance of the virgin Mary on December 9th in the year 1531 near what is today Mexico City.

I was still facing the task of finding a place to stay in Ozuluama, a picturesque little town. After crisscrossing the downtown core I found two hotels and decided to ask around for rates. The owner of the first one was a real businessman and talked me into staying at his place for what he called a special rate, it came up to the equivalent of about $ 25 and supposedly included hot water. Tired and desperate for my shower, my decision was quick.

The weather outside was on the chilly side, so hot water was important. My rude awakening came when the shower was cold. *This guy had bragged about his hot water and I had paid extra for it!* After braving the ordeal to get rid of the grime and dust that eight hours of riding the bike had left on my skin, I was shivering and probably near hypothermia. Not even my hoodie and sweatpants were helping. I decided to crawl under the covers and watch some Mexican TV to warm up before heading out to grab a bite. Disappointment number two was that the TV was just a piece of decoration. That was enough!

"Donde es el señior?" I asked the girl at the reception after trying to explain to her that my shower had been freezing, the blanket on the bed was too thin to keep me warm and the TV didn't work. I was pissed. The girl did not loose her composure despite my angry complaints. She truly seemed to relate to my pain as she explained, slowly in simplified Spanish, that her boss had gone out and wasn't coming back till morning, while handing me a thick wool blanket with a heart warming smile. I realized that she was doing all she could and suddenly couldn't be angry any more. As my attitude changed she turned even friendlier. The ice between us was broken and we went on conversing in a very slow Spanish. She liked the idea of cycling across Mexico, but thought it was too dangerous. She thought I'd fall in love with Veracruz. She also recommended some local food vendors who would be out till late in the evening. We must have chatted for half an hour or more, just like old friends and I was grateful for every second of it. How many more awesome people would I meet on this trip? The fact that I was touring by myself had actually multiplied my odds of making meaningful connections with complete strangers. Not having a travel destination was turning out to be a huge asset, it meant unlimited possibilities.

Surprisingly, I was not cold any more when I stepped outside. I found a typical small town taco stand, right outside on a sidewalk. The tacos were delicious. Even though it was dark outside now there were lots of people at the town's central park. The Guadeloupe parade had long been wrapped up and, but the atmosphere in this little town retained its magic. I was tempted to explore more of my surroundings, but fatigue was catching up, so I went back to the hotel, cuddled up under the thick blanket and passed out.

The next morning, the owner of the hotel was back behind the reception desk. As soon as he saw me he started playing his role of good hotel host. "Good morning sir, how you like it?" I remembered the shower and the

TV that wasn't working and could not resist mentioning it. "Aaaw", he responded with a grimace that was supposed to convince me that he actually cared. To be fair, the hotel was well cared for, but this guy had bragged about stuff he didn't deliver. I still had to get used to the standard of Mexican budget hotels. By the end of the day this one would seem like the Ritz Carlton to me.

    The weather had improved considerably; it was once again warm and sunny and riding was a pleasure. I didn't eat much along the way, but stopped a few times to make my own sort of taco with tortillas, fresh tomatoes, avocado and refried beans. My diet had changed in Mexico. Many of the food choices available in the US just didn't exist here, but there was still plenty of excellent food available. Most of it was locally grown and lacked the fancy packaging we tend to expect in North American supermarkets.

    It didn't take me long to reach a small town by the name Naranjos. Once again it was time to look for a place to sleep. There was a small, but inviting looking hotel by the side of the road, quite a distance from the center of town. A lady showed me the room that was available. It was tiny, with just a bed, but there was an even smaller private bathroom attached. It seemed fine to crash a night. I was just about ready to settle in and spend the rest of the day relaxing and perhaps take a stroll through the little town, but walked out when the hotel lady told me that there were no room keys. She reacted annoyed, exclaiming: "No hay problema!" Everyone was honest here. I could lock my room from the inside by using the little button on the doorknob, which resembled a typical bathroom privacy lock. Not good enough! What I really wanted was a room I could lock so I'd be able to head out to explore and grab a bite to eat before bed. I was not naive enough to trust the entire town based on a suggestion by a business owner I had just met. After pushing the bike down the road for a few hundred meters I came across another hotel. An elderly man answered the door after I had rung the bell several times. This time, the first thing I asked was if there were room keys. "No problem" was the answer. It sure sounded like a yes and momentarily lifted my spirits. My jaw just about dropped when I was shown a filthy little key that was probably more than a hundred years old and likely hadn't been used for fifty. I asked to see the room anyways. The man led me to a tiny room quite similar in design to the one at the first hotel, but this one looked badly neglected. The bare concrete floor was dusty, and green paint was peeling off the walls. There were spider webs. The bed was sagging and I could not even imagine sleeping in it. I thanked the man who just nodded as if he had expected a rejection all along.

What was I going to do? Feeling somewhat defeated I decided to go for an early supper. Thankfully that was easy to find in this village. As I was enjoying what seemed to be the typical Mexican cuisine, my thoughts drifted back to the challenge of finding a decent hotel. Perhaps there was one a bit further down the road, but a look at my map revealed slim odds for that. Perhaps the first hotel would do for just one night. Who needed a key anyways, just to sleep? My decision was made and about an hour later the lady at that place seemed very pleased to see me return. "No hay problema!" she proclaimed again as she accepted my hundred pesos. It was relatively early, the sun was just setting, but I was tired. After a quick cold shower I crawled under the covers and passed out.

I woke up abruptly. Someone was at my door! I heard knocking, then the knob was being turned and the door opened. I was shocked. Hadn't I locked it? A voice yelled "lo siento!" and the door shut again. Next I heard someone banging on the door next to mine, voices I couldn't understand and shuffling. *So much for no problema!* There was music and laughter coming from outside through the window that was behind my bed. How was I going to fall asleep again? A quick look at my watch revealed that it was only eleven o'clock. I had to make sure the door was locked, before anything else. I got up and threw on some clothes, just to check out the lock. Everything seemed fine. Why had it failed me? Somewhat annoyed, I decided to put it through a test. Sure enough; a gentle turn of the knob wasn't going to release the latch, but a strong grip and a bit of force was doing it every time, no tools needed. The lock was totally useless: cheap to begin with and also worn out. I felt at the mercy of a bunch of intoxicated strangers who were still drinking at the bar next door. To top things off, there were no numbers on any of the doors. All of them looked exactly alike. Who could tell the difference, especially under the influence of Mexican booze? I felt totally lost, but what could I do? Once again I locked the door, hoping for the best, and tried to fall asleep, but to no avail. The door opened two more times before it finally got quiet outside. After a long period of tossing and turning I eventually passed out again.

Despite accumulating fatigue, my next day started relatively early. Around eight the sun was up and I was wide-awake. After last night's adventures I could not get out of the hotel soon enough. A look at my map revealed that I was going to be able to reach a bigger city that night: Tuxpan. I remember very little about the trek from Naranjos to Tuxpan, except that the weather was bright and sunny, which allowed for a good ride. Weariness was building up, but surprisingly it wasn't affecting me physically. Instead I was riding in an almost trance like state. I took a lunch break at some roadside food stand on the outskirts of Cerro Azul, a little town I had passed without paying much attention.

Arriving in the city was quite a change. Suddenly I was challenged to be alert and deal with traffic. I remember a left-turn off the main road that almost had me hit by an oncoming car. Unfamiliar cities are dangerous for cyclists, no matter where. What struck me about Tuxpan was how beautiful the city actually was. It took a bit of asking around to find a hotel, but my Spanish was already improving by leaps and bounds. I had recently learned words like "economico" and "barrato", which helped me find hotels that were right within my budget, instead of getting sent to the Hilton or whatever other luxury hotel might be in town. Locals tended to assume I was a typical American tourist, with pockets full of dollars. My appearance, I thought, was far from that.

I ended up at a cheap hotel. The lady in the office didn't try to promote the more expensive rooms. Later I found out that all rooms were pretty much alike, except that they were undergoing renovations, one at a time and the rate was higher for the newly remodeled rooms. I was handed a towel, bar of soap, a remote control that was held together with tape, and a brass key with a chunky key chain on it. The lady was polite, but seemed very detached and cold. The hotel was a concrete building that resembled a prison more than a hotel. There were steel bars on the windows and even the door to my room was solid steel. I had to drag my bicycle, and then the panniers, two at a time, up as set of stairs. The building was showing its age, but there was rebar sticking out of the roof giving it the appearance of a construction zone that had long been abandoned, leaving it incomplete indefinitely. My room was very plain. There was some writing on the dirty yellow walls. In one corner was a cheap TV, encased in a steel cage. Besides that, everything was plain concrete; the floor, the night table, even the bed was just a block of concrete with a mattress and some bedding on it. There wasn't a piece of actual furniture in the room. I quickly proceeded to the bathroom, which was equally plain, but actually had hot water. After a very pleasant shower I felt rejuvenated and decided to get out of the concrete cell, before it would start to depress me.

The charm of Tuxpan came from the river that was winding through town and old streets that resembled a maze. I enjoyed wandering through the streets and got lost a few times, first when trying to find a place to eat, then again later when trying to return to the hotel from a grocery store. It was dark already, but I was still enjoying my seemingly endless walk around the quiet city streets. Eventually I had enough and opted to walk back to the store, only a few blocks. The manager, whom I had conversed with earlier, would surely be kind enough to give me some directions. Sure enough, he didn't mind and we ended up spending another half hour chatting. As it turned out, there was a turn I had missed twice, from where the hotel wasn't even half a block away. It all sure looked different in the dark, almost a bit spooky. When I walked past the reception, the lady who had checked me in earlier, barely acknowledged me. I stopped half way up the stairs to look across the small yard. It was quiet, except for a tired looking man sitting across the yard, smoking a cigarette and drinking a bottle of Dos Equis. I shut the door behind me and locked it well. Within a few minutes I was asleep.

I was up early again the next morning. The hotel was quiet for Mexican standards, but there were people rushing down the stairs and a cement mixer was chugging along in the yard. Efforts were under way to transform this sad old place. Even with fresh cement and paint, it would be hard to shake off that prison atmosphere. I did not spend a minute more than necessary in my room, so my cycling day started relatively early. Breakfast was "Huevos a la Mexicana" at a sidewalk eatery on the outskirts of town. It came with the usual tortillas, beans and hot salsa and Nescafe, typical for Mexico as ironic as it may seem.

My goal for the day was to reach Poza Rica, another city. The ride was just over 50 kilometers on a smooth highway, which seemed like a breeze that barely tapped into my energy. I arrived in the city just in time to look for a place to have lunch. After what seemed like an endless odyssey into the center of town, I finally found a market that was way too busy to explore while pushing a loaded bike. After spending some time trying to shuffle my way through the crowd, bumping into people constantly, I decided to start looking for a place to spend the night, so I could return later, without my bike. The city had already captured my curiosity and I wanted badly to explore it. With some luck, I'd be able to check into a hotel early, which would then free me up for the afternoon.

Once again, hotels were easy to locate, but many of the places I passed looked too shabby for even my standards. I wasn't looking for a luxury hotel, but in this part of town, all I could find were a bunch of filthy old brothels that were renting rooms for five dollars an hour. They all had a line up of young girls waiting in the lobby, many of whom looked awkward in their lingerie, smoking cigarettes or chewing gum. Most didn't look a day over sixteen. I felt out of place and kept pushing my bike along the sidewalk. A stranger noticed my helpless expression and tried to direct me towards the more expensive hotels on the main drag. I explained to him that I had already passed those, but was looking for a budget option. He volunteered to guide me to a place, which felt pretty safe because the streets were bustling with all kinds of people. After a couple of blocks we arrived at a purple colored building that looked newly renovated. A sign over the door indicated "Hotel". I thanked the man and offered him a tip, but he wasn't interested. Instead he told me that he worked at the store across the street and that he could also hook me up with a real woman if I was interested. I laughed it off, but couldn't deny some temptation.

The room was more expensive than I had hoped, but came with free Wifi and a functioning hot shower. The entire hotel looked exceptionally well kept. After crashing at a string of low budget places that had all failed me in basic ways, it was impossible to pass this one off. At the equivalent of thirty dollars it was still a bargain. Here too, I was handed a towel, a bar of soap and a remote control, free of duct tape this time around. The room was such a treat that I postponed lunch in favor of a prolonged hot shower.

There was still plenty of time left in the afternoon to go for a late lunch at the market and then wander around downtown. I felt more and more comfortable, even in Mexican cities. To my surprise Poza Rica even felt a lot safer than most cities in Canada or the US. People were out in the streets, going about their business and nobody was out to get me. Instead there were signs of a very rich and beautiful culture around almost every corner. Parks appeared meticulously well maintained, the market showed a huge variety of goods and locally grown food, and there were all kinds of food vendors in the streets. I was enjoying an afternoon in paradise.

I felt the need to go back to my hotel shortly after sunset. Once again I had got lost and expected to take a while finding my way back, but this time my sense of orientation was right on. I stopped by the store across the street to pick up a couple of beers and some tortilla chips. Sure enough, the guy who had walked me to the hotel was there and we talked for a while. As it turned out he had only recently started to work at the store. "I used to be a bouncer at a hotel around here", he explained. "I got beat up pretty bad one day by a jealous boyfriend. That hotel is not the same kind you'd spend a whole night in". He smiled and went on about how he still knew most of the girls and that some of them were really nice. Prostitution was apparently perfectly legal here, but the problems that are usually associated with it still seemed to exist anyways. Obviously, my new friend was trying to tempt me, and quite possibly earn a commission. I called him on it and told him that I wasn't interested. He responded with a smile and shrugged.

Minutes later I was alone, sitting in my room, suddenly feeling very lonely. I couldn't stop thinking about girls. Had the conversation with the store guy brought this on? I had not made any real friends in Mexico yet and the temptation to experience a connection, even if purely physical, was getting stronger. It seemed like my dream of constantly being on the move, without a firm destination, was starting to rob me of the best opportunities. Was I running away from everything that truly mattered?

I spent the rest of the evening relaxing in doors, enjoying a functional TV and researching the Internet about various things, including my route to Veracruz, the port city. The next few days were going to be interesting. I was only a few kilometers from a world famous archaeological site: Tajin, a place I absolutely wanted to visit.

The ride to the pyramids was surprisingly quick. For a few pesos the parking lot attendant agreed to watch my bike. There was a ticket booth and a small entry fee, but viewing the ancient pyramids was definitely worth it.

El Tajin had been a big city, hundreds of years before the Europeans ever set foot on American soil. It had long been abandoned by the time of their arrival. For over 500 years it had been hidden in the jungle. Today the pyramids and several other buildings have been restored, and new discoveries of ancient ball courts and other structures continue to be made. They are all even older than the Mayan pyramids in other areas of Mexico. To top off the attractions, a group of acrobats in traditional outfits performed a kind of dance, while hanging from a rotating pole upside down, resembling a unique type of carousel. The spectacle was quite impressive and definitely worth attending. There were many tourists at El Tajin, most of who seemed to be from within Mexico. A Canadian couple stuck out and I got to talk to them a bit. Sheila and

Tom were not typical tourists. Both had jobs in the oil industry off the Gulf of Mexico. They pretty much wrote me off as crazy after they heard that I had arrived in Mexico by bicycle, but it still felt good to have a conversation in English after living completely in Spanish for quite a while now.

The visit of Tajin took up more than half the day and it was time well spent. I even decided to ask at the exit gate if there was a hotel nearby. Sure enough, one of the guards said there was, but the rate was much higher than my budget. His collegue read my mind. "Go to Papantla!" He said. "It's not far at all".

I had already read about Papantla the previous night and knew it was a town, not even five kilometers away. However, getting there was challenging. For the first time since the begining of the trip I encountered a hill too steep to climb with my loaded bicycle. I ended up pushing part of the way, which seemed just as hard. It took a lot of effort to make sure the bike wasn't rolling backwards! Baby-steps turned out to be the trick, but I was soaked in sweat by the time I arrived in town. Papantla was a picturesque little town. There was a big festival going on and I found out that it was all part of "La Guadalupe". The event seemed to have an impact on hotel rates, but thanks to a helpful local man, I was once again successful in finding a very cheap place to crash. It was a far cry from the relative luxury I had enjoyed in Poza Rica.

The room was a good size, but filthy despite the fact that the floor had just been mopped and was still sopping wet. I had to put my panniers on the bed. The place must have been truly pretty at some point. It was so colorful; bright yellow walls and a tile floor that was nothing short of artwork. The bed appeared to be ancient, with a detailed wooden frame and a saggy mattress. Without a doubt, all of it had seen better days. Even the shower looked like a museum piece. My jaw dropped about an inch when I noticed the light-switch hanging loosely from two wires; way too close to the showerhead to be safe. Skipping the shower was not an option, but I cut it short. Those wires were hot and making me very nervous. I had no intention of ending my life here by electrocution. After surviving the scariest shower of my life, there was absolutely no reason to stay inside. Daylight was still bright outside and there was plenty of fresh air, while this room reeked of cleaning products, without actually being clean; it wasn't a comfortable place.

Papantla had a very unique topography. It was made up of two hills that were quite steep, even for walking. Exploring this place felt like an adventure, as the views were truly spectacular. After leaving my hotel, I first discovered the main plaza with its beautiful ancient church. I was hungry, so I went down the main street in search of a place to eat. There were plenty of choices, among them fried chicken and pizza, but I decided on a typical local eatery, serving "comida del dia". Once I had filled my stomach I decided to walk some more. It seemed like only a few turns, but suddenly found myself on another hill in the middle of a residential area, looking at the church from a distance. The sun had set and it was about to get dark. There were a few puffy clouds, reflecting the remaining light in various reddish colors, which made for a stunning view. How lucky I was to experience this evening, right here and now! I was almost ecstatic when I returned to the main plaza, where hundreds of people had gathered for the Guadeloupe celebration. Many were wearing traditional costumes. The church was packed and the service was about to begin.

I spent the better part of the night in and around the plaza, observing the festivities and enjoying the atmosphere. Even though I had no connections here, it was impossible not to feel as part of the crowd. Once again, Mexico had cast its magic upon me. So many people were gathered here, I was grateful to find a bench to sit down on at the edge of the plaza, and do nothing but watch the crowd. In my mind I had become part of the local community, belonging here just as much as anyone else present. But of course I stuck out; I was a tourist! There were no other foreigners around as far as I could tell.

An elderly man suddenly appeared, and sat down beside me. He started talking to me in Spanish. "Americano?" he wanted to know. "No Canadiense!" I replied. He didn't seem to realize that Canada was a country and continued to address me as American. He may have thought Canada was a part of the United States. Next he asked me how I liked the town and continued on how peaceful and quiet it was. "Tranquilo aqui, no hay violencia!" I nodded and confirmed my enjoyment. Instead of leaving it there, the man went on about how violent he thought the United Stated was, talking to fast for me to understand completely, but his gesticulating and his imitation of gun shot sounds left no doubt and made me quite uncomfortable. My five minutes of feeling at home here had come to an abrupt ending. Perhaps it was time for a nap. "Voy a dormir, buenas notches señor." I told the man as I got up. He got up too and we shook hands. "Ven aqui mañana al medio dia!" he said. I understood that much, but had trouble following the rest of his words. Had he just invited me for lunch the next day? As if he had read my mind, he repeated "si, ven aqui!" while nodding intensely. I promised that I was going to consider it and thanked him. On my walk back to the hotel I replayed the conversation in my mind. I did not feel comfortable about the invitation. Nothing this man had said to me had made sense. All his ideas were based on assumptions from a perspective that was foreign to me. Quite obviously, his view of North America was distorted, but the more I thought about it, the more I realized that my own view of Mexico had been far from accurate as well. Perhaps it would have been interesting to meet him again, but I decided against it in the end.

   Upon my return at the hotel, the floor in my room was still damp. For the lack of a TV or anything else to do, I shut off the light and went to bed. I was tired enough, but for some reason could not fall asleep right away. At one point I had almost dozed off, but then there was someone in the room next door. A couple! Suddenly I was wide-awake again while witnessing a special kind of entertainment purely through my ears. They were getting it on! The wall separating us was thin. The squeaky bed, the throaty moaning and laughing, it was all just as clear as if it were happening to me. My mind was racing. What did she look like? Had I seen her in the crowd earlier? I was jealous. I had seen many attractive women in Papantla that night, yet all I had come up with was an encounter with an elderly man who seemed to assume I had escaped the gang violence he had seen in Hollywood movies. Eventually the activity next door subsided. Minutes later I heard the door open, then footsteps down the hallway before it got really quiet.

I left Papantla the next morning. The road led me back to the coast, which meant some amazing descents. A bike loaded with luggage is incredibly fast, going downhill. It was a beautiful day and the beach looked simply irresistible. There was a string of hotels right by the ocean. Originally I had planned to reach the town of Nautla, but now I was reminding myself that my trip had no deadline or destination. The idea was total freedom and I had adapted to it well. Why not go swimming in the ocean? I started looking for a place to park my bike. There were several campgrounds, but some asking around revealed that none of them even had a bathroom. Finally I decided to pull into the yard of a beautiful hotel. Everything looked spacious and well kept. Some people were sitting outside at a patio table. Before I could locate the office, a man identified himself as the manager and asked if I was looking for a room. "Si señor, busco una habitcion" I managed to reply. Even in Mexico hotels right by the ocean come with a surcharge. In this case the price for a room was 500 pesos, not bad, but still outside my budget. I figured that here had to be a more economical alternative along the way, so I thanked the manager and told him my limit was 200 pesos. I was surprised when he asked me how many nights I wanted to stay. It turned out he had a vacant room with a defective air conditioner. I was welcome to it, but would have to vacate it by noon the next day, because the repair was scheduled already. This turned out to be a really sweet deal. Even without air conditioning the room was perfect and definitely worth more than I had paid. It was easily three times the size of the room I had occupied the night before and spotless. Another perk of the hotel was a common room for people to play games and watch TV. However, I used the rest of the afternoon to go swimming and walking on the beach; it was paradise!

When I returned shortly after dark there were several people hanging out in the common room. Two of them turned out to be Canadians who had jobs at off shore oilrigs. Both seemed dumbfounded when I told them about my trip. "Isn't it dangerous to ride a bike here?" the older one wanted to know. "It is, just about as dangerous as riding your bike at home in Canada", I shrugged it off. To both my new friends, this confirmed that I was completely insane. After thoroughly laughing at me, they started to tell each other horror stories about gang violence that was supposed to be rampant "right here" in this coastal area.

"They're using the beaches around here for smuggling drugs at night!" the younger one finally lectured me. I assured him that I wasn't going to walk the beach at night and went on about the families that were enjoying themselves out there, but that I hadn't come across anything suspicious. This only raised eyebrows and made me feel even more out of place. The conversation wasn't going anywhere and I was hungry, so I got up and left.

There was nearby grocery store and I decided to get some tortilla chips and beer. I thought of going back into the common room to rejoin the two Canadians, but it was quite comfortable outside. A mild breeze was blowing from the ocean and the temperature was perfect. I noticed a couple sitting at one of the tables, enjoying wine. Both looked up as I approached and asked about my bicycle tour. "We saw you arrive" the lady said in very good English. The thin white blouse she was wearing over her bikini top was completely unbuttoned, revealing her slim torso. She had my attention and apparently I had hers too. It was reason enough to sit down, especially since her husband didn't seem to mind. We talked for a while and it turned out that both were teachers in a nearby town. They were regulars at the hotel and good friends with the owner. When I told them that the objective of my trip was to learn about Mexico, they had many recommendations. By the time we split I had a list of towns to visit, both their email addresses and an invitation to stay at their place, should I pass through their hometown. I knew that I probably wouldn't be able to visit half of the places on the list, but was blown away by the hospitality and grateful for the conversation that didn't revolve around drug cartels and violence. As a result I slept really well that night. My room had a king size bed and a large TV that I tried watching for a while, but I passed out in the middle of a program.

As planned, I left before noon the next day. After only a few kilometers I reached a police checkpoint. Men in riot gear, armed with machine guns were checking documentation. Others were tending to barriers made from sandbags. The whole scene looked like something from a movie and it reminded me of the conversations I had had with the two men from Canada the night before. Was I too careless on this trip? Those cops appeared to be ready for battle and there had to be a reason. The fear I had put behind me after leaving the border zone behind was suddenly back. What were the odds of getting caught up in something, out here on my bike with no protection around me at all? I had to remind myself that the odds were on my side and that this was probably just a routine check. It turned out to be just that and I didn't even have to show my passport. While I was at the checkpoint, talking to an officer, a minivan pulled up beside me. There were three people inside: A blond lady behind the wheel and a young couple. The window rolled down and the driver yelled: "Hey! How's it going? I'd love to talk to you after we clear the checkpoint!" A few minutes later we were both sent on our ways and I saw the van pull over just ahead of me. The blonde introduced herself as Penny and told me about a turtle rescue station her and her friend were operating. "It's not too far from here, but the road may be a bit rough for a bike. Why don't you take your time and stop by for coffee?"

An invitation that was too good to turn down. I made my way along a rough, but paved coastal road, through a village called El Raudal, and finally down a gravel road until I arrived at a gate. At first I was a bit hesitant; there was no sign on the gate. Had I found the right place? Then I saw the van. A few seconds later, Penny appeared. "Hey cool, you made it!" she said. Now the young couple I had seen with her also came out and introduced themselves as Julio and Lucy. It turned out that Penny and her boyfriend were running the turtle recue station here, while Julio and Lucy were volunteers who worked here for food and a place to sleep. Both were from Uruguay. They spoke

Spanish with a dialect I had a hard time understanding. Penny was originally from Finland. The reason she really wanted to chat with me was that she had done a bicycle tour across China several years earlier. We had indeed a lot to talk about.

I felt right at home with my new friends who gave me a tour of the turtle rescue operation, including a photo op with some baby turtles and a visit to the beach. "We walk the beach, sometimes all day, and look for turtle eggs in order to pick them up and bring them to safety." Penny explained. " This way we can make sure they actually hatch, before a predator can get them."

I liked the idea and wondered if more volunteers were needed. Penny must have sensed that just looking at me. Before I could even ask, she explained that the season had just about ended. "However, you're welcome to stay here for the night if you want!" I simply could not say no.

The evening that followed was one of the most memorable experiences of my tour. Julio, Lucy and I walked back to the village in order to find some fisherman who was willing to sell us a good part of his catch. It was surprisingly easy, so about half an hour later we returned with a huge bag full of fresh fish. The beach near the turtle rescue station was full of driftwood. Penny had explained earlier that part of their job at the station was to keep the beach clear, to provide a safe path to the water for the young turtles once they were old enough to be released. That was why a lot of wood was piled up in one spot already. Driftwood is an excellent fuel and the sand makes a perfect base for it. We made a fire on the beach until there was enough glowing charcoal to barbecue the fish. To go with it we had rice, vegetables and tortillas. It would have made a great meal anywhere, but on a private beach after dark it tasted just so much better. After the meal we shared some wine Penny had brought out and just sat there, chatting and gazing at the stars. Besides our voices the ocean waves and some crackling from the fire were the only sounds to be heard. El Raudal had not even been on my map, but now it felt like I was always meant to be here, perhaps indefinitely.

I would have been content to fall asleep right at the beach, but that wasn't an option. We eventually had to gather our dishes and wash them at the station. After it was all said and done, I got to set up my air mattress in a room that was normally reserved for turtles, but was empty now at the end of the season. The floor was concrete, which didn't really matter to me. It seemed just like camping, minus the tent.

I left El Raudal the next day around the noon hour. Everybody at the turtle rescue station assembled around me and it felt like I was leaving a group of close friends. Even after just one day it was hard to say good-bye. "We might go to Veracruz tomorrow, perhaps we'll see you on the way." Penny said when I left. I liked the idea, so for the next couple of days I kept my eyes open for the grey minivan. I didn't see it again on the way to Veracruz. It took two more days to reach the port city, but they went by quickly. It is hard to beat riding a bike in the sunshine, eating at roadside mom and pop food stands without a worry in the world. Somewhere along the way I even found a hotel with a pool.

When I finally got into the outskirts of Veracruz I was blown away. The suburbs seemed endless, and strangely different from North American cities. At one point I had to cross a huge overpass. I remember stopping for a few minutes to take in the view. Every house had a water tank up on the roof and they all looked identical; there had to be thousands of them! I had been warned many times not to drink, or even brush my teeth with tap water in Mexico, but had become a bit careless in that regard. It seemed overcautious. While I was still drinking only bottled water, it was way too inconvenient to brush my teeth with it. So far I was doing fine, except for some occasional rumbling in my stomach and a very mild case of diarrhea.

I worked my way toward the center of town, all the while keeping my eyes on whatever hotels popped up. One of them was an ugly blue motel that looked like it was in my price range, but it turned out to be more expensive, unless I wanted the room for just an hour. The lady at the reception encouraged me to move on to "el centro", where hotels were abundant in all price ranges.

I eventually found a great place called Hotel Monaco. My tiny room was on the fourth floor. At the reception I was told that there was no space for my bike except in my room. The clerk, an attractive young lady, seemed surprised when I didn't mind hauling my bike up all those stairs. After my shower I went out, exploring the city till dark. I liked Veracruz instantly. This city had character and I decided to stay at least a few days. I had already paid the room for two nights, but there was no way that could be enough to satisfy my curiosity.

After enjoying a good supper in one of many restaurants to choose from, I returned to my room with a bag of corn chips and two cans of beer. There was a TV and Wifi in my room. Why not watch some Spanish language TV to help me get fluent? My stomach was bothering me; it felt like it was simply refusing to digest the meal. Certainly a beer would solve that! I had just a couple of gulps and suddenly realized that I was really sick. What was I thinking? The beer pushed me over the edge. I barely made it to the toilet!

I woke up the next morning with the shivers and a headache that made it almost impossible to move. I was shivering and sweating at the same time. This wasn't good! The TV was still going from the night before and provided an additional incentive to stay put. I stayed in bed like this until early afternoon. It took that long to gather enough energy to get up for a while, and go outside for some fresh air. There had to be something I could eat to nourish my aching body!

It was pretty painful to descend three flights of stairs as my head was pounding like if my brain was slushing around inside my skull. Once on the street I felt better, but I only walked to the nearest convenience store, picked out some plain cookies and a bottle of Pepsi. I was too sick to go for a real walk, so I returned to my room to rest some more, after paying for an additional two days stay.

The next morning I was well enough to explore the city on foot, though in slow motion. I also ate a ton of "safe" food, including oranges and bananas, bread and tortilla chips. It wasn't exactly the greatest diet, but my stomach still didn't feel right. Over the next two days I covered a lot of ground walking around downtown Veracruz and along the boardwalk. The two long piers, where people went fishing with just a line and a hook, using little pieces of fish for bait became my favorite hangouts. Giant Pelicans were always nearby, watching for unattended pails. I witnessed them steal several little fish right out of a man's stash. Further down the boardwalk was the aquarium, a big complex that housed several museums and a mall besides the aquarium itself. The mall was free to explore and interesting enough. Further away from the shore was a downtown shopping district and finally a huge market. It all was new and exciting to me, so I spent hours wandering around, barely satisfying my curiosity about this great city.

On what was supposed to be my last day, I finally felt confident enough to resume my tour the next morning. I was planning to continue on to Alvarado, a town 70 kilometers further south. Nestled between the ocean and a freshwater lake, it promised to be an interesting place. There would also be a small fishing port and, just like Veracruz, the town had a lot of history.

As it turned out however, I wasn't done with Veracruz yet. The city still had a surprise in store. Once again I had walked to the aquarium and enjoyed watching the crowds along the boardwalk. This time I decided to take a different route back to my hotel. Veracruz is very old. Streets don't run parallel or in any particular pattern. It was almost inevitable to get lost, which made it all the more interesting. I was completely disoriented when I saw a big picture window, featuring the Toronto skyline, CN tower and all. I had to check this out! It looked like a store, but there was no looking inside through the picture window. Perhaps the door was unlocked?

I opened the door and stepped inside a large foyer with a reception desk. A young man in a neat uniform greeted me from behind the desk. He saw that I was curious and, without even asking, I got a tour the entire place. Kiosk International was a private language school with ties to a Canadian company by the same name. There were several classrooms that were all named after

Canadian provinces. While it was truly impressive how clean and organized this place looked, it also gave me an idea. Why not play teacher for a while?

I already had a certificate that qualified me to teach English as a second language. A while back I had considered the idea of finding a contract for a couple of years in a foreign country. *Could this be the place? Would this be my opportunity to pick up the idea once more?* I was in conflict. Part of me resented the idea of staying put and just wanted to carry on with my bike tour, but another voice inside my head begged to stay in Veracruz. The city was awesome and after four days of exploring the streets I barely knew any of it. Suddenly it seemed like the perfect challenge to find out if I'd be able to get shot at teaching English at Kiosk International, possibly making me a resident of Veracruz for a while.

"Do you sometimes have openings for teaching positions'" I heard myself ask. The young man who had given me the tour smiled as If he had known it all along. "Yes, sometimes." he answered in perfect English. "We might have some openings here for the new semester. You'd have to come back Monday afternoon, when the coordinator is in."

I walked back to my hotel, as it was getting dark, contemplating my options. What was I to do? Part of me was restless and wanted to move on. But I also really liked Veracruz and the prospect of calling it home for a while. I had no idea, which was stronger. The only decision I could make at the moment was to stop for a good meal somewhere, now that my stomach finally felt better. For the rest of the evening I tried not to think about what I was going to do next. I would just have to sleep over it.

Chapter 19

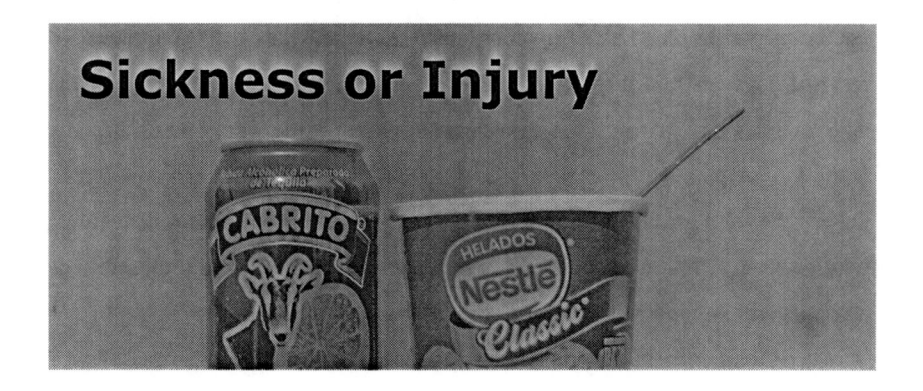

Sickness or Injury

Prevention is key

Bicycle touring for extended periods of time, covering long distances is not for the faint of heart. However, that doesn't mean that only a handful of super healthy elite athletes should do it, quite the contrary! Even those who are somewhat out of shape can go on tour, as long as the trip starts off easy enough to have fun. This leads me to the first and most common kind of discomfort; fatigue related conditions. There will be sore muscles, aching joints and a raw butt. You may even get cranky and irritable if you take on more than you can easily handle, without recuperating properly. How much pain you go through will be a good indicator of your physical condition, which will then allow you to custom-tailor your tour. Cycling is always more enjoyable if you pace yourself. Over time your tolerance level will increase and rides that once seemed to require huge effort will become easier. When I first started to rediscover the bicycle for transportation, a six-kilometer ride to the gym and back seemed like an accomplishment. Shortly after that, I started to use the bike for more and more errands and the distances grew almost daily. There were days when everything seemed to ache, but they were relatively few. Riding was soon too much fun to give up.

151

Once you set out on a tour, spending up to eight hours a day riding your bike, it may seem like there is no bicycle seat in the world that can make you comfortable. The key to overcoming those challenges is to take plenty of rest and never overdo it to the point of resentment. It is always a good idea to take an extra day of rest after an especially excruciating ride. Over time, you body will adapt, even the raw skin on your butt will heal and become tougher. Other aches and pains will diminish and soon you can cover more mileage with relative ease. A few weeks into the trip, what may have seemed impossible on day one, will be the equivalent of a walk in the park to you.

Of course, there will always be good days, and some not so good ones. For example, the wind alone can make all the difference. We tend to set deadlines for almost everything we do, including the completion of a bicycle tour. It is easy to look at a map and figure out how many days it would take for a certain route, just by assuming you can ride x- number of kilometers each day on average. Most of us will plan like that to some extent, because we often don't have a choice. The key to making the most of your time is not to get too ambitious. Remind yourself of why you're touring in the first place! Is it to earn bragging rights about how fast you can cycle, or to have an unforgettable experience? Give yourself plenty of time and don't plan rest days too far in advance. Your body will know when its time to rest, so listen to it! It can be very tempting to pick certain places of interest for rest days. There is nothing wrong with that, as long as you have still enough time to take unplanned days off too, whenever you need them. You can significantly cut your risk of injury and fatigue related illness, just by doing that. Spending too much time on your bike, always trying to ride hard becomes dull pretty soon. It will leave you more vulnerable to injury and can even make you sick.

Along those lines I'd like to go back to one of the criteria for a perfect touring bike. If your bike is not comfortable, the tour will inevitably turn into torture. An uncomfortable seat for example will do more harm than just a sore butt if you ignore it and keep riding. You can literally burn your skin off. Even the most comfortable seat will leave you with a sore butt after long rides, but if your bike is a good fit it will allow you to slightly change positions during the ride so that you're not applying excessive pressure to the same spot all day. I'd like to mention that, after trying out a variety of different saddles, I have found an unpadded leather seat, like a Brooks, to be the best choice for me. While it is not padded at all, it seems to be molded to a good shape and is reasonably comfortable, even when new. Over time the seat will break in, which means the leather will adapt to your individual shape and you will barely feel it at all. If your bike is well fitted, you will be able to ride completely pain free for extended periods, which is essential for the enjoyment of your tour.

A sore butt may be among the most common, however is by far not the most serious problem you may encounter. Riding a bike all day means exposure to the elements. As much as you may like sunshine, your skin is probably not prepared for it. The result can be sunburn so bad, it can land you in the hospital. The best weapon you have against it, as far as I know, is sunscreen. Some cyclists avoid riding around the noon hour, which is a smart strategy if you can stick to it. The sun is usually most intense between eleven am and two pm. So if you get up early, ride till about 11, then take a lunch break till two, you avoid a lot of UV-rays to begin with and cut your risk of skin damage a great deal.

Riding in the rain can pose another problem all together. When your skin is wet your body will loose heat a lot faster than normal. Ad to it the wind, perhaps even from descending some hills at a good speed, and you can end up with hypothermia. I had a little taste of this on the very first night of my bike tour when the temperature in near Gravenhurst, Ontario, dropped to - 7 degrees Celsius after dark. It goes without saying that the right clothes can go a long way in preventing hypothermia.

Even hot climate is not without its unique challenges. Dehydration can sneak up on you without much of a warning. Riding a bike is a very intense activity. You will absolutely sweat and secret gallons of water. Along with water your body will loose important minerals. Neglect replenishing either of those and trouble will catch up with you before you even know what happened. I found electrolyte drinks, Gatorade for example, to be helpful in preventing dehydration. While they may seem the easy way out, they're far from perfect however, as they're usually packed with sugar and artificial color. Of course, as a cyclist you will burn the sugar in no time, but your body needs a lot more than what is in those drinks, which aren't the cheapest and may not always be available.

The key to preventing dehydration is balanced nutrition. Besides drinking a lot of water, you will also have to eat mineral rich foods. In hot countries, the local food is usually sufficient to keep your minerals balanced. If you're sweating all day long, a bit extra salt may not be a bad idea. Go for the soup before your main course once in a while! Bananas and nuts are also rich in minerals and make great snacks.

In some places it can be a challenge to find clean sanitized water. In Mexico for example, the local tap water is generally not suited for drinking. While locals might be unaffected, you could get sick for days, even just from brushing your teeth with it. Thankfully bottled drinking water is available at every store and relatively cheap. It makes sense to carry a few bottles on the bike and buy drinking water by the gallon whenever possible. Many food stands and restaurants will serve a jug of purified ice water along with their meal. Your best policy is to take advantage of it. Water and food are important; we already know that. During any extended bicycle tour you are at risk of suffering some form of food poisoning, along the way. Every time you eat a meal, or have a drink, you put your faith in the hands of the strangers who prepare those things. Most of them do their job properly, but it doesn't take much to contaminate a batch of food and it happens all the time. As a foreigner you may not be able to spot the bad apples. If a meal just doesn't taste right, the better option may be to lose a couple of dollars and leave it on the table. If you are forced to buy from a store that looks poorly attended to, go for the stuff that is unlikely to perish. I have made the mistake of buying ice cream from such stores and paid the price, more than once. How can you tell if ice cream was put in the freezer promptly after the delivery? You will know soon after consuming it, but cycling with diarrhea is no fun and it will quickly dehydrate you much worse than sweating alone.

I am no physician, but as you may have noticed in the previous chapter, I have way of dealing with minor illness that does not involve doctors or medication. I might slap on a skin cream for sunburn and eat vitamin rich food to help my body deal with other problems, but in general I believe in plenty of rest. This means when overcoming a sickness, I will not cycle until my strength is back. Even then I start off easy.

Except for food or water poisoning and some minor scratches from a fall (don't ride in flip flops!), I have been spared major illness or injury during my bike tours. I take precautions to ensure it stays that way, but cycling can be a dangerous activity. A collision with another vehicle can land you in a foreign hospital or, worse, like the morgue. There is always some risk, but don't forget; it is possible to get in trouble anywhere, cycling or not. It might be a good idea to read up on vaccinations that are available to protect against common disease, such as malaria and yellow fever. Some countries even include those in their entry requirements. Consult the Internet for up to date information!

Many diseases are transmitted via insects. Mosquitoes in swampy tropical areas are known to transmit yellow fever, malaria and dengue. I personally have not suffered from any of those, but know that they are all serious enough to seek medical attention, as well as they require you to rest until completely recovered. You don't want to catch any of them, so take precautions against insect bites and the odds are in your favor. Diseases are a fact of life. They can sneak up on you any time. As a cyclist your body is in better shape than most, so you will likely recover quickly. It might be a good idea to have travel medical insurance, or at least a budget that allows you to visit a doctor when needed.

Chapter 20

Decisions

What is it really all about?

Up to my stay in Veracruz I never gave much consideration to the possibility of interrupting my bike tour for an extended period. Even places I truly enjoyed visiting, I generally left after a day or two. They never had quite the same appeal as the open road. I loved the freedom that cycling without a destination seemed to give me. What kept me going was my appetite for adventure and curiosity about locations I had not seen yet. Then something changed. By the time I was ready to leave Veracruz I was having real trouble deciding what my next step should be. All of a sudden I was wondering what I might miss if I left Veracruz too soon. A four-day stay, that probably wouldn't have happened, had it not been for food poisoning, was enough to make me fall for this city.

All those things went through my head while I was pedaling south on Mexico 180, with destination Alvarado for the day. After being sick and off my bike for a few days, the urge to ride the bike had been won out against the temptation to stay in Veracruz, at least for now. In the back of my mind was an idea however. For the first time I was seriously considering to backtrack.

The day was Friday. I could still be back in Veracruz for Monday if I decided to turn around. I had simply put off the decision. First I was going to explore Alvarado!

Even with a view of the ocean for much of the way the ride was almost boring due to the straight road and the lack of hills. I remember stopping at one convenience store along the way, an Oxxo, where I bought some Gatorade and cookies. By late afternoon I was in Alvarado, looking for a hotel. The one I eventually found was an ancient family run business that had probably seen better days. About thirty rooms were accessible via a large yard. The sign in front of the building claimed to have hot water for all of them, but the gas-operated water heater was way too small. When I took my shower, only cold water was coming out. Later, on my way out to explore the town, I noticed the owner trying to ignite the pilot light on the ancient water heater with a burning piece of newspaper.

I enjoyed my evening in Alvarado, a beautiful and relatively quiet place, especially compared to Veracruz. I could walk all over town in about an hour. There was a park by the city hall, almost right next to my hotel. It seemed like this was where things were happening in this town. Not only did entire families and groups of teenagers hang out there, it was also a gathering place for hundreds of birds. The chirping sounds added an unforgettable touch to the atmosphere.

The port was just a short distance away. I noticed a handful of small wooden fishing boats anchored here. The interesting thing about this port is, that it isn't exposed to the ocean, but a freshwater lagoon on the other side of town. Alvarado has a truly unique location on a narrow strip of land, nestled between the ocean and the lagoon, that ads a lot to it's character. There is absolutely no room for expansion either, so the town is made up of very old buildings.

After some wandering around, I found tacos for supper from a street vendor. It was really easy to connect to some locals here. Later, I ended up in a bar, where I had a couple of drinks and a lot of fun with complete strangers.

Just a few weeks earlier, the thought mingling with people in a Mexican bar would have freaked me out. Now I was quite comfortable here, speaking even better Spanish after a few drinks, with only the occasional English word thrown in.

That Friday night turned out to be the best of my time in Alvarado. When I woke up the next morning, rain was pouring hard outside. At times it was so heavy, that the roof of the hotel looked like it had waterfalls running down in a few spots. There was no way I could walk around outside in the streets, not even to buy some food. All I had was a bag of chips, some oranges and an avocado; barely enough to keep me fed for a little while. The TV was old and had a fuzzy picture, but it had several movie channels to keep me entertained.

I still had a decision to make. Being stuck in my room was bringing back all the thoughts of indecision. Perhaps the rain the rain was going to keep me in Alvarado longer than planned! Where was I going next anyways? Part of me wanted to go back to Veracruz by Monday, the other part just wanted to enjoy total freedom and bum around the country or find a deserted beach. It also became quite evident that there was no real conflict. I couldn't help think that there might be some great experiences still in store for me, if I chose to return to Veracruz. I had not made a lot of lasting connections on this trip so far, but living in the city I had barely begun to explore could change that. There was still time to think about it, so I put the decision off once more.

The rain had tapered off, but occasional showers kept me wet despite some periods of picture perfect sunshine. It was Monday morning and I was riding my bike again, fighting a strong headwind. I had finally decided that I was going back to Veracruz. There was plenty of time to get back into town, find a hotel within walking distance of the language school and drop in there late in the afternoon. My mind was made up: I was going to start a new adventure. It would leave me time to get to know Veracruz better. I felt that I had a good shot at gaining some experience as a teacher and meet some new friends. I had never worked as a teacher before, so there was no guarantee this was going to happen, but what did I have to loose? Even a good, honest effort at a short and challenging teaching career, would certainly mean a personal gain.

Later that day I walked through the door at Kiosk International and was greeted by a young lady.

"Who were you talking to the last time you were here?" she wanted to know.

"I'm not even sure what his name was" I responded.

Before she could ask me anything else, the young man who had told me to come back appeared behind her. "Jorge is my name!" he said. "Please sit down, I will tell Lucy that you're here."

I waited patiently for about fifteen minutes or so, when a young lady with glasses showed up in front of me and introduced her self as Lucy.

"I'm the coordinator, Jorge told me about you. Let's go to my office and have a chat!"

I followed her to a tiny office that had a huge bookshelf on one side, packed with language books, dictionaries and other learning materials.

"Tell me about yourself" she started the conversation.

I rattled down my story, starting with the course I had taken to prepare me for teaching English as a second language, months earlier. Then I went on about my bike tour and my first experiences in Mexico, finally ending by telling her how I had discovered the language school by accident.

"I would like to give this a shot. This place looks really well organized and made a huge impression on me last week. Here I am, applying to you for a teaching position!"

Her look was encouraging. "We actually do need a few new teachers. Can you come back on the 4th of January, in the morning?"

There we go again, was my first thought. The date was December 21st, 2009. I had already decided and wasn't about to give up on this teaching opportunity now. There was still no guarantee of employment and perhaps not even a very good chance, but I already knew that nothing was going to keep me from appearing at this place again on the requested date. In the meantime I had two weeks to do whatever I wanted and a head full of ideas.

Chapter 21

Leaving the Coast

Learning about hills

I did not stay in Veracruz the next day. Two weeks was all I had for some inland exploring and I had a rough idea of what I wanted to see. I still had the must see list the friendly Mexican couple at the hotel near Nautla had given me. The next two weeks would give me a chance to check out at least some of them. To start off however, I wanted to ride to Cordova, a town I had heard about on the Spanish language TV.

The trip started off awkward. It had been fairly easy to follow the coast so far, but now I was looking for the best road to Cordova. Could it be the toll highway or should I take the free route?

Still unsure about toll roads, I decided to follow the scenic route, which lead to problems right off the bat. I had not been overly fussy about following a specific route since my arrival in Mexico, but followed a main highway in a general direction. This was why I was unprepared for the poor signage. I was trying to follow a highway now too, looking for signs to confirm my direction, but all the while believing to be on the right path to Cordova. When I finally realized that I was way off track, it was too late to correct the course without loosing almost the entire day, so I decided to adapt my tour and go towards Xalapa first. I would go on a big circle tour and visit Cordova on the way back; problem solved!

Soon it became evident that there was something else I wasn't prepared for. During my entire tour, up to my arrival in Veracruz, I had not climbed a real hill. Sure, there had been a few around Papantla, and yes, I had used my lowest gear and even pushed the bike on a couple of occasions. Now I was finding out what it felt like to climb long hills. Not only did I have to use the lowest gear; it was also taking all the energy right out of me. In order to keep moving at all I had to use a simple little strategy: Never look too far ahead! By looking down on the road, at least I had the illusion of rapid movement. There is one upside to climbing hills though: You gain elevation and eventually you have to come back down. Of course, compared to the long and grueling climb, the pleasure lasts merely a few minutes, but there is no better feeling than to descend a hill with a loaded bicycle! The weight makes you gain speed without effort. Warning: Make sure your brakes are in top working order!

On this first day of my mini tour the descent lead me into a valley and a beautiful little town by the name of Paso de Ovejas. It was still relatively early in the day, but I decided to stop here and enjoy the small town atmosphere along with some good local food. I had no trouble finding a hotel, better and even cheaper than anything available in the city. I then spent the rest of the afternoon doing what I love to do: wandering around, taking photographs and finally eating a huge supper at a busy local restaurant. Later I discovered that my hotel even had wifi. I stayed up late I checked out whatever I could about Xalapa, the capitol of Veracruz, online.

The next day was, once again nothing but a steady climb. I had figured that it would be a relatively quick trek to Xalapa, but my legs got tired early on and the entire day felt much like riding on a stationary bike that was set at the highest level. To top it off it was a hot day, probably amounting to one of the toughest ones of my journey so far. Not only was I constantly climbing, but the road was pretty boring too. Besides struggling up ever longer and steeper hills, I remember stopping at a place where I could take a break while leaning my bike against a guardrail. I had a quick snack and peed in the ditch. The little breather was cut short when I noticed that I had stepped into an anthill and had come under attack by thousands of aggravated little buggers.

When I finally reached Xalapa as darkness was setting in, I was exhausted, hungry and lost. It was not too hard to find a hotel, but the first few that I saw were simply out of my price range, a somewhat familiar problem! I was in the wrong part of town, but after some searching and pushing the bike along sidewalks I finally found what I was looking for: An inexpensive, older hotel. Even though the price was still double what I had paid the night before, I booked two nights. It meant that I was going to stay in Xalapa till Christmas morning.

For two days I did a lot of walking around, just like I had done in every other Mexican city I had visited so far. Contrary to popular North American beliefs, Mexican cities had turned out surprisingly safe and visitor friendly. Besides exploring Xalapa, I did one more pivotal thing: On Christmas Eve I went to an Internet cafe and booked a flight from Cancun to Orlando. Up to this point, my return to Canada had been uncertain. While I did have a return ticket for a flight from Orlando back to Buffalo, on April the 16th, The deciding question had been, if and how I was going to make it back to Orlando by that date. When I found an extremely cheap flight out of Cancun for April the 15th, my problem was solved. My tour had just become a lot more defined. I was eventually going to continue on, all the way around the Gulf of Mexico. It would keep me in the eastern part of Mexico, with some variations here and there, as time would allow. I would have to leave Veracruz about a month before the flight, just to avoid a big rush toward the end that could potentially take the fun out of the experience. I went to bed happy that night. My return to Canada was now secured without having to backtrack all across northern Mexico, but it was also still three and a half months away.

Christmas day started out cloudy, with a lot of moisture in the air. I had decided to continue my trek toward a town by the name Perote. On the map it looked like a relatively short trip, but I still had no real concept of hills. This day was going to change that for good.

The ride started out relatively smoothly, up to Banderilla, which was still a suburb of Xalapa. I passed a couple of hotels that looked perfect for spending a night, but it just wasn't the right place nor the right time, or so I thought. I left the suburb, energized by two days of rest and the prospect of exploring more interesting places. Barely noticeable at first, conditions changed ever so gradually, for the worse. First the clouds thickened and turned into dense fog, then it got colder. I was also still climbing hill after hill, telling myself that a long descent could not be too far off. Of course it was in part the increased elevation that led to the change in climate, but I was inexperienced in that regard. What kept me going steady was the firm belief that I would get rewarded for my hard work with a long descent some time that day. No, I had not checked the map for altitudes, which would have seemed like Chinese to me anyways; how much worse than the ride to Xalapa could this possibly get?

After nearly reaching a state of complete exhaustion, soaked all the way through from the fog, that had evolved into steady drizzle by then, I eventually reached a roadside food stand. The older lady, who was running the place, shook her head when she saw me. Where was I trying to go? She wanted to know. Perote? Well that was going to take me many hours by bike. It was an hour or so by car, but on a bike it would be just brutal. I would have more hills to climb and yes, they were pretty steep. This simply wasn't the day; it was way too wet!

I bought a sandwich, as this was pretty much the only quick item on the menu. While I was sitting down to eat, I was contemplating my next move. Perhaps this really wasn't the best day to try and get to Perote? Maybe I had started too late, or planned too long a ride without considering the altitude. The weather was shitty too, but that was eventually going to change and I'd get another shot. I thought about turning back and how it would mean that I had muscled my way up all those hills, basically for nothing. What was I going to do?

Finally I asked the lady, who was now smiling at me, how much time she thought it would take to get to Perote, riding my bike. She replied that it would take about three hours on a good day, but that today wasn't a good day. I thought about it for a while as I sat shivering. As if she had read my mind she finally said that I could make it back to Banderilla in about twenty minutes. I thought of the hotel I had passed earlier. The idea seemed inviting, not only because I would finally get out of the rain, but also because I would get my long awaited descent down those hills. It had taken me a few hours to get where I was. Going back down would mean that I would have to repeat the brutal climb again if I wanted to stick to my route, but for now I would be able to hammer down into town at breakneck speed. Under the circumstances and after thinking about it for a few moments, this was a no brainer. I turned the bike around and started the descent, looking at my watch just for the fun of it.

Barely fifteen minutes later I was in front of the hotel in Banderilla. Never before had I experienced such speed on a bike. The only thing that had slowed me down a bit was the wet condition of the road. The downside was that I was shivering even more than before, probably from hypothermia. After checking into the hotel I took a shower that lasted exactly as long as the hot water supply. It wasn't enough to warm me up, but it helped enough to get me motivated to leave the room for one last time that day. I walked to a nearby store where I ended up buying some cheap Tequila. If this wasn't going to get me warm and fuzzy, then nothing else would!

When I returned to my room I got comfortable in bed, found a movie channel on TV and got plastered on the nasty liquid that probably wouldn't be approved for consumption anywhere but in Mexico. Finally I passed out for the night.

I woke up late the next morning, feeling drained, partially due to a bad hangover, but also from exhaustion. The weather outside was grey and wet. There was no way I was going up those hills again right away anyhow, so I decided to take a true rest day and stayed in bed, eating whatever I could find in my panniers and watching some more movies.

I didn't even peek outside until later in the afternoon. That's when sunshine was finally back. Hunger had started to bother me, so I decided to go outside and find a good place to eat. Downtown Banderilla I found a promising looking restaurant, after passing several people selling food on the sidewalk. Thinking that I was going to treat myself to something special that day, which was actually Christmas Day, I took a seat in the restaurant. After a long wait it turned out that the food was more expensive than I was used to, but mediocre at best. Perhaps it was best to support small food vendors outside after all!

Since it was nice outside now, I spent the rest of the afternoon wandering around town in slow motion. Much later I had a couple of quesadillas for supper; the kind you get in the street from mom and pop, usually always great and this time was no exception. It was just after dark when I returned to the hotel. My determination to ride to Perote the next day was now stronger than ever. I would have to get up early the next morning and tackle those painful long hills once again, but there was no way around it; I was going to get there!

Morning came and I woke up well rested and early. This time I knew what to expect; this wasn't going to be a picnic, but nothing was going to stop me! The change of attitude made all the difference. Instead of expecting a pleasant descent around every curve, I simply accepted the fact that this was going to be an entire day of climbing steep hills and paced myself accordingly. The key was to move slowly, but steadily. Soon I passed the sandwich place from the other day and it seemed like no big deal, so I kept going. Even when the incline wasn't really that bad, I stayed in the lowest gear and kept looking down on the pavement to fool myself into thinking I was moving pretty fast with minor effort. It worked.

This time the weather didn't let me down neither. I arrived in Perote, a beautiful little town, late in the afternoon. The search for a hotel didn't take long as there was a place right on the main street. What struck me right away about this hotel was the facade that was decorated with hundreds of small tiles, forming a sort of mosaic. The look was unique and it really made me want to see the rest of the place. I rang the bell and after a few minutes a lady answered the door. She appeared to be in her mid forties and was quite attractive, with long her long dark hair and slim build. Her presence left no doubt that she was also the owner of the hotel. Unfortunately she was either too busy to chat or just not interested, but she did help me locate the nearest laundry service.

I did not have any clean clothes left and some of my stuff was still damp from my first attempt to reach this town. Now was the time to deal with it all. Even before supper I gathered all my dirty clothes, stuffed them in a plastic bag and went over to the laundry. As it turned out, it would take an entire day to get it done. The lady who ran the service and a couple of young girls seemed to have their hands full. Perhaps most people in Perote didn't do their own laundry. I was handed a piece of paper with a hand written number on it. This was not exactly what I had hoped for. It would mean I had to stay an extra night in Perote; another day of rest and with it, some time to roam around. I even toyed with the idea of asking the hotel owner out for supper, but changed my mind when she was busy talking on the phone, barely acknowledging me upon my return.

A while later I went out by myself to find a little restaurant that advertised comida corriente and sat down for a meal. I had come to love Mexican food by now and this place was no exception. The meal came with a desert and a drink and it cost only about two dollars; simply amazing! After supper it was still nice outside, so I decided to go for a stroll and explore my surroundings. Perote had a very beautiful central park, municipal building and several churches. There were quite a few people of all ages outside, engaging in various types of activities, but the most noticeable sound came from the many birds in the park. It gave the place such a calming and natural atmosphere. Time went by fast. I barely managed to grab a few fruits and a couple of cans of beer before the local stores closed.

There was a small old TV in a cage on the wall in my room. It sure reminded me of the setup I had seen in Tuxpan. To my surprise, this one worked really well and also had the movie channel.

The weather stayed really nice the next day. It helped me to thoroughly enjoy my extra day in Perote. Despite the relatively small size of the town it definitely had character. The streets were bustling with people all day long and it felt like I was the only tourist in town. I was like a kid in a candy store, taking pictures of everything that caught my attention. Small town Mexico can be incredibly colorful, despite its simplicity. Later in the afternoon I ended up in the town square, right next to the park. It was a great place to sit around with a bag of pastries; pan dulces, from the local bakery. I had discovered those goodies first in Veracruz, but they cost much less here and the calories were just what I needed to keep riding strong.

To my disappointment I never got my laundry that day. I went to check for it twice and was turned away as many times. This wasn't a good sign! Perhaps someone was messing with my stuff? Indeed, it was much later down the road, somewhere else along my route, that I tried finding a certain shirt I knew I had, but wasn't anywhere in my luggage. At this time however, I could not do anything except be patient, when I was told to come back the next morning.

That morning went surprisingly smooth. The weather was still beautiful, I went for breakfast at a local eatery and successfully picked up my laundry right after. By eleven o'clock, I was checked out of the hotel and back on the road.

Not to far from Perote I crossed into the state of Puebla. The terrain looked much different here. Gone were the steep hills and instead I was moving through relatively flat terrain that also looked very dry. The highlight of the day's ride was El Salado, a crystal clear lake that had formed in a volcanic crater. It simply looked amazing. Of course it was a perfect place to take a break and observe a fair number of tourists stopping by to snap pictures. The rest of the day turned into a pretty nice ride on some not so smooth roads. At least I was done climbing mountains for a while! Late in the afternoon I arrived in a place I'll just call El Seco. The full name is actually San Salvador el Seco, another beautiful little town with historic churches, a row of run down hotels, local shops and small manufacturing operations. There was also a little store with an open front, that sold liter bottles of beer and provided plastic cups to enjoy it right on the spot. I made the decision to return later and have some beer, but first I had to find a room. To start off, everything went exactly as planned. I found a nice hotel and got a sweet deal on a room. But then, when unloading my bike, I discovered that the rough road had taken its toll on my equipment. The front rack was broken on the left side, just about ready to break off completely. While it had held up well enough to get me to El Seco without even noticing the defect, it was not likely to survive even another day. This meant I had to find a way to fix it, but I was at a total loss as to how. Perhaps there was a shop in town that was equipped to weld aluminum. Even though that seemed like a bit of a long shot, there was not much else to do, so I took my bike back outside and approached a nearby truck repair shop.

To my surprise the workers did not shy away from the challenge. A lady, who was dressed in coveralls and appeared to be in her forties, dismounted the rack and took the first shot at welding it back together. The problem was that the material was really thin and had broken right where a bolt was meant to hold it to the bike. The woman was an excellent welder. Minutes later the rack looked almost perfect, except that the hole that was meant to hold the bolt was completely obstructed. After an attempt to drill through the brittle aluminum the weld broke again, revealing that it hadn't been all that strong after all. I was half expecting the welder lady to give up and tell me the rack couldn't be salvaged, but I had no idea how much pride the people of El Seco took in their work. Even after numerous attempts and involving pretty much the entire staff at the shop, she did not give up. It took a whole hour to fix the rack. The end result was a repair that didn't exactly look beautiful, but was, without a doubt, way stronger than the original part. When I asked how much it would cost, the lady charged me 100 pesos, which was equivalent to about eight dollars. I was happy and thanked everyone who had helped with the repair. We ended up chatting for a while and I found out a few things about the town of El Seco.

The name El Seco came from an old legend. When Spanish settlers first arrived here, there used to be a huge dried up tree in front of the town entrance, which became a reference point for travelers on their way to or from Veracruz. El Seco has numerous antique churches. I decided to tour the town a bit more the next morning before my departure.

Now it was finally time for a beer. I went to the store across from the hotel and purchased a big bottle. The clerk poured about a quarter of the content into a plastic cup. This wasn't really a bar, but there was already one other client drinking beer from a plastic cup. When his beer ran out we ended up sharing the rest of mine. Before I knew it an attractive woman, who appeared to be in her in her late 20's and was wearing very short cut-off jeans, had joined us. The other guy pulled some change out of his pocket and bought another bottle for all three of us to share. It seemed like he had come to this place simply to unwind after a long day at work. Now things were starting to get interesting, as he was slowly getting drunk and making a fool out of himself, trying to impress the young lady by cracking some dirty jokes. Then the situation got a lot weirder. My new drinking buddies suggested we'd all get a room together where we could drink more beer and, from what I understood, have a threesome. I would have been quite inclined to spend time with the young lady alone, but by now it was evident that she was a prostitute. I wasn't exactly up to sharing, nor paying money for sex, so I declined, telling them I was tired. The guy did a short "come on my friend" song and dance, but soon they both disappeared and I stayed behind shaking my head, while the store clerk, who had followed the entire conversation, was having a good laugh. I really was tired and just went to my hotel to get some rest.

I left El Seco relatively early after enjoying a good breakfast at a little restaurant, just down the street from the hotel, and chatting with an ambitious used car salesman who must have thought I might buy a car. I was unsure how far I'd take it that day, but it was a toss up between Cuidad Serdan and somewhere near Orizaba. I just had to see how the day was going to shape up; at least there were places to stop within reach. Cuidad Serdan looked imposing from the perfectly straight road leading up to it. Some beautiful old buildings were way up on a hill, while other parts of the town were down below. When I finally arrived there, it was time for lunch. I found a little restaurant and sat down for a meal.

Then something out of the ordinary happened. Three men walked in and approached me in an awkward fashion. At first, a feeling of being in trouble came over me. Perhaps they were cops, or criminals who had their eyes set on me? As it turned out, they were a crew working for a local TV-station. Somehow they had spotted my loaded bike in front of the restaurant and seen the potential for a story on the television news that evening, New Years Eve 2009. I agreed to an interview once I was done eating. Of course my Spanish wasn't really fit for a TV interview, but the man in charge said it didn't matter and his crew proceeded with the interview.

"Where had I come from, how many kilometers a day, what was my motivation?" And so on. It was not easy answering those kinds of questions in Spanish, but somehow I managed to pull off a pretty good interview and my insecurity changed into a form of pride. People actually thought my trip was newsworthy! At the end of the interview the leader of the crew passed me a business card and asked if it would be all right to follow me for a few kilometers and shoot some footage of me, cycling. Of course I agreed, but at the same time I was still nervous those guys might turn out to be kidnappers after all. Everything had been so random and their equipment, including the car they were using, was not top of the line stuff like you would expect from a TV station. I asked what station they worked for and man pointed to the card in my hand. Yes, it had to be legit, I told myself.

We left the restaurant and the crew stayed with me for about five kilometers or so, filming me going up some mild hills that somehow seemed much easier to climb, knowing I was on camera. The whole thing gave me a boost for quite a distance.

Then I reached the point where a boost was no longer needed. All I really needed were my brakes, and for the bike to be in top shape. When I had started my little round trip in Veracruz, I had been baffled by how many hills I've had do climb. It had seemed that this was not going to end. However, as mentioned before, the advantage of gaining altitude is that a descent always follows, somewhere, some time later. This one was long overdue!

I was on a smooth toll road with a wide paved shoulder that was leading back toward Veracruz. For lack of a working speedometer I cannot say how fast I was going, except that I was keeping up with the cars nicely. Thankfully there were not too many of them or this would have felt like a suicide mission. It was also impossible to tell how much distance I covered in a minimal time frame, but as soon as the steep descent ended, slowing me down to a disappointing normal bicycle speed, I felt how tired I actually was and decided to take the next exit. It turned out that I had not quite reached Orizaba, the large nearby town on my map, but a charming community called Cuidad Mendoza. After some searching I found a great little hotel in my typical price range; fifteen dollars.

It was a nice place. Access to the rooms was via a good size yard, featuring a pool in the center. Unfortunately the pool was out of service. The staff, all members of the same family, also had some problems with the water supply. In order to have enough water for the showers, they had a little pump puttering away in the yard, pretty much right in front of my door. After the usual routine of checking in and making myself at home, I had a shower and then tried to watch TV for a bit, but fell asleep almost right away.

When I woke up it was dark outside. This was New Years Eve and not even seven o'clock! I felt an urge to get up and check out some festivities, meet some locals and have fun! At that moment it was easier said than done. Not much was going on and I didn't even know where the town center was yet. I took my time exploring my surroundings and was prepared to hop into a bar with local people, or anything that would give me access to a cool way to ring in the New Year. Eventually I found a busy hamburger stand on one of the sidewalks. It reminded me that I was also very hungry.

"Una hamburgesa por favor" I asked the guy when it was my turn. He unwrapped a patty for me and threw it on the grill. "Americano?" he asked. "No" I replied, "Canadiense".

He went on to tell me his name was Miguel and that he had just returned home from working in the US for twelve long years. He and his wife had run a bakery in Seattle. They had saved their earnings and were now building a nice house of their own in their hometown. He had liked living in the US, but life was better here. People were different, less in a hurry and more genuine. We continued the conversation as I was standing there enjoying my burger. He wanted to know what brought me to Cuidad Mendoza. I told him about my bike tour and about the teaching job in Veracruz. His eyes lit up and he promptly invited me to a new years party at his dad's house. "Can you come back around ten?" he asked. As it turned out, that was when he was shutting down the burger stand. Of course I accepted the invitation.

When I returned at ten, Miguel was busy loading up the burger stand onto his little pickup. We then went to his house where I first got to meet his wife and two kids. The house was not quite finished, but it was a large beautiful place that would have fit into an upper-class neighborhood anywhere. Miguel and his extended family had done all the work themselves, which I found truly impressive.

The celebration however was taking place at Miguel's dad's place, which turned out to be just across the street from where the burger stand had been set up earlier. When we arrived I was introduced to the rest of the family who all welcomed me with open arms. They asked me questions about what I thought of Mexico and how I had managed to come so far on a bicycle. We were still chatting as we were setting up plastic tables and chairs in the yard. Everyone was contributing in some way. The women were in the kitchen preparing food.

The meal that followed was a bit of a surprise. There was chicken, a variety of vegetables, black beans and Kraft dinner a la Mexicana! Macaroni and cheese was a welcome change from the typical Mexican diet of rice and beans. I found the combination of Kraft Dinner and black beans to be especially delicious.

After the meal the entire family turned their attention to a colorful piñata, a cardboard replica of Winnie the Pooh that was hung up on a clothesline. Family members would take turns trying to hit it hard with a broomstick while their eyes were covered and after being led around in a circle so they'd loose all orientation. The kids got their shots first, but then everybody in the family, including Grandma and I, got to take a turn at beating Winnie. The idea was to destroy the sculpture and get out the candy that was hidden inside of it. It all seemed easy at first, but turned out to be difficult without vision or orientation. The game went on until the piñata was completely destroyed and there was candy all over the floor, enough for the whole family.

When midnight finally came the adults got to enjoy a couple of shots of tequila, which was the only alcohol at this party. Outside there were fireworks everywhere. Pretty much everybody in the family party was joining the fun by lighting up and throwing something; firecrackers, sparkling sticks and what have you. It was fun. Everybody was having a good time in the family atmosphere. The party ended shortly after twelve thirty. I said goodbye to everyone and a big thank you to Miguel, the guy from the hamburger stand, who was now my friend. We exchanged contact information, but to my surprise he did not have an email address. Looking back, New Years in Cuidad Mendoza was definitely one of the highlights of my tour. I had stumbled into it totally unexpected. Cuidad Mendoza had not even been my original destination for that day, but I had ended up here and found what I had been missing for much of my tour, which was quality-company for an unforgettable evening.

The surprises continued through the next morning, when after getting up and taking yet another cold shower, I walked across the town some more in search of a place to eat breakfast. On one of the narrow sidewalks I literally bumped into a very attractive woman, who didn't seem to mind, and asked me what I was up to. For a few seconds I wondered if she might have an agenda, but when she came across as genuine, we started chatting. "Desayuno?" she asked. I nodded. "Ven conmigo"! We went through a few narrow streets as she led me to the local market, where her family was running a food stand. Within minutes I was introduced to everyone and invited for breakfast. They were all curious about where I was from and what had brought me to their town. When I explained that I was from Canada and had arrived on a bicycle, they had a lot of questions. Once again I didn't mind telling my story, including the part about possibly landing a teaching job in Veracruz. When I offered to pay for the meal for both Veronica, the girl who had invited me and myself, the lady in charge declined. As it turned out, she was Veronica's aunt.

After the breakfast Veronica showed me around town some more. It was New Years Day and she had the day off. It was almost painful when I had to tell her about my plan to leave Cuidad Mendoza that day due to the deadline for my return to Veracruz Looking back on it now, I could have stayed another day without loosing out, but I had no idea what the road ahead had in store for me and wanted to spend an extra day in Cordova. We finally exchanged email addresses, and hugged each other. While we were still basically strangers, it felt more like saying good-bye to a friend. To this day I have not heard from Veronica again.

I hit the road again a little later that day, destination Cordova. It was a relatively short ride, along the same toll road that had led me to Cuidad Mendoza. Cordova was a much bigger city and that meant much more traffic. After getting lost in the outskirts for some time, I eventually found a hotel downtown; not exactly a nice place, but the rate was only around twelve dollars.

Some would find Cordoba ugly and dirty. To me, the city had a lot of charm and I didn't regret having planned for an extra day to explore it. In the evening it became apparent that there were plenty of bars in this town, which all seemed to do pretty good business. That was when all my usual caution went out the window and for the first time since coming to Mexico, I went bar hopping till late at night. It was worth it, even though I remember very little of the people I met and talked to. The change of scenery and the interaction with random strangers for no specific purpose felt great. Even much later, when I walked back toward to my hotel, a little under the influence, the city was still busy. While the stores were closed, some bars seemed to be busy all night and outside was a freak-show made up of food vendors and prostitutes that could have been either male or female. One middle aged black woman acted insulted after I turned her down, telling me that she was an actual woman. She seemed like quite the character, so I offered to buy her a taco in exchange for a few minutes of her time, just so I could chat with her some more. She had other ideas that involved more of my money, so I left.

I did a lot of walking on my extra day in Cordova. My curiosity had me all over town once again. It was fun to explore yet another Mexican city on foot, my way and at my own pace. I have always enjoyed watching people go about their business and it tends to be most interesting as an observer, somewhat detached. I did plenty of people watching in Cordova and found out that Mexicans generally don't rush around like their neighbors to the north. Many actually took the time to say hello and engage in a little chat. Even some of the most attractive women were open to a random conversation. Cordoba was a good time.

On January second I had to leave Cordoba. The plan was to make it to Veracruz in one shot, so I could show up at Kiosk International for my interview early the next day. It should have been an easy ride on a mostly flat or descending toll road. That was how it started off, but then something unexpected happened. First I noticed that my front tire had developed a little bulge in one spot that I could feel on the road. While still wondering how long the tire would last, I heard a pop and a hissing sound. There was my answer; the tire was in pieces!

I had no choice but to push the bike and get off the main highway to look for a town that would hopefully have a bike shop. Thankfully there was one not too far behind me. The highway had bypassed it completely, but there was an alternate road that ran parallel to the toll road. All I had to do was to push the bike off the next exit and follow that road back about half a kilometer.

Within fifteen minutes or so I was on the outskirts of a town called Cuitlahuac. Someone had already noticed me and motioned for me to come over. He was a relatively young man who had been distracted from washing his car when he saw me push my bike.

Yes, there were several bike shops nearby, the man told me and immediately offered to give me a lift back to town, which was only a kilometer or so. Even when I declined because I figured I could easily manage, he insisted. I finally accepted and told him I'd need a couple of minutes to take the wheel off my bike and he might as well finish washing the car. Minutes later I got to ride in a shiny 1986 Volkswagen Beetle, complete with a Superman sticker on the windshield. The front-wheel of my bike was resting on my lap. There were three bike shops in town, Antonio, my new friend told me. It seemed like a sure thing that one of them was going to have the right tire. While he was well intentioned and convinced, we both didn't know that the 700 series tires were not common in Mexico. We did the tour of all the bike shops in town and every one of them made an effort to find something that would fit my rim, even if it wouldn't be an exact fit, but ultimately they couldn't help me; the right size tire just wasn't available.

Finally, at the last tire shop we stopped at, an older man wasn't going to let me walk out of his shop without some kind of solution. Antonio explained to him that I was from Canada and had come here on my bicycle, and how there was no way the trip would end here; he had to try something! The man agreed and over the next half hour or so we got to watch him repair my blown out tire in a most creative way. Several inner tubes were cut into pieces and an old tire from a kid's bike was converted into reinforcing patches. By the end of it I owed the equivalent of five dollars and had a tire that held 35 pounds of pressure. I was not convinced that it would make it to the next town, let alone Veracruz, but I had little choice, so I was going to try.

Antonio drove us back to his house where I immediately installed the wheel. When I tried to give him fifty pesos to compensate him for all the help he had given, he declined. Instead he invited me to stay for lunch, which his wife Juliana had almost ready. Once again I was blown away by the hospitality. Not only was the food excellent, so was the company. I could have easily stayed the entire afternoon and Antonio probably would have driven me somewhere to make up the lost time, but I was determined to reach Veracruz by that night and do it entirely by bike. Shortly after lunch we said our goodbyes and I hit the road.

At first I rode the bike very carefully, expecting my tire to burst at any moment. My confidence went up with each kilometer I completed. Every pothole, no matter how minor was testing my nerves as well as the tire, but contributed to my growing optimism when I left it behind. After about ten kilometers or so, it was pretty sure that I was going to make it to Veracruz and my focus shifted from merely arriving, to reaching the city before dark. I didn't exactly accomplish that, but at least I got close enough to town to find my way around. Once all daylight was gone I resorted to riding the less traveled streets or pushing the bike on sidewalks and through narrow laneways.

I still had no clue where I was going to stay this time around and nor was it a good time to be too picky. The cheapest hotels were in a shady area around the market, so that was where I ended up.

Chapter 22

Living in Veracruz

So much more than a visit

It was Monday afternoon and for the third time I had returned to Kiosk International for an interview. It went well and very smoothly. The management liked me, and I knew right from the start that they were ultimately going to hire me. There were some more hurdles to overcome however. I was sent home, or back to my hotel with an assignment. I was to teach a test class the next day, in front of faculty members who were then going to decide weather they thought I was fit to teach English to their students, mostly wealthy people who paid a substantial tuition. I took it seriously and spent the rest of the night preparing a lesson, just like I had learned during the 60-hour course I had taken to get certified.

When I stood in front of the group of four teachers and the coordinator the next day I was nervous, but not enough to let it truly sidetrack me. I had nothing to loose and a whole lot to gain. All I had to do was demonstrate that I was able to present the course material in an easy to understand manner without putting everybody to sleep. The key to accomplishing that was in the so-called icebreaker activity at the beginning of the lesson. I had decided to start off with a game called packing, basically a memory challenge. The idea was to get everyone to imagine they were packing their suitcase for a trip to Canada. They were to take turns saying the following phrase: "I am going to Canada tomorrow and I'm packing _____." At each turn they not only had to fill the blank with their own item of choice, but also repeat all the items that had come up prior, in the correct order. Eventually the chain would get too long to remember and somebody would screw up. In the meantime everyone was having so much fun that they became a lot less focused on my shortcomings. I went on to teach a lesson about things being tall, taller and tallest, basically using the word tall to demonstrate a grammatical principle. After the test lesson I was invited into the coordinator's office and hired on the spot. I was going to teach a four-hour class of fairly advanced students every Saturday morning, and a small class of TOEFL students Monday to Friday mornings for one hour starting at seven am the following week. For now that was going to be all. I walked away happy that day. I had enough time to get settled in Veracruz before the new challenge was about to begin.

First I had to look for accommodation in close proximity to the school. I was considering renting a small apartment or a room in someone's house. In the end however, a family run hotel turned out to be the best option. The key to a good rate was some negotiating. After spending quite some time searching ads in the paper and walking all over the area surrounding my new workplace, I was able to rent a room with Wifi, cable TV and full bathroom including a "hot" shower for 3,000 pesos a month. This meant only 100 per day, the equivalent of about eight dollars. The only catch was that I had to pay the money up front; cash. It seemed worth it and I had found a place! I moved the next day and somehow it seemed like a huge deal, despite the fact that I had done it pretty much every day up to this point.

The rest of the week went by in a hurry. Suddenly it was Wednesday and I started to realize that there would hardly be any time to take it easy before starting my new job. Bit by bit I found out how much preparation was involved in getting myself ready, even just for the first lesson, never mind the rest of the program. Besides having to prepare lesson plans, there were mandatory staff meetings, held entirely in Spanish. The little free time I had left was spent looking for a bike shop that carried 700 series tires, since I still needed one for my bike. Even in Veracruz it turned out to be harder than expected. Sure, there were plenty of bike shops in the city, but they all carried pretty much the same standard assortment of utility bikes, mountain bikes and children's bikes, which all had the same limited number of tire sizes. Soon I was convinced that nobody in Mexico had ever even heard of 700 series tires. It was frustrating, but didn't really matter immediately, because I wasn't going anywhere for a while. There surely had to be a way to get the darn tire by March, even if I had to order one from Canada. For the moment, the defect did not even prevent me from using the bike for local transportation. The patched tire was still holding up and would last for a while, especially without having to haul any luggage. As soon as I had stopped worrying about the dilemma and had basically put off dealing with it, I met someone who had his own boutique, selling high-end bicycles and triathlon gear. He was friend of someone else I had met during my search for a place to stay. Jorge was his name. Not only was Jorge able to get the right tire for my bike within a week's time, he soon also became my main contact for everything that had to do with cycling and other aspects of my trip, like exploring the surrounding area. Jorge and I had a lot of interesting conversations and remain friends to this day.

    Friday afternoon finally snuck up on me and it might as well have been Saturday morning. I ended up spending the entire afternoon in my room, trying to build a lesson plan. The task was daunting and I could not seem to focus on it long enough to actually pull it together. I dismissed my troubles as inexperience and vowed to get better, but for now I had to overcome this first major challenge: teach a class of about twelve students for four hours. The lesson included two grammatical principles that I had never consciously analyzed, besides applying them for some conversational practice. Of course I was nervous about teaching my first class. I had no experience with timing the activities beyond teaching a twenty-minute test class, which seemed like a piece of cake by comparison. To get my mind straightened around, I finally left the room and the unfinished work, after dark. A long walk would surely put things into perspective and perhaps give me some insight into what obvious piece I was missing to the puzzle. Within minutes of walking along the boardwalk, I totally forgot my dilemma. The weather was perfect; a light breeze was blowing from the ocean, providing relief from a hot sunny day. There was always something going on along the shore, across from the port. I became absorbed in watching the street performers and a group of people who seemed to be practicing dance moves for an upcoming performance. This kind of simple, yet joyful and wholesome nightlife did a lot to shape my perception of Veracruz as a beautiful cultural city. I didn't return to my room till about one in the morning.

I had not used my alarm clock in quite some time, but thankfully it still worked. It was Saturday morning and I was awake! I realized what I had done to myself, but dragged myself out of bed trying to think positive. What was I going to have for breakfast? Was there going to be warm water for my shower? Twenty minutes later I was at the nearby Oxxo convenience store, picking up a sandwich and a coffee. It was still very quiet outside.in the streets. I was not used to being out and about this early. Since the beginning of my tour I had usually slept in and completely missed the calm of early mornings.

The school was still locked up when I got there, but I wasn't the only one arriving early. A young girl, from Canada out of all places, was already waiting by the door. Minutes later Lucy, the coordinator, showed up too and let us in. It was only around 7:30, but teachers were expected to arrive half an hour early on this first day of classes. We first had a short meeting and all of a sudden just a few minutes of preparation time remained before the students were let in. My class was an interesting bunch. Some students were teenagers, but I also had a handful of older people in business attire who seemed very serious about perfecting their English.

I started the class with an icebreaker activity once again. It was a game that was going to help me remember everyone's names, while helping the students to get acquainted with each other. Once I got comfortable speaking in front of the entire class, teaching the lesson plan was actually quite easy. There were unexpected challenges however. A few of my younger students proofed very hard to engage. A guy named Jesus was much more interested in the girls sitting next to him than the lesson. I tried to ignore the disruptions at first, but then it started to affect other students and I had to put my foot down and politely threaten dismissal from the class. I made it through the first four hours of class quite easily with only some minor improvisation. In the end I was happy with my the first day of teaching. At the same time it was a big relief when it was done. None of my students really had an attention span of four hours, so I had explained all the grammar during the first two while the latter two hours were spent practicing conversation and playing games within small groups. After school I celebrated with a huge chicken dinner and some Corona at one of the fancier local restaurants. I was a real teacher now! The next day was going to be Sunday and I had nothing on the agenda at all, except to sleep in until noon.

    That was exactly how I started my Sunday. The temperature in my room was hot when I finally got out of bed. Outside was picture perfect sunshine, so I decided to take the bike to the beach and go swimming. Veracruz had a beach right in the city, but the nicer stretches of sand were a short bike ride away, in the suburb of Boca Del Rio. It was easy to reach via the boulevard that follows the shoreline. I spent the entire afternoon at the beach and almost forgot that I had a lesson to teach at seven o' clock the next morning.

    I had been told the TOEFL class was easy; advanced students who already spoke English fluently. The only thing they were missing was a certificate that would qualify them to attend an English speaking university. Still, I was a bit nervous about teaching them, because I was unsure of what to expect. What was I going to do with them? The class was supposed to consist of four or five students, some of which would not be able to attend every morning. All I had for preparation was a book Lucy, the coordinator, had lent me. It was full of test questions. She had suggested I'd use the computers in the language lab to run the students through test after test, using a program with the same questions that were also in the book the book. I had a slightly different idea.

Getting up at six am on Monday was rough, but I managed. I walked through the deserted streets to the convenience store, bought junk food and coffee just to tie me over, and continued on to the school. My classroom was called Alberta, after the Canadian province. It was the only one that was equipped with computers that I had not had a chance to try out. It was a good thing that I had arrived a few minutes early, as it gave me a chance to get acquainted with the equipment. I didn't really mind it, when no students had showed up yet at ten past seven. Finally, at quarter past, I had three students and simply started them on the same exercises I had been playing with for the past half hour. By 7:30 I actually had four students. After letting them answer test questions for another ten minutes or so, I decided to search the Internet for a Canadian radio station. We caught a discussion on CFRB 1010 in Toronto, which dealt with problems of snow removal. My students, who had never seen snow in their lives, were instantly hooked. The program lasted exactly up to the end of our lesson. At eight o'clock I simply sent them off, asking them to prepare a short summary of the program they had listened to. I felt pretty good about my idea and went for breakfast at a nearby outdoor cafe.

For the next month and a half or so, the pattern didn't change much. I got used to getting up early, spent most of my Fridays preparing lessons, attended meetings and probably became a much better teacher. When the weather was good I took bike rides to various beaches in the region. The rest of the time I took walks around town and spent visits to Jorge who had already supplied me with a new tire and had become my best friend in town. I totally fell in love with the neighborhood around my hotel. There was a large park and a market, all within one block. Right outside my door were a bakery, a sidewalk restaurant that had the best quesadillas in town and a laundry service. A fruit store was just a few steps away and beer could be had at two different outlets, depending weather I wanted Corona or Sol (the two major breweries in

Mexico). The famous Aquarium of Veracruz was only a five-minute walk away and along the route were a number of really good eateries. It didn't take me long to feel totally at home in Veracruz, almost ready to settle here for the long haul.

One evening, on one of my walks, I made yet another discovery. Less than a block away from the hotel I noticed what looked like an open garage door. I walked in and saw that there were people inside working on paintings. At first nobody paid much attention to me. There were many beautiful paintings on display on the walls, some of which had prices marked beside them. I got a bit lost admiring the pieces, when a lady approached me with a big smile and asked if she could help me. That lady's name was Gloria. She was an accomplished artist and was holding workshops here. Right off the bat, Gloria struck me as a passionate woman who was living her dream. She didn't mind my curiosity, when I asked her everything that came to mind. By the end of the conversation I had given her the last 300 pesos in my wallet as tuition for my first month of classes. This was a commitment I hadn't planned for. It was going to affect my routine. Painting class was twice a week in the evenings, Mondays and Fridays, four hours each. It meant that I had to prepare for my Saturday classes by Friday afternoon. I didn't mind any of it and for the next two months I got right into acrylic painting, which came to me quite naturally.

The first payday at the school was rather disappointing. Of course it was in part because I only taught a total of nine hours a week, but the pay was the equivalent of just four dollars an hour for classroom time. Neither the preparation, nor the mandatory meetings were compensated for. When the German teacher, a young guy from Austria, quit his job, I picked up his class as well, which took place Saturday afternoon and gave me some extra paid hours. However, a short time later I was replaced as the teacher of the morning TOEFL class, which had been my favorite one. My replacement was to a Mexican lady whose English was impeccable. What ticked me off about the entire situation was, that nobody had bothered telling me, until she herself showed up one morning, ten minutes after the beginning of the class, to tell me that she had been assigned to take over. I was not impressed, but let her teach while I waited around for Lucy, the coordinator, who was due to arrive shortly. Lucy seemed to be caught off guard when I approached her, even though it would have been her responsibility to inform me of the change. I expressed my disappointment and went home to my room. I had to make a decision and it was an easy at this point: I simply logged on to the Internet and wrote my first ever resignation email in Spanish, giving a week's notice. I would teach my upcoming classes the following Saturday and that would be the end of my career with Kiosk International. The Carnival of Veracruz, Mexico's biggest, was about to begin and I would enjoy it to the fullest, not having to worry about classes!

Just in time for the Carnival I had received a message from the Couchsurfers of Veracruz, who were organizing a get together to attend the first parade. It seemed interesting enough, so I went to join them at the meeting point on the specified evening. A group of about 20 people, a mix of Mexican locals and international travelers of all ages showed up. We hit it off immediately and took over a section of the bleachers that lined the boulevard as a group of friends. The parade itself beat all my expectations, but the party that followed was even better. I got to meet several people who remain friends to this day. Somehow we all ended up on the beach at Boca Del Rio, drinking beer from the 24 hour Oxxo store there. Before we knew it, the sun was rising. I had no responsibilities at all, so it didn't matter when I only returned to my hotel around lunchtime in a condition that could best be described as completely wasted.

The carnival had caused some last minute changes at the hotel. I had been asked to move to another room, so that my regular room could be given to a family of six. The room I was provided with was much smaller, but for the duration of the celebrations I had to pay triple the regular rate. Of course I wasn't too happy, but there were simply no other options. Veracruz was packed with tourists from all over Mexico and I had to consider myself lucky to have a room at all. It was only after I woke up from my long sleep, when I realized that the room reeked of sewage. The ceiling fan was out of order, probably intentionally, so the smell couldn't travel through the vent above the door, into the lobby. What was I to do? The situation had not bothered me while under the influence, so once again I ventured out into the craziness of the biggest carnival I had ever seen, in search of more beer. There were special sales all over town, even outside on the sidewalks. A bottle of more than one liter sold for just sixteen pesos (not even $ 1.50) and it came with a huge paper cup that fit the entire content. I took advantage and drank way more than I'm even going to admit here, which is why most of the Carnival is a bit of a blur. I know I had fun while it lasted and sobered up as soon as it was over. That was when I got to move back into my regular room.

Even after the carnival, for a few weeks I became the perfect beach bum, often taking the bike to a deserted place by the ocean, spending the entire day building sandcastles and swimming in the ocean. Later I'd go to an outdoor restaurant for supper, before returning to my neighborhood for a stroll. It was a fantastic life, completely without worries, at least for a while.

Things got even better one evening at the painting class. I was hard at work on a painting, when I noticed that someone was looking over my shoulder. She was an attractive woman, right around my age. As a single guy I was immediately interested in her and apparently she loved the attention. Muriel, as I'll call her here, had walked into the painting class, exactly the same way I had done weeks prior. I had never seen her there before, and now my Spanish was coming in quite handy. Before I knew it, we were engaged in a conversation. Suddenly Gloria stood beside us and asked her to kindly leave the studio, as to not distract her students from their work. Muriel handled the situation gracefully, but before she left, she passed me a note with her name and email address on it. I winked as she left and she responded with a smile. Later that night I sent out an email to her, just to let her know that I had enjoyed our conversation and would like to meet her again. The response came almost right away, confirming that she too, would love to meet again. I almost jumped up and down on my bed, but then she messaged that she had only stopped in Veracruz for a few hours to visit her daughter. She had discovered the paint studio on her way back to the bus depot and had decided to step in to kill some time. For the next few weeks Muriel and I exchanged emails and made plans for when we would meet again. It turned out she lived in Coatzacoalcos and frequently traveled to Xalapa for business. Eventually the emails became sporadic. I pretty much lost hope that we'd ever cross paths again.

Weeks had gone by, seemingly in a hurry. All of a sudden I had to think of leaving Veracruz to make it to Cancun in time for my flight. During the first week of March I had a visitor, my daughter Jennifer. She had decided to come down to spend March break. We had a great time together, packed with daytrips to attractions, ranging from the mall to the beach and the aquarium. Jen had even got to use a bike that Jorge had lent us so we could cycle together. The highlight of her stay though, was a daytrip to Catamaco, a town that was a four-hour bus ride away. Catamaco is famous for the lake by the same name and an annual festival of witchcraft. We got to take a tour of the lake that led us to an island called Isla de Monos. It was completely populated with monkeys, which was the result of someone, long ago, dropping of a couple of monkeys there to get rid of them. Jennifer arrived on a Sunday, and left the following Sunday, which was also going to be my last day in Veracruz. After sending her off at the airport, I pretty much spent the day walking around town before I started packing. When checked my email late that night, there was a message from Muriel. It was just a couple of lines. She was letting me know that she was coming to Veracruz in the morning and asking me to confirm if I'd like to meet up with her. I responded that I was still in town and told her which hotel I was at, adding that it was going to be my last morning there.

I was still in bed when I heard voices in the lobby. It had to be Muriel, asking for me. The lady at the front desk seemed surprised and had almost sent her away by the time I had thrown on some clothes and opened my door, which was just across from the reception desk. There she was, dressed all in red and looking pretty darn hot. When I caught a glimpse of her top that was quite revealing, I noticed that it had "Born to be Sexy" printed across her chest and a picture of Mini Mouse underneath it. She was wearing dark sunglasses and her black hair looked fantastic. Still stunned by the sight, I asked her to give me five minutes, and suggested we'd go have breakfast together. She was fine with that.

When I came out of my room she was sitting on a chair in the lobby, her tanned legs crossed, chewing gum and looking slightly bored. We hugged and kissed each other on the cheek. She smelled as good as she looked. I tried to conceal my excitement, but must have looked quite awkward. We went, hand in hand, to my regular breakfast place, the little restaurant on the sidewalk with the awesome quesadillas. The food was as good as always, but I could tell that the environment was not what she had expected. Her behavior was not exactly first class, especially when she acted rudely toward the waitress. That embarrassed me, because I had come to know and like the staff at this plaand knew that they were all part of the same family. Muriel seemed to sense my unease and attempted to make up for it by cracking awkward jokes. She was talking a lot, about everything and nothing. She was obviously nervous, perhaps even more so than I. After breakfast we returned to my room. Muriel wanted to spend time with me alone. We barely knew each other enough to get comfortable and all of a sudden I forgot how to speak Spanish. It mattered little for the twenty minutes that followed. For all I cared, we could have talked in Chinese. Body language is international and we hit it off quite well. Perhaps there was even hope for us to get to know one another more. The thought of that prospect almost made me burst from excitement. Before we parted Muriel invited me to contact her at her home when I'd be passing through her town, Coatzacoalcos. Sure thing I thought. Perhaps I wasn't going to Cancun after all.

Chapter 23

Goodbye Veracruz

Back on the road

After Muriel left I had only an hour or so before checkout and just half a day to actually get somewhere. The plan was to start off easy by going to Alvarado. I had liked that town the first time around and could barely wait to see it again. Just packing everything back onto the bike and getting out of Veracruz turned out to be a major ordeal. While going through my little duffle bag that was supposed to have all my paperwork, including the electronic ticket printout for my flight back to the US, I noticed that my Canadian money, about $ 150 in cash, had gone missing. While this wasn't enough money to break the bank, it was still annoying and completely shook my confidence in the staff at the hotel. Someone had been entering my room on a regular base for cleaning. Of course, the money could have disappeared at any time during the past two months. I had pretty much forgotten about it, thinking that no one would go to the trouble of having to exchange the foreign currency. Instead of finding a secure manner to store the cash, I had simply trusted the hotel staff to keep their fingers off my belongings. As it turned out now, I had been mistaken and it was time cut my loss.

I reported the issue to the front desk during checkout. Body language often speaks louder than words. The reaction of the woman at the front desk let me know me where my money had gone, even without an admission. There was no proof, but after spending two and a half months as a guest I left the hotel on less than good terms. I made it perfectly clear to the hotel manager that I was never going to return because the place obviously wasn't secure. Besides, I was still mad about the sewer smell I had been subjected to during the carnival. The woman listened to my little rant and then replied that Muriel must have taken my money that morning. That response only confirmed what I already knew. The hotel had been a bargain for a reason (I will refrain from mentioning its name here).

On my way out of town I stopped at Jorge's Store for one last time. He and a friend were present. Before we said our good byes we took pictures outside the store. Then it finally sank in; I was leaving Veracruz behind. The city I hadn't known anything about just three months earlier had become my home for a time. I was going to miss it. There were tears in my eyes for the first five kilometers or so, while I was paying little attention to the road, but reliving some of my fondest memories. The consolation was that I had over a month of cycling adventures ahead of me. Once again I was free as a bird, even if it was temporary.

The first day went by quickly. I reached Alvarado late in the afternoon and found a hotel right off the highway. I had considered going back into town to stay at the same hotel I had already spent two nights at on my first visit, but then I remembered the shortcomings and thought it might be worth to try some place else. The little hotel I chose to check out offered a room that was clean and well equipped, for a great price, so I took it. After taking a much-needed shower and a short nap, I ended up taking a walk back into town in search of a good place to eat. Even though Alvarado was pretty quiet compared to Veracruz, I had no trouble finding the perfect outdoor taco stand. The food was great and cost way less than in the city. After the meal I roamed the dark streets of Alvarado once again. It was a joy to revisit the park, the port and other vaguely familiar places. I skipped the bar this time around. Instead I came across a language school that looked like a simpler version of Kiosk

International. The door was locked and the shutters were down, but it still made me stop and wonder if I could have found work here too. One of Alvarado's perks was that it seemed completely untouched by tourism. Of course this made me stick out like a sore thumb, but at the same time the experience was truly authentic.

    I didn't waste a lot of time the next morning and only had a quick breakfast in my room. The goal was to reach the town of San Andres Tuxtla, or perhaps even Catemaco. The weather was hot, even early in the morning. I rode non-stop, all the way to a small town called Lerdo de Techada, where I found a small market and decided to have lunch. It was pretty much the usual comida del dia, this time empañadas de pechuga (chicken breast rolled up in tortillas and fried) were on the menu. I was told that it was a local specialty. I stretched out my lunch break, chatting with the ladies who were preparing the food. There were three of them, a mother with her two daughters.

    When I finally decided to hit the road again, I noticed another cyclist coming up in the distance, also traveling in my direction. I almost couldn't believe my eyes when I realized that this wasn't a local cyclist. As the bike was getting closer I recognized the panniers. Curious and eager to meet another cycling tourist, I decided to wait up. Minutes later a young lady in a cycling outfit was standing in front of me. Anna was her name and she told me that she was from Sweden. Her trip had started in Vancouver, British Columbia six months prior. We had a little chat and decided to ride together for a while, since we were both headed in the same direction, without having a defined destination. We stayed together for most of the afternoon, alternating the lead. Anna was in top shape and giving me a run for my money as we were starting to encounter some hills. After a couple of hours of rather intense cycling we came up on a roadside restaurant. We were both overdue for refreshment and decided to stop for drinks. We sat down for a while and talked cycling. It turned out that Anna had started her ride very early in the morning, so she decided to call it a day and order supper. It was a bit too early for me to do the same, but I stuck around for a good hour, swapping stories with Anna. I learned that she was constantly in touch with a radio station in Sweden, which would put her on the air live, several times each week. She already had a regular audience, back in her hometown, who were interested in her adventures and were virtually experiencing them through her eyes. Anna eventually decided to ask the restaurant owners if she could pitch her tent in their yard and stay for the night. When they agreed without a fuss, I was tempted to do the same, but then I thought of San Andres de Tuxtla and changed my mind. There were still a few good cycling hours in the day and the sun was much less intense now. When we said good-bye, Anna gave me a business card with her contact info. We both figured that we would probably see each other in Catemaco the next day. Anna's business card described her as a writer and photographer. It meant we had something in common, even though I was just beginning to consider writing in a serious manner.

    The ride to San Andres didn't take long, but finished with a killer hill. I sure was glad once I had put it behind me. The town was as pretty as I had come to expect. Despite considerable fatigue I spent the evening hours exploring. At the town square I even bumped into an American couple from Illinois who were exploring Mexico by car and had seen me ride my bike earlier in the day. Both seemed to love the idea of traveling by bicycle, but confessed that they could not even start to imagine how to go about doing it. My response to them was, for lack of a better insight, that I had been a total novice at it too a few months earlier and that things always tended to fall in place quite nicely, wherever you went. While they were staying at a gorgeous hotel right by the park, I had found another bargain hotel right on the main road. My room was on the second floor. Leading up to it was an external spiral staircase that had made it particularly tough to get the bike up. Needless to say, I was very tired. After finding out that he TV in my room sucked, I took a long shower and went to bed.

    The next day I didn't have far to go, but the climb to Catemaco was brutal. Not only was it very steep, the road was also perfectly straight, which made it seem endless. I had no plan to continue on much further that day. My idea was to stay somewhere close to the lake and enjoy the afternoon by going for a swim before spending the night. That was why I took my sweet time in the picturesque town. I found an excellent place to have lunch and did some snooping around afterwards, pushing the bike. Eventually I decided to start looking for a hostel. There was a billboard at the shore, advertising a place called "Hostal Catemaco". It appeared that the place was located across the bay and could be reached either by boat, or via a trail that branched off the main road a few miles down. I wrote down the name and what little directions were provided on the billboard and started cycling.

The ride turned out to be much longer than expected. A few times along the way I wasn't sure the place even still existed, but there was always another banged up sign, confirming I was on the right track. After a turn off, away from the main highway, a secondary road first led me through a village and then turned into a dirt trail. It eventually got so rough that I crashed while descending a hill. Luckily I had only scraped part of my right hand, but now I was pushing the bike. There was supposed to be a hostel here? Where the hell was it?

I almost convinced myself that those stupid old signs had led me on a goose chase for a place that didn't actually exist, but finally I ran into a young couple that were on the trail, exploring. They were definitely not Mexican. Perhaps this was a good sign? When asked about the hostel, they just pointed in the direction they had come from and said that it was "right there". Sure enough, I just went around another bend and there it was. The place looked exceptionally well kept. It had a main house with a large kitchen and a few private rooms, a separate dorm and outhouses for the toilets and showers. The owner was Swiss. It turned out he was running the hostel together with his daughter and had been at this location for fifteen years. The couple I had met on my way in was also from Switzerland and they were the only other guests beside me. The hostel had an option for every budget. People with money could rent a private room. The less well off could sleep in the dorm, or if they had a tent, camp. For fifty pesos, that was definitely the perfect option for me.

For people who were really broke however, there was the possibility of working in exchange for the accommodation. The owner was operating a small organic plantation that grew coffee among other things.

There were just five of us, including the owner, Phil and his daughter Mona. Paul and Emily were the other two guests. We spent a great night together in the big open sunroom of the house that was well screened to keep the bugs out. Phil was supplying locally made rum for free. When asked about if there was a limit on how much to consume, he shrugged and said he didn't care. The gang who supplied the stuff was using free booze as their sales pitch for the bottled stuff. Needless to say, none of us stayed sober for very long. Phil was a motorcycle guy. He seemed knowledgeable about the road ahead and kept assuring me that my next day was going to be a pretty smooth ride along the main highway. "It's all rolling hills man!" I remember him saying. By the end of the night I was drunk and even ended up smoking a couple of Emily's hand rolled cigarettes. The buzz was pretty intense. I don't remember too much of the night after that, but I eventually ended up in my tent. At least that was where I woke up the next morning.

The hangover was nasty. I seriously considered staying at the hostel for another day, but after half a gallon of coffee and a hefty bacon and eggs breakfast decided that I was good to carry on. Perhaps the free rum was meant to keep people here long enough to get them to work on the plantation? Hostal Catemaco was my very first introduction to a typical party hostel. The place catered mostly to a young audience who simply liked to get hammered while on vacation in a beautiful warm place. That was just fine, but more than one night at a time might carry serious health risks, so I had to get out of there. Besides that, I was hoping to get to Coatzacoalcos by the next weekend, so I could hook up with Muriel.

A seriously rough day awaited me on the road. No, drinking rum by the beer glass and smoking unfiltered cigarettes is never a good idea, but if you're trying to undertake a 100-kilometer ride across rolling hills the next day, it is downright stupid. The term "rolling hills" was stupid too. Sure, on a motorcycle it would have felt great to cruise on this winding road, simply twisting the throttle a bit further at each incline. On a bicycle however, it meant hours of grueling climbs, in exchange for a thirty second-descent every so often. To top things off, it was one of the hottest days of my trip. I could feel the sun burn up my skin right through the SPF 30 sunscreen, while I was battling dehydration. At one point I stopped at a store and drank an entire liter of ice cold water in one shot, only to buy a bottle of Gatorade immediately after. Eventually the sun lost its intensity, daylight wasn't going to last much longer

Just before dark I arrived at the outskirts of Acayucan where a four-story hotel caught my eye. The place seemed to be brand-new, but at the same time it looked so typically Mexican that it almost intrigued me. To my surprise, a room was just 200 pesos. Considering that everything was new and the place had AC, free Internet and cable TV, this was a bargain! After checking in I walked to a store to get a ready-made sandwich and some junk food for supper. Forgotten was the hangover, so I also bought a couple of cold beers to enjoy before bed. I didn't have enough energy left to venture out into the town. Instead I decided to watch a movie, but passed out in the middle of it. Later I found out that the hotel had a flaw. Sound was traveling in strange ways across the stairwells. One of the rooms had a party going on. I knew from the sound that it had to be almost all young girls. They were loud enough to wake me up in the middle of the night, but I didn't get to see any of them. After a small eternity turned quiet. The place was spooky at night. Some weird shadows were dancing around on my wall. Eventually I fell asleep again.

The next day my ride was much easier. The road was much flatter and the sunshine never got too intense. I had no problem making it to Coatzacoalcos by late afternoon. Now the only thing on my mind was my next encounter with Muriel. I had to locate her address! I would just show up at her place and the rest was going to be just peaches. I was convinced that Muriel was a single woman in her mid forties who had a thing for me. It seemed a pretty safe bet that all I had to do was find her, to ensure a good time and a place in her warm bed. Finding the place she had written down was easy enough. After some asking around and walking the bike across town, I was standing in front of a stationary store. Did this mean she worked here? Or perhaps her apartment was in the building above the store? It was time to find out, so I stepped inside. The man behind the counter asked if he could help me. "Do you know Muriel?" I asked in Spanish. He nodded. When I went on to ask if she was around, his expression changed. His eyes were staring me down, but he remained calm and told me that she should be around the next day.

Of course I was disappointed, but I still had plenty of time to find a cheap hotel, something at which I had become good-at. I found a twelve-dollar shack right smack in what was probably the least secure part of the city. Then I went on a hike across town that led me to a great little restaurant for supper, and finally an internet cafe where I sent an email to Muriel. Coatzacoalcos reminded me a lot of Veracruz, so I immediately liked it here.

After a night in a sticky, windowless room with a noisy ceiling fan, I checked out of the hotel right away. There had to be a better place than this, even if Muriel wasn't going to accommodate me. I headed back toward the stationary store once again. I still had no idea why the man in the store had stared at me. When Muriel was still not around, I left the place without asking about her again. I walked around the neighborhood, contemplating on whether, and when to return for a third time, when one of her neighbors chatted me up. I am pretty sure the young lady was trying to sell me some marihuana. However, she quickly changed her tune, when my reaction wasn't favorable. She was an attractive looking blonde (probably fake hair color) in her late twenties who also spoke decent English. Local information, she had meant; "dope, you know?" We started chatting and I asked her about Muriel. Of course she knew Muriel. She was older, and did I know she was married?

Shit! I shook my head in disbelief. Yes, she was talking about my Muriel, who was a bit older, had a nice slim build with curves in all the right places, beautiful long black hair and was as pretty as she was intelligent. She was even a "licenciada", but definitely married! The girl went on to show me some hairclips that Muriel had sold her. No, she didn't really know her that well, but well enough to know her husband. Yes, he was the man in the store. Yikes! I was crushed. What was I going to do? Go to Muriel's husband and ask him if he wouldn't mind me hanging out with his wife for the weekend?

The girl introduced herself as Bonnie. She must have sensed my confusion and said something about Muriel being of an older generation and very career minded. I ended up spending my day with Bonnie, which wasn't too shabby at all and came with a few surprises as well. Bonnie didn't mind showing me all over town. We drove to the beach in her dad's minivan. There was a boulevard all along the beach, several monuments, a promenade and a bicycle trail. Some apartment buildings across from the beach were painted very colorful, in artistic fashion. I liked "Coatza" even more now. On the way back to Bonnie's place we first stopped to pick up some beer. Afterwards we had to pick up her son Bernie at a friend's house. Bonnie's friend Margarita was quite attractive and dressed to highlight the shape of her body. She made it a point to let me know that she was wealthy, single and lonely. Besides that she was going to get butt implants. I could hardly believe my ears and probably rolled my eyes a few times while listening to Margarita. I had her email address and her user name on some dating site when Bonnie and I left. Yes, Margarita was rich, Bonnie confirmed. Besides that she was also a very nice person, if a little insecure at times. Sure I was interested, but had she really said she was getting butt implants?

Bonnie drove us back to her family's place where we shared the six-pack of beer. They were jumbo cans of Sol. we each had three in a relatively short time and I definitely felt the effect. I was surprised when Bonnie left the house again to drive her son to soccer practice without even hesitating. Driving under the influence was perfectly acceptable to her, "as long as you were careful". I stayed behind with her parents who also seemed fine with the idea. I was secretly shaking my head in disbelief.

Later, Bonnie's Dad took us on a little sightseeing trip of Coatzacoalcos. There was an impressive new bridge nearby that had a bronze statue of a naked man, complete with all the small parts, at its ramp. Perhaps there was something in the city's drinking water that had an ever so slight effect on people's psyche. I was fine with most of it, except that, as a cyclist I have a pretty strong opinion about drinking and driving. Bonnie's family was very hospitable and I was offered a place to sleep in a patio chair on the porch. It sounded pretty good to me; I was due for a free night! After dark, I told Bonnie that I needed to take a walk to the Internet cafe, in order to check my email. I still had a glimmer of hope that Muriel might have responded to my message. Bonnie told me I was welcome to use her computer and I gladly accepted. Unfortunately there was no message.

We talked some more before everyone went to bed. Mine was just a lawn chair, which I thought was fine. In the end it turned out to be a terrible idea. At night, the porch was infested with mosquitoes. I was sitting in the chair, wrapped up in my sleeping bag, which was way too warm, just so the buggers wouldn't eat me alive. All the while I was wondering about Muriel and what could have been. It was by far the most uncomfortable night of the trip.

Chapter 24

Social Stuff

On making connections

Often people ask me why I tour alone. They can't seem to imagine being by them selves most of the time while on the road. There are good reasons to travel alone however. Remember what I said about cycling at your own pace? Unless you have a partner who is close to you and whose fitness level is comparable to your own, touring with someone else is going to be a compromise in that regard. That's not to say you can't make it work. The thing is, traveling alone gives you unlimited freedom, which has been one of the main perks of bicycle touring for me so far. Yes, it is a form of escape and a pretty complete one at that. I withdraw from my usual world for the duration of the tour and it is entirely up to me how much or how fast I want to cycle. Whenever I see something that interests me, I have the option of adapting my agenda without consulting anyone else. It makes touring easier in a lot of ways once you're comfortable with the idea. Does it make it a selfish pursuit? Possibly, but that doesn't make it any less worthy.

By going it alone you're definitely more open to your surroundings, including the people in them. It is surprisingly easy to pick up a new language, when there is nobody around to talk to in English or help you translate. It is much easier to make new friends. As a cycling tourist people will approach you. Often they will start a conversation just for curiosity's sake. If you give them enough time and focus, many of them turn out to be good friendship material. In general, I believe that the more persons are traveling with you, the harder it becomes to make meaningful connections with persons you meet along the way. Your focus is simply not on them as much. More often than not, people are open minded and friendly. While some will just pop up and disappear again, the minute you turn around, others may turn into lifelong friends. The amazing thing is that they don't necessarily have to have a lot in common with you. They may speak a different language, be of different race and live in a very different social system. It doesn't matter how wealthy or poor they are, give them due respect and you will make a connection. The key issue to understand is that no matter where you go in the world, there are always more good people than evil ones. Sure, if you listen to the news and some travel advisories, you may not necessarily be convinced of my last statement, but isn't the idea worth giving a chance? Bicycle touring is still an unconventional way to travel. It takes you off the beaten path and provides you with opportunities to connect with many different individuals and gain insights into their way of life. No school or university can duplicate that.

    Once you've been on the road for a while, you will, on occasion bump into other touring cyclists. Needless to say that when you do, you almost always have a lot of information and stories to exchange. Bicycle tourists are few and far between, so nobody understands you better than they do. If you meet someone who happens to move into the same direction, you might decide to ride together for a while, which also has its perks. The nice part is that there doesn't have to be any commitment to stick together. You can just enjoy the company for a while and then go back to riding by yourself when it suits you. There were times on my trips, when locals told me about other cyclists who had passed through. Sometimes I would just keep hearing about someone, without ever meeting them, but on occasion I'd bump into those people somewhere further down the road.

Meeting new people who are different in some ways is not only fun, it is also a great way to learn about different cultures. Virtually all cultures have their own customs that they are proud of, but that aren't widely known beyond where they live. If you are by yourself and take the time to stick around long enough to talk to someone, chances are you will be introduced to some interesting stuff, ranging from tasty food, to alcoholic beverages and perhaps even parties. My personal experiences have included all of the above and they are perhaps the number one reason I love to go on bicycle tours in foreign countries. Yes I love cycling, but there is more to it than that.

The best moments of any bike tour cannot be planned for. They just happen. That's why it's so important to have enough time and keep an open mind. Sometimes a change of plans is the way to go. When you meet someone interesting and perhaps get an invitation, you have to decide whether to take him/her up on it or not. After a while you will develop a pretty good intuition about when it is safe to do so (more often than not). If you hit it off with a member of the opposite sex, enjoy with caution! They may not have the same idea as you do. It is really easy to develop a crush on somebody while you're on your tour of a lifetime, far away from your usual day-to-day responsibilities. Best-case scenario; you fall in love and find your soul mate, but all kinds of other outcomes are equally possible (remember Muriel from the last chapter?).

Ultimately I believe that making friends in unlikely places, as tends to happen on long bicycle tours, has huge potential to make the world a better place. We all have different backgrounds. Opportunities are far from equal, depending on where someone grows up and lives, but give others a chance and you'll see that we're not so different after all. Better understanding ultimately leads to a more peaceful world. It helps to put religions and political systems into perspective. We're all human; the rest is trivial.

I hope my enthusiasm for going it alone on most of my longer tours won't discourage those of you who would rather cycle with a group or a partner. In recent years I have discovered, and come to enjoy something entirely new to me. Lately my now wife, Barbara and I have been touring together, mostly on weekends. Barbara used to cycle for basic transportation in her younger years, but hadn't been on a bike for decades. We started off with very short trips, entirely on trails. At first I was not convinced we'd ever go on any more serious tours together, because our fitness levels were quite far apart. Now, two years later, Barbara is an avid cyclist who has no problem keeping up for trips up to 50 kilometers long and she enjoys it enough to keep going. Thanks to her, I have discovered how much fun it can be to share the experience of even a day trip on bikes. Barbara's bike is now equipped with a luggage rack and she has a set of panniers. Can you see where this is going? We are looking forward to many more trips together, and who knows, some day we might go on a multi month tour as a couple. Whatever your preference, alone or together, bicycle touring always has potential to broaden your horizon in some way. All you need is an open mind. You can then focus on what truly matters, which is of course the entire journey and not just some ultimate destination.

It is still a dream, but there seems to be some interest in bicycle touring everywhere you go. Perhaps some day even people in countries where the average citizen cannot yet afford to go on extended bike-tours, will take to the road in fair numbers. I know from personal experience that I have inspired a few, at least for a period of time. It is worth advocating for bicycle culture, including respect from motorists and perhaps, some day, safe bicycle paths and trails everywhere. We are inching closer toward those ideals as more and more people discover the joy of touring for themselves.

Chapter 25

Tabasco & Campeche

Mexico at its Best

It was Sunday morning. I left Bonnie's house after I was treated to some coffee and breakfast. I felt tired. The patio chair I had slept in had left me with a sore back and I had been awake on and off throughout the night. It didn't keep me from leaving Coatzacoalcos right after saying good-bye to Bonnie and her folks. I had enjoyed my stay here, but there was nothing more for me here. I was still recovering from the disappointment about Muriel. What a letdown!

Traffic was light, so it was a quick and easy ride out of the city. I had originally hoped to follow a secondary road away from the main highway, staying closer to the shore, but it turned out to be almost impossible without getting lost. According to the map, that road led to a little town; Aguadulce. I loosely envisioned it to be my destination for the day. This didn't change at first, even after I ended up on the main highway almost by default. Aguadulce would have been just a bit off my route that way. I eventually changed my mind when I reached the turnoff early in the afternoon. Why bother going five kilometers off my route, when the same distance would take me right into the State of Tabasco, if I followed the main road? Half an hour later I was posing and taking pictures of myself by the big sign on the highway that indicated the border. I was finally entering a new stage of my tour, leaving the state of Veracruz behind.

The first town in Tabasco was called La Venta. It was also about five kilometers off the highway, in the same direction as Aguadulce, toward the shore. Upon arrival I found a tiny hotel on the outskirts of town, right next to a large industrial plant. The owner told me in an almost apologetic way, that his hotel only had the bare necessities and catered primarily to the workers of the plant next door. I told him that, as long as he had a room available, I didn't care how simple it was, as long as it was clean. He assured me that all rooms were attended to daily, so I checked in. It turned out the room was better than many I had slept in during my tour so far. The rate was around twelve dollars. There was a small TV that could receive two channels, but no Internet.

I was tired from riding in the heat, so, without planning for it, I ended up taking a nap while it was still broad daylight outside. The room was hot and sticky. A dusty old ceiling fan provided just enough air circulation to make it bearable. When I woke up an hour later I was drenched in sweat. The sunlight outside was slowly fading. It would have to be cooler outside now than in my room.

I was thirsty and somewhat hungry too. There had to be a perfect place in town to take care of those needs. It was only a five-minute walk to the town center and there I had the choice between several restaurants. The one I picked turned out to be great, like most mom and pop eateries in small town Mexico. After stuffing myself with chicken, rice, salad and tortillas, besides a big jug of water, I was almost too full to walk. The sun had completely set by now and there was just a little bit of daylight left. Across the street I saw a sign that said "Cafe Internet". The light shining through the windows revealed that it was open. I walked in and was greeted by a girl behind a counter. I asked her when was closing time. They'd be open for another hour, she told me. For ten pesos I could use one of the terminals. It sounded good, so I took her up on it.

The first thing I noticed when sat down and logged into my email was a message from Muriel. Wow, now she's getting in touch! Of course I had left

Coatzacoalcos behind hours ago, so whatever was in that email was irrelevant at this point. Or was it? When I opened the message I almost fell off my chair because it was so funny. This woman actually suggested that we'd meet at some park, within a few blocks of my hotel at around seven that night. I looked at the time. She'd be there waiting for me! Perhaps she had figured there was no point because I had not responded? It didn't matter. While I had enjoyed meeting her, she certainly wasn't worth having some angry husband come after me. I sent a reply anyways, explaining that I had already left town and how I knew she was married. It sure felt like this was going to be the end of the story.

Almost half an hour had passed by the time I finally got around to reading up a bit on La Venta on various websites. An article on Wikipedia revealed that this area had once been the center of the Olmeca culture. There was a huge archaeological area within the town. I made the decision to check it out the next morning.

Since I had no plan to stay in La Venta, I got up fairly early the next day, which was a Monday. The town was busy with lots of people already. I had no trouble finding a place to have breakfast. My checkout time at the hotel was only at one, but I was planning to hit the road, way before that. I walked to the archaeological site right after finishing up my coffee and "Huevos a la Mexicana". It cost a few pesos admission, but seemed well worth it. Besides pyramids and ancient sculptures there was a museum with many artifacts that were over 2,000 years old. What amazed me even more, were the professional guides. Two young boys, who could not have been much older than ten, offered their services for fifty pesos. It seemed like a good deal and turned out to be just that. These guys knew their stuff.

About an hour later I was on my way out of the museum, still mesmerized by the idea of an ancient civilization that had once inhabited this area, when I saw a familiar figure walk through the gate. There was Anna, the woman from Sweden. She was still wearing the same cycling outfit. With her was a local family who had accommodated her for the night. Now they were all going to check out the pyramids together. We said hello and talked for a while. Anna had stayed in Catemaco for a couple of nights, but had skipped right through Coatzacoalcos. Once again we parted ways, thinking we'd probably bump into each other again.

I left the hotel less than half an hour later. My destination for the day was Cardenas, a small city, about 80 kilometers away. I had to pick between route 180, and a toll road, route 1800. I was more out of curiosity that I took the scenic route, but in this case it turned out to be a good choice. Traffic was light and the road took me through some untouched wilderness. It was eventually going to meet up with the toll road again anyway, leaving my options open. Just in time for lunch I found a restaurant at the side of the road that looked both inviting and inexpensive, it was an easy decision to stop. The daily special was "Empañadas de Pollo", a typical Mexican dish with chicken and corn as the main ingredients, topped up with plenty of veggies and salad. I washed it all down with some Coke and lots of cold water. Once again the restaurant staff took great interest in my tour and even supplied me with some fresh oranges, free of charge, for the road. Cardenas was still a good distance away, but soon I ended up on the toll road, which allowed me to cover a lot of distance in a relatively short time due to a strong tailwind and the wide, smooth shoulder to ride on.

Cardenas was a beautiful city. I found my way to the central square and a Hotel by the name "Hotel Yax-ol" pretty quickly. When I asked for a low priced room, I was offered a special deal for 160 pesos a night. The hotel was undergoing renovations, but some of the rooms had not been done yet, so they were cheaper. I got what I paid for; the room was all right, but the walls were dirty and the furniture was barely holding together. There was no TV, nor Internet. It was fine by me, because the city was so interesting that I didn't want to spend time in my room anyway. I went exploring for most of the evening and found a great place to eat. After supper I walked into a store to pick up a can of beer. A young man who looked like a tourist himself approached me and began a conversation in English. It turned out he was the owner of a hostel in Campeche. Of course he recognized me as a traveler right off the bat and tried to pitch for his enterprise. Once he understood that I was touring the entire country by bike, he readily offered me a free stay. "We would love to have you stay at our place as it would be great for promotional purposes." Wow I'm a celebrity! I took his card and thanked him, without promising to stay at his hostel. I was just going to check it out once I reached Campeche, in a few days. I walked back to my hotel and settled down, falling asleep quickly. There is nothing like daily long bike rides to ensure quality sleep.

The next morning I wandered around town some more, before and after breakfast. It was almost tempting to stay in Cardenas another day, but in the end I decided to move on. Cardenas was a sort of crossroads for me. The options were to either keep following route 180 into Villa Hermosa, Tabasco's largest city, or to follow route 187 back to the coast. A lot of people had recommended I'd go see the ruins of Palenque, which would have required me to stick to route 180, but I wasn't exactly thrilled about passing through the big city on my bicycle. Besides, the ocean had always had a special appeal to me, so I decided to head up route 187, without really knowing where I'd end up in the evening.

The first town on my route was Comalcalco. While it took the rest of the morning and a good part of the afternoon to get there, the ride didn't seem long at all. I found an inexpensive place to eat that had great food. You can always tell a good restaurant by how many locals are eating there during off peak hours. The waitress was a friendly young lady, who was very helpful and knowledgeable about the route ahead. She told me that there were some good budget places to stay in the next town, Paraiso, which was only about 20 kilometers away. It seemed good to me. The ride to Paraiso went by really fast. Route 187 did not really go straight through town, but before I even realized that, I had basically passed right by. I considered turning around to find accommodation, but just kept pedaling as I was contemplating. It felt good and I had a tailwind. Why stop now? I had reached a point that some cyclists call "the zone". It felt like I could just keep going forever and nothing hurt or even tired me. Fatigue no longer seemed to exist. I had super powers. The magic lasted another ten kilometers or so. That's where I found a turnoff that would most certainly lead to the shore. Perhaps I'd be able to camp somewhere for free. I decided to turn off the main road, onto the roughly paved secondary road. As soon as I changed direction, every bone in my body started aching. I had a full day of intense cycling behind me and was starting to feel it all at once. I wobbled my way down the road and eventually reached the beach. The place was beautiful, but there were some people fishing. I wasn't sure if it was a good idea to set up camp, especially since it was still broad daylight. After a while I decided to backtrack toward the main road. Perhaps there was a campground or a small hotel nearby.

When I had almost reached the highway, I noticed a middle-aged couple working on a property on the left side of the street. They recognized me from before, when I had turned off the highway. Both were eager to talk to me. They were Pedro and Maria and it turned out that they had lived and worked in the United States for about eight years. They were wondering if I was American. When I said I was from Canada, they at least knew right away where Toronto was. We chatted for a while and eventually I just had to ask if they knew of any good places to stay for the night, within reach. Pedro looked at his wife first. When she smiled he turned to me and said that I was welcome to stay right there. He was pointing at what appeared to be a garage. As it turned out, the building had been his parent's house, but they had passed away recently and the building was to be torn down to make room for a store. Before I knew it, Maria was sweeping the floor inside to make the place suitable for my air mattress. Pedro explained to me that he had just disconnected the power, but for tonight it was no problem to reconnect it, so I'd have light. I was amazed by their willingness to help me out. I would have been happy with just a place to pitch my tent, but now I had a small house. I was set up within minutes and Pedro even gave me a key. They were going out to visit relatives. Maria encouraged me to go down to the beach and told me about a nearby store, in case I needed some food. She told me to check back with them later if

I was still up when they'd come back. "Come over and visit" she said, pointing across the street. "Our house is over there".

After they left I went back to the beach, now without any luggage on the bike except a towel. This time I had the place all to myself and went for a swim in the very calm water, which was actually part of a lagoon called "Laguna de Chiltepec". When it was almost getting dark I decided to return to my house. On the way back I stopped at the store to get some snacks and a beer. Upon my return the place was extremely quiet. I was grateful for the light as it allowed me to sit down on my mattress and study the map for the road ahead. There was really nothing else to do, so I almost nodded off. Suddenly there was a knock at the door. It was Pedro. He invited me to come to his house, where Maria had some snacks and a glass of wine for each of us. I gladly accepted.

Pedro and Maria had worked in Tennessee for about eight years. They showed me photo albums of another life, made up of company picnics, trips to the mountains, and their apartment building in the US. They reminded me of Miguel and his family in Cuidad Mendoza. They too had saved all their money to build their house right here in the rural part of Tabasco, where they had both grown up. Life in Tennessee had been good and their employer had been like family, but after eight years they had been deported back to Mexico. Their stay in the US had started out legally, with one-year work permits. Their employer had liked them and tried to extend the permits, but been unsuccessful. They had managed to stick around and work for seven more years anyway. After their return to Mexico, both Pedro and Maria had put all they had into their new house. It showed. They had a beautiful home and were now building their own store across the street. We chatted for a couple of hours and then parted ways. I could just leave the key in their mailbox, they said. Pedro was going to be up and gone to work early and Maria was going to visit her mom. We said our good byes before I went across the street to sleep. Where was I going to end up the next day? Cuidad del Carmen was in the state of Campeche. Could

I make it all the way there in one day? I fell asleep with that question still on my mind.

I got up earlier than usual and even met up with Pedro and Maria, as they were getting ready to leave their house. Maria was kind enough to provide me with a sandwich and a cup of hot coffee. I was all set to start my ride and determined to keep riding until I was in Cuidad del Carmen. On the map it looked like a 100-kilometer ride, but in reality it was actually 140. The flat coastal road and a strong tailwind both worked in my favor that day. The road would have been pretty boring if it hadn't been for the fast and easy ride. For much of the trip I was in the "zone", feeling like Superman again. Nothing could bother me and no matter how hard I pushed myself, I didn't get tired. I only made two stops the entire day. One was for lunch at some roadside place, where the waitress had trouble making change for a hundred pesos. The other was to take a dive in the ocean at a deserted stretch of white sandy beach. The only other problem I encountered was a brutally hot sunshine that caused me to slap on extra sunscreen more than once.

Finally, late in the afternoon, I arrived at a long bridge that led across a lagoon, to the island Isla del Carmen. There was a police checkpoint at the entrance to the bridge. I had seen plenty of those checkpoints before. Usually the officers didn't bother with a touring cyclist and would just wave me through. This time was different however and an officer waved me over.

"Passaporte por favor!" I pulled out my passport and handed it to him. The officer, who couldn't have been more than twenty years old, appeared to study my passport intensely and then looked at me. "The picture didn't look like me.", he argued in Spanish. I wasn't sure what to tell him. Perhaps I had lost weight from riding the bike, but I was pretty confident my appearance had not changed that much, especially since I had maintained a clean-shaven look throughout my tour. Perhaps that guy was fishing for a bribe? I told him to take a second look and reassured him that I was the guy in the passport. Don't believe me? I got other ID to back it up! When the kid started to lecture me about how I was responsible for my passport picture being up to date, a supervisor walked over to join us. "What seemed to be the problem?" He wanted to know. After the first officer showed him my passport he laughed and asked me how many kilometers I had cycled so far on my trip. I told him that I wasn't sure, but that my trip had started in Canada. He then smiled and turned to the other officer. As far as I understood he told him not to bother me and let me pass, adding that it was normal to loose some weight during a long bicycle tour. "Have a great day and stay safe, sir!" he addressed me in English.

What followed next was a ride across a three-kilometer long bridge called Puente el Zacal. It was only a two-lane roadway with a narrow shoulder. I was nervous the entire way because cars were passing me frequently, just inches away from my handlebars. As soon as I entered the city I was basically lost. At first I was just looking for a store that would have some snacks and a cold drink. As usual on hot sunny days, I was feeling very thirsty. Once those needs were met, the search for an inexpensive room had me running all over town. I actually found a place that would have charged only fifty pesos for the night, but it just wasn't sufficient for me that day. It was a private residence. The owner, a lady was renting out her spare bedrooms. The one she showed me was dirty and cramped. There wasn't even enough space for my bike, so I passed. Eventually I found a very nice hotel with all the amenities for 180 pesos. I did not hesitate.

Before even checking out more of the town, I decided to check my email, using the hotel Wifi. There was a surprise from none other than my old friend Muriel. Perhaps she hadn't liked the comments about her marriage that I had made in my last email. Her reply was brief and stated that she was married only for appearances. Whatever she did on the side was nobody's business. What freaked me out was the attachment she sent along with the text. It was a slideshow. The images started out with two masked men, holding a third man captive, whose arms and legs were tied up. In the subsequent images the captive was relieved of his clothing, which were cut away with a knife. The blade must have been hot, because after removing the man's clothes, the perpetrators cut into his flesh, along his limbs and torso, without causing a lot of bleeding. All this was taking place somewhere outside, in an open and hilly area, much like some of the ones I had passed on my trip. The following images showed vultures, first just one, then three, ten, and still getting more. It was clearly visible what was happening to the captive man: His body was getting consumed by the birds; little by little. A shiver and cold sweat ran down my spine, but I could not resist watching the rest of the pictures. Sure enough; at the end the two masked men appeared again, carrying a bare skeleton. Muriel's comment to it all was that this was what happened to "narcos". I could not help but wonder. Perhaps she was angry with me? Did it mean she was angry enough to get someone to chase after me to finish me off? I didn't really think so, but the attachment sure gave me some insight into her character and I was glad we hadn't met up in Coatzacoalcos. The last thing I needed was an overly demanding female trying to chip away at my newfound freedom. As terrible as those images were, they were just pictures. Who knew where she might have gotten them? I made the decision shrug it off and forget about the email. Screw Muriel! -Simple enough.

  I had another surprise that evening. This time it was a good one. Just before sunset I decided to take the bike, loaded only with my camera and my bathing suit, to the beach. Quite amazingly there was an actual bike lane all along the shore. Cyclists with all sorts of bikes, even high-end road bikes were on it. The road it was on was practically free of other traffic. Cyclists had completely taken it over. The beach I went to was called Playa Norte, due to its location at the north side of the city. I pushed my bike onto the sand and went for a quick swim before returning to my hotel via the port area. Of course the port was fenced in, but there was enough to see from the outside to get the impression that it was a major one.

  I stayed in Cuidad del Carmen for an entire day and a second night. The city was worth exploring and I really needed a day of rest from cycling. I was blessed with a picture perfect day of sunshine. In the morning I spent a few hours taking photos of pelicans, which were strategically hanging out around the fish-market. In the afternoon I just wandered around town with no specific goal other than to see and experience all I could. At one point I was sitting down on a park bench, eating an orange, when a big squirrel jumped right into my lap and stole a piece of the orange right out of my hand. Wow, that little bugger had nerves! He wasn't afraid of my camera either, so I caught some great shots of him eating pieces of my fruit.

I went to bed not long after dark that day. My room had cable TV and I found a movie channel, which helped me unwind along with a cold beer. The next day was going to take me further along the coast, without having a more defined destination.

I left Cuidad del Carmen early in the morning. The road along Isla del Carmen was close to the shore the entire way and it seemed like the perfect opportunity to make another stop, somewhere along the beach, to go for a mid day swim. When I finally found the perfect spot, the weather was scorching hot and the sunshine so intense that I could feel the burn right through the layers of sunscreen. The slightly cooler water was crystal clear and felt great, but I didn't stay in it very long. All I really wanted was a short dip to cool off, so I'd feel refreshed for the road ahead. Before jumping back onto the bike I slapped on more sunscreen and ate some oranges and tortilla chips I had in one of my panniers. While the beach was always close by and the scenery was quite beautiful, the ride was quiet and lonely for many more kilometers. To make matters just a bit more difficult, the wind had picked up and was certainly not blowing in my direction. At least the road was flat and had a good shoulder to cycle on. I would just take my time. According to the map there was just one town within my reach. Sabancuy looked like it was rather small, so I couldn't be sure what kind of accommodation would be available, but its location across a lagoon looked quite promising. It took a small eternity to reach the turnoff, but it was a great relief when I finally did. Turning away from the coast made a difference immediately as I no longer had to work against the wind. After crossing a narrow bridge I arrived in Sabancuy. A sign was letting me know that there was a hotel here. It took only a few minutes to find and offered a comfortable clean room at a price cheaper than expected.

The first thing I did after checking in was take a shower. The water was not heated, but nor was it cold. After the long ride in the sun it felt just about perfect. I was tired, but also very hungry, and thirsty. Still torn between the options; bed or food, I decided that a good supper would be essential for refueling my energy reserves. I put on a fresh pair of shorts and a shirt and left the hotel. Like usual, I walked around more than I really had to, to find a place to eat. There was a lot to see. People were busy in this little town. Finally I picked a restaurant with a huge charcoal barbecue and ordered the daily special. It was mostly rice and beans with a good chunk of beef; enough to satisfy my appetite. Along with it I gobbled down close to a gallon of water.

I liked Sabancuy and even to this day I could envision going back to spend an entire vacation in this picturesque little town. Due to my looming deadline to reach Cancun however, I decided to move on the next day. After a night of solid sleep I felt up to the task of reaching the city of Campeche in a day's ride. I only had a rough idea of the distance as my map of the region was not very detailed and I hadn't looked it up on the Internet. Once again my sole insurance of making it was an early start. Fatigue was showing its face early that day. As soon as I left the town, the wind was non-cooperative, as if it was trying to keep me in Sabancuy for a bit longer. I have always been a bit stubborn by nature, so I fell into a rhythm of labored pedaling until I reached the open highway; Mexico 180. The right turn I had to make to follow the coast only brought temporary relief. The wind was even harsher near the shore. Even though it was now pushing sideways with all its force, it wasn't helping my efforts at all. Occasional gusts were strong enough to force me off the road. The wind persisted pretty much throughout the entire day, making the ride seem incredibly slow. I remember the ride to Campeche as one of the toughest ones of the entire trip. It was already past my usual lunchtime when I arrived in Champoton, a small town along the route. I was happy to find a simple eatery that was serving nothing but grilled chicken with rice, vegies and tortillas. It felt a little to have chickens strut around my table, while I was chewing on a piece of, - well, chicken! The meal however, was exactly what I needed to get reenergized and it was delicious to boot.

After lunch I allowed myself a little bit of time to explore Champoton and even asked around for a hotel. When it turned out there weren't any, I just hopped back on the bike and headed for Campeche. I was just taking it a bit slower, in a slightly lower gear, to make up for the heavy wind. Once close to the city of Campeche I somehow ended up on a bypass route first. It took me up a hill unnecessarily, but the descent into the downtown core eventually made up for it.

Of course, I had to find the hostel my friend in Cardenas had told me about. It was easy enough, since it was located right across from the downtown park. The setting was beautiful. The municipal building and a huge cathedral were also situated around the park. Plenty of people were walking around and many of them appeared to be tourists. However, the hostel was upstairs in an old building. The staff was young and seemed inexperienced. I had the feeling they didn't care about their job. None of them had any suggestions on where I could keep my bicycle during a stay. After a while I was getting nervous because I had left it unsecured, downstairs on the sidewalk. I simply needed t get out of here and find another place!

I walked around for about an hour, pushing the bike through old streets with cobblestone pavement. What struck me as very unusual, even for a Mexican city, were the higher than normal sidewalks. Using them to push the bike was pretty much impossible. The city had plenty of hotels and several friendly tourists eagerly told me where they were staying and how much they liked it. Eventually I found a place all by myself that was right in my price range. As a bonus for me, it was also beautifully kept. My room seemed like it might have been 100 years old. The walls and furniture were all painted in bright colors, which complimented the old tile floors nicely. The entire hotel had a unique kind of simplicity about it.

I was tired from the long ride, but Campeche was a unique and interesting city. As usual, after a shower and a short nap, I was back out in the streets to witness the sunset. There was a long boardwalk along the shore, just outside the historic gate to the old city. It was easy to find great places to eat, but the prices were slightly higher than in other parts of Mexico. Campeche was a tourist hotspot, more so than any other place I had seen up to that point. It was a sure sign of my proximity to the Yucatan Peninsula, but at the time I didn't know it yet. For me it was a big change from being the only tourist in town. At first I enjoyed the change, but even before the night was up, two things were on my mind: First, where was the beach? Second, where was the market? All other coastal cities I had visited had beaches within city limits, but not Campeche. An inquiry at a busy tourist information office revealed that I would have to backtrack several miles along the shore to find a place called Playa Bonita. I decided to check it out the next day. "Why do you want to go to the market?" the tourist information lady was wondering. I explained that to me, the market would be the perfect place to experience the local atmosphere outside the typical tourist attractions. This included mostly food and conversation with people. The lady gave me rough directions. I decided to go to the market for breakfast the next morning.

  The market was everything I had hoped for. The food was simple, but tasted better than fancy restaurant food. I got to enjoy it in the company of local, working people and was the only tourist among them. They didn't mind and nor were they shy when it came to cracking jokes about "gringos". I can completely understand how some tourists would be intimidated by that alone, but I had long ago become accustomed to it and knew it was good-natured. If I had ever suffered true culture shock, it must have been somewhere in the north of Mexico. A long time had passed since then.

  The Playa Bonita was a disappointment. The beach was man made, with sand that was unusually rough. There were some places to camp and set up beach gear. Besides a large Mexican family whose action revolved around a cooler full of Corona, I recognized a young tourist couple I had seen in town the night before. They had arrived at the beach via rental car. I went swimming for a good while, then found a place to eat lunch and finally decided to return to Campeche early.

Somewhere during the twelve-kilometer ride back to town, my rear derailleur hit a curb, got bent and as a result got caught in the spokes of the rear wheel. I got off the bike, wondering what had happened. When assessing the damage, I thought this could have meant the end of my trip. What were the odds that someone in Campeche had the parts to fix that? I tried to bend the parts back into shape, but having left my tools at the hotel, I didn't accomplish much. The only way to go was to push the bike. I guessed that I still had seven or eight kilometers to go. This could take a while!

To my surprise, an old Datsun pulled over just in front of me. Two young guys got out. At first glimpse they looked like gangsters. Both had their arms completely covered with tattoos. For a moment I wasn't sure what to expect when both of them marched toward me. Then the taller one of the two asked me if I needed some help. I explained the situation and showed him my derailleur. "No problem", I was told. It turned out both the guys worked at a bike shop in town. "We can fix that for you right here!" I just stood there in amazement. The shorter one of the two went back to the car to get some basic tools, while his companion started to carefully realign my derailleur. Within a few minutes the taller guy was trying out my bike, riding up and down a side-street. "Works pretty good!" He said with a big smile on his face. "You try it!" I did, and the result was definitely better than I had thought possible. I tried to give the guys a tip, which they both declined. "We have to go, good luck amigo!" was all they responded.

Minutes later I was riding my bike again in direction Campeche, pedaling carefully at first. I was fully expecting my problem to return, but eventually arrived at my hotel in the city without further incident. Once again, I had been blessed with more luck than I deserved. By now I was truly grateful for having picked Mexico for my first ever long distance bike tour. What an awesome country!

I spent the rest of the afternoon and a good part of the evening outside, sightseeing. This was going to be my last day in the state and the city of Campeche. The atmosphere in town was almost like magic. Besides many people, locals as well as tourists, there were hundreds of birds at the park. All one could hear were their chirping-sounds. After dark the temperature outside was extremely pleasant. Even though I was by myself, it remains one of the most memorable evenings of my life. I fell asleep easily that night. The next stop on my journey was going to be Merida, the capitol of Yucatan.

Chapter 26

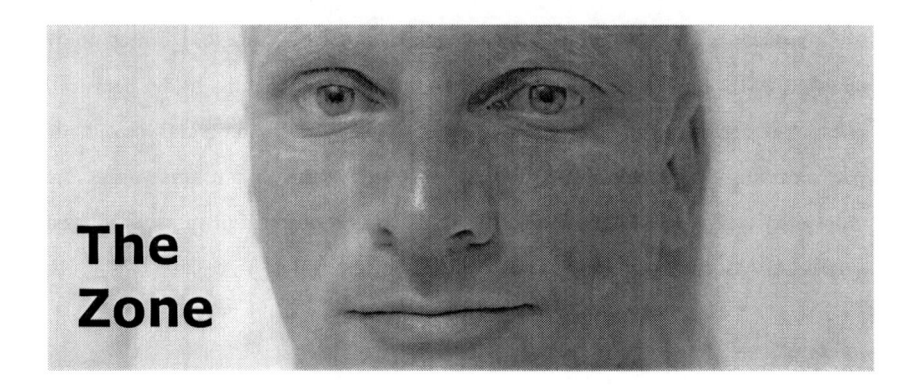

The Zone

It's all about feeling good

Often people ask me if I ever get really tired when on tour. I think they mean a kind of fatigue that is so overwhelming that it makes it almost impossible to carry on. To be honest, there have been moments when cycling felt just like that. However, what are you supposed to do when you're somewhere in the middle of nowhere, in the height of, say the afternoon, and you know you have to go on at least another thirty kilometers to find a decent place to stay? You find a way to carry on! While this does not sound like a lot of fun, those moments never last very long. Some long distance cyclists and even runners call this condition "hitting the wall". The good news is that you will eventually break through the so-called wall. In the previous chapter I described how I was cycling, beyond my daily destination on one occasion, seemingly without effort. After many hours of cycling I had entered a different state, many call "The Zone". At that point cycling feels great. Your body just seems to have unlimited energy to keep going, despite actually being very tired from miles and miles of cycling. I'm not a doctor, so whatever I tell you about this state is based, to some degree, on assumptions. I believe the cause for what we call "The Zone", is in the brain. After hours and hours of cycling, the body seems to have a mechanism to make us cope with the fatigue and the reality that we may still have many more miles ahead of us. It releases brain chemicals called endorphins. Those are some of the same chemicals that keep drug users addicted to their drugs of choice.

Does that mean you can become addicted to cycling? I would say you probably could in a way, but since the definition of an addiction includes some kind of negative effect on your life, you would probably have to become extremely obsessed with cycling in order to qualify as an addict. Another significant difference is that cycling gives you a sort of natural high quite easily. You do not need to cycle more and more to get the same effect, like you would if you were taking a drug or drinking alcohol to achieve a similar state. The only side effects I can think of are positive ones and might include finding a way to remain on tour indefinitely. I have a really hard time to see anything wrong with that. As a matter of fact, I'd rather be on tour than not!

Speaking of addictions; perhaps you have some that keep you from enjoying your bike rides to the fullest? Or do you have some that are severe enough to keep you from cycling all together? Granted, if you're into hard drugs, such as crack or heroin, then cycling is probably the last thing on your mind, unless it's the only way to get to your next fix. However, plenty of people smoke, or drink excessively. Is it possible to start cycling and enjoying the benefits, without giving up your vices first? If you happen to be in that situation, I'd encourage you to try it out. Don't even worry about that cigarette you might want twenty minutes into the ride. If you think you must have your smokes, bring them along. Who cares what anyone thinks or says? But here is the thing: twenty minutes into the ride you may not want to light up. If you ride your bike at your own pace without trying to push it too hard, you might enjoy it enough do it again. After a while riding the bike becomes even more fun as your condition improves. Without even trying to quit smoking, you might cut down significantly on the habit. The same is true for consumption of alcohol. As a result of cycling, your body will crave water, not beer. Alcohol dehydrates the body and so does intense cycling. My point is, the more you cycle, the more likely you will be to cut back on those bad habits. Regardless of how far you go, the effect of cycling on your health will be a positive one. For some, this can go as far as a complete transformation, from chain smoker and heavy drinker to very fit athlete with none of those vices. Others will never give it all up, whatever the reasons may be. There is no doubt in either case that your physical condition will improve as a result of cycling.

I myself am not a smoker, nor a heavy drinker, but I do not mind a beer or two on occasion before bed and have on rare occasions smoked a few cigarettes, even while on tour. While I don't claim to be a super athlete, the good feeling I get from riding the bike is so much better than anything I could ever get out of those vices. Riding the bike intensely can give you a natural high, without having any negative effect besides a sore butt. If you've partied a bit too much one night, you will probably feel the effect the next morning when you get on the bike, but intense cycling allows you to get rid of a hangover quicker; feel better much sooner.

The long-term result of cycling regularly is, more likely than not, that you get your vices and/or addictions under control, simply because they will eventually start to interfere with your enjoyment of cycling.

Whenever I hear someone complain that their doctor told them they should exercise in order to loose weight, or strengthen their heart, but they really don't enjoy exercise, I wonder if they've tried cycling. Like in the first chapter of this book, I like to remind people of how much fun it used to be when, as kids, they first learned how to ride a bike and enjoy the freedom that came from it. For most people, I would imagine, that is a positive memory. So why is it that so few people stick to the bicycle for regular exercise or transportation? I believe the bicycle industry is partially to blame. When you walk into a bicycle store it can be intimidating. Eager sales persons are intent on selling you a bike that costs close to or over a thousand dollars, along with accessories that are at best non-essential. Who hasn't seen those bicycle clothes that have advertising printed all over and can make even the most athletic person look kind of ridiculous? This is not what cycling is about. One aspect that makes riding bicycles so great is their simplicity, and the fact that almost anyone can learn to ride one. You don't need the lightest, or most sophisticated bike to enjoy a good ride, in fact, a heavier steel frame bike will generally give you a more comfortable ride than a lighter one with a frame made from aluminum. The effort it takes to ride either one is about the same, because the weight difference is just a few pounds; too little to notice even when climbing a hill. A bike with inexpensive components made from steel is also generally more durable than the more expensive ones. Higher end bikes have many parts; derailleurs and sprockets for example, that are made from lightweight alloys. Sure, the result is a lighter bike, which makes it easier to ride, at least in theory. In reality however, the difference is minimal and you will likely not even feel it, especially not when you are carrying panniers with fifty pounds of luggage inside. Yet, we are often being told that we need to invest in a quality bicycle that costs at least seven or eight hundred dollars. This, my friends, is deception. While there are store brand bicycles on the market that don't ride well because they're poorly made, you can still buy a decent bicycle for around four hundred dollars, much less for a good used one. Forget the accessories and the bike specific clothes, unless you really like them or are planning to go into racing. Just focus on having fun. Cycling is supposed to feel good. You don't have to be an expert or own a high-end bike to experience that. If riding your bike doesn't feel good, perhaps you're pushing yourself too hard too soon or you just haven't found your ideal pace yet. I would encourage you not to give up too soon, because it can take a while to become entirely comfortable on a bike. Perhaps you need to find a route where you're away from cars, so you can focus more on riding than on traffic. Whatever the case may be; give cycling a chance! The benefits are many.

      The good feeling that comes from a bike ride doesn't just last for the duration of the ride itself. Even hours later I tend to feel great. My muscles relax easily and blood circulation is at its best. It is much easier to get a good night sleep as well.

      Strangely enough, riding a stationary bike at the gym doesn't work as well. It simply does not have the same effect and is also very boring by comparison. That is a bit unfortunate where climate in the winter makes cycling difficult. How can you get that same great feeling when cycling outside is just not an option for you? I my experience, the best way is to go on tour in a country where climate is not a problem. I realize that this is a tall order, but it is something I would highly recommend for your bucket list once you have found the perfect bike ride feeling, or "zone" for yourself.

To conclude this chapter I would like to remind you of not trying to accomplish too much in too short a time. Even when you are on tour and cycling feels great most of the time, your body will eventually need a break from it. One thing that I've learned from my tours up until now is that you cannot really take too many rest days. One reason for this is accumulating fatigue. After cycling 100 or so kilometers per day for four or five days in a row, you may feel great when you're on the bike and going strong, but that can be deceiving. Your body may actually become run down to the point where everything else starts to bother you. I have experienced this a few times myself. The solution is a day off, or better yet, two. I cannot brag about my own planning, but one way to get the most out of a tour is to plan for plenty of extra time. One of the few regrets of my 2013 tour of Central America is that I took way too few days off. There were so many places that I could have spent a few extra days, but I had a deadline. The entire tour could only take about twelve weeks. For a 4000 km trek across a variety of different terrains this is not a long time. Think about it, to truly experience a place you've never been to, it takes more than a day. Pick the places that you are curious or intrigued about and spend some time there while the bicycle is getting a break. You will enjoy the tour more and perhaps meet new friends. When you are ready to get back on the road the cycling will feel even better. It will be even easier to find your pace and experience the great feeling that comes from riding.

After being on tour for a period of a few weeks or months it can be hard to reintegrate into what most of us call a normal life. Having a regular job and live in the same place for an undetermined amount of time can start to look like a step down from a great adventure. In the next chapter I will tell you about my last few weeks of touring Mexico and how I felt about the prospect of returning to Canada

Chapter 27

Yucatan Peninsula

The final weeks in Mexico

It took two days to reach Merida, the capitol of Yucatan, from Campeche. The first day was so uneventful that I barely remember anything about the ride. What I remember clearly is an evening in Calkini, a small community somewhere along the road, roughly half way between the two cities. There were just two hotels in town and neither of them was really well marked. I had to ask around to find a place at all. The one I finally ended up at was old, family run and cheap. The rooms were all accessed through a small rectangular yard that had chickens running around in it. After checking into a room I went for my usual stroll around town, finding a good place to eat supper and checking out the surroundings.

Calkini had a beautiful park where many locals were spending their evening. Once again I was amazed by the sound of the birds that were also gathered around the park. The mild temperature of the early evening contributed to the atmosphere that seemed almost magical. At one point I noticed a bunch of school-aged girls sitting on a bench, gathered around a laptop. I walked over and asked if they had Internet at this park. "Si" one of the girls replied. "Es inalambrico."

I had not really planned on logging onto the net at all that evening, but since the park apparently had free Wifi, I decided to get my laptop and check my messages. There were none worth mentioning, except another message from my friend Muriel, who was trying a much gentler approach this time. She was going to get a few days off around Easter, so perhaps we could meet somewhere. I dismissed it, but replied with a brief note telling her that I'd probably be in Cancun by then.

The next day is very clear in my memory, but sometimes I wish it wasn't. On my ride to Merida I got attacked by five or six dogs, which kept running after my bike for at least a kilometer. They belonged to a lady who was hanging up laundry in her yard and had failed to restrain them. For a short time I was struggling to keep the bike straight on the road, all the while quite nervous about getting bitten or worse. The dogs eventually abandoned their chase and the incident ended with one of the dogs getting run over, and killed, by an oncoming truck. The only relief I felt after looking around me was that I didn't loose control of my bike during the chase, which could have easily caused me to get run over. The picture of the dying dog was grueling. There was blood and flesh all over the road and a couple of the other dogs were gathering around their companion. I still have a hard time thinking about it, even today.

As a result I arrived at the outskirts of Merida somewhat numbed out. Without noticing it, I ended up on a major bypass route around the city. After a compete circle on this road, I realized that I wasn't going to arrive downtown anytime soon, unless I made a turn somewhere. It was dark by the time I found my way to an area downtown that had any hotels at all, none of which were in my price range. Finally, after what seemed like an endless odyssey around the worst parts of a fairly large city, I found a place for a hundred pesos. It was not nice by any standard, but there was an old squeaky bed and a shower. The staff seemed trustworthy enough. Despite my fatigue I didn't feel like going to bed right away. The dead dog was still fresh on my mind. A cold Mexican beer or two would certainly be a good remedy for that, so I wandered out into the night.

Finding the heart of the inner city was surprisingly easy; there was a big church, the municipal building and a park full of people, many of them obvious tourists. I stayed out till late at night, simply because there was so much to see. Numerous vendors were placed all around the park, offering handcrafted goods. Street performers and buskers were present, entertaining the crowds. I had not seen such an active place at night since I had left Veracruz. Merida also seemed to attract a lot more tourists than any other place I had already been to. Before going back to my gloomy little hotel room by myself, I spotted an Oxxo convenience store. A tall, blond woman, who was obviously a tourist, went in just before me. Our eyes met briefly at the beer cooler as she seemed unsure what to pick. When I pulled out two cans of Sol she smiled and asked me to pass her two of the same. I gladly complied and told her it was good stuff. She smiled again and replied with an accent that nothing here came even close to German beer. I laughed in agreement and told her that I too, was of German origin. We had a brief conversation, in English strangely enough, until it was her turn at the cash. Besides the beer she bought a pack of unfiltered cigarettes. Before leaving the store she turned around briefly and said "good bye" with a smile, before disappearing into the darkness.

I walked back to my room, turned on the ceiling fan and took another shower to make the humid heat more bearable. Before I went to sleep I downed the two cans of beer, while they were still cold. Sweat was pouring over me almost right away, but I fell asleep within minutes.

The next day my goal was to get to Progreso, a nearby town by the ocean. As much as I liked Merida, I could barely wait to see a real beach again. The ride was only about 30 kilometers, so it was pretty quick. What took a lot longer was the search for a good hotel. I had thought of spending a few days in Progreso, but hadn't completely made up my mind about it. When I found a hotel for about 150 pesos I checked in just for one night. Progreso was a small town, but it had lots of good places to eat and a nice beach. Most impressive was the huge bridge that connected the town with a nearby island. I found out that there wasn't a lot to see over at the island besides port installations. The one attraction that was located there was the dock for an restored pirate ship, that would take tourists on a three hour cruise in an attempt to take them back in time to experience a by gone era. Hundreds of years ago, pirates ruled the waters around the Yucatan. I seriously considered taking the cruise, but decided against it when I saw the price of a ticket. Instead, I treated myself to a great barbecue fish on the patio of a little mom and pop restaurant, overlooking the beach.

The next day I was already done with Progreso. After a relatively late breakfast I checked out of my hotel and hit the road, going east along the coast, which felt more like going south because of the slow and steady curvature of the Gulf Coast. The next significant town was supposed to be Dzilam de Bravo, but even as I started my ride I didn't really believe I was going to get that far. I had started too late in the day, the sun was very intense and didn't even feel like riding the entire 85 kilometers it would take to get there, according to my map. Still in the outskirts of Progreso, I saw some vehicles with Canadian license plate pull up in front of me. One of the drivers, a lady, waved to me. It was a good reason to stop for a few minutes and chat with her. Two families from Alberta had driven all the way down, across the US and most of Mexico from their homes in Calgary to escape what was left of the winter. They owned a little house down here, right on the beach. "We bought it dirt cheap" the lady told me. It was a welcome disruption of the ride that would soon turn quite monotonous, despite the beautiful natural vegetation and occasional view of the beach. Suddenly it dawned on me that I couldn't afford any more delays if I wanted to get to Dzilam de Bravo before dark. The realization actually took some of the fun out of riding. I was starting to wonder why I hadn't taken an extra day in Progreso.

A little over two hours into the trip I spotted a banner that had been placed between two fence posts. It said "Hostal" in big red letters. The place looked like private property, without any buildings on it besides some simple cabañas, traditional houses of the region; erected from nothing more than tree branches and palm tree leafs. My curiosity was awakened, so I stopped and pushed the bike across the road toward the dirt driveway. A hostel, out here in the middle of nowhere?

A young man with blond, shoulder length hair, walked towards me from one of the cabanas. "Hi, my name is Klaus." He announced in English with a slight German accent. "Welcome to Hostal Zocalo of San Crisanto!" We chatted for a few minutes before he told me that, if I decided to stay, I could either pitch my own tent, or share one of the cabanas with another traveler. "It's up to you, man." He declared in a casual, but friendly tone. The decision was easy. Each cabana had two hammocks and a sand floor. There was no real door or windows to shut, but the climate was so warm that it seemed way more comfortable that way than my tent would have been. To top it off, the cabana next to the one I was assigned, was occupied by two young ladies. A brief look revealed that I had met one of them before. She was the tall blond woman I had followed into the convenience store in Merida a couple of nights before. It turned out that her name was Angela and she was traveling across the Yucatan Peninsula with her friend Britta, another tall woman with a very slim build and short dark hair. Sharing my cabana was a young lad from Sweden who called himself The Pirate. The most amazing aspect of this hostel were not the young guests from Europe however, it was the location. Just a few feet down from the cabanas was a beautiful beach, with palm trees and picture perfect white sand ending in crystal clear water that had a turquoise tint to it as far as one could see. If there is a paradise, this place had to be pretty close! It was an easy decision to pay for two nights.

I spent most of the afternoon with my new friends, Angela, Britta, Pirate and his travel companion Agnes. We went to the beach together where, to the amusement of the rest of us, Pirate was trying to climb a coconut tree and pick fresh coconuts. We all went swimming in the ocean and eventually ended up at the main cabaña, a slightly larger building that incorporated a dining area, consisting of one long table, and a kitchen. There were two refrigerators, one of which was stocked with beer. Klaus was selling it pretty much at cost, another nice feature of this hostel. There was clipboard circulating around the table that had a description of a delicious dinner. The price would be 100 pesos per person. Guests were asked to enter their names on the list below, if they wanted to take part. Klaus would go to town shortly to get all the ingredients and cook the meal that included barbecued fish. It would all be served around eight. Since there was not much else in terms of food, and the meal involved barbecued fish, I added my name to the list. As it turned out, this was a good decision. The food was excellent and plentiful.

After the fantastic meal I ended up spending the evening drinking beer and playing cards with the rest of the guests. Two more young women from Germany eventually showed up. The atmosphere was very relaxed. There was now a majority of Germans around the table, yet most of the conversation was in English. Later I found out that this was typical for most hostels. As it turned out, Hostal Zocalo was a well-established hostel in Merida. The San Crisanto branch was relatively new and was receiving most of its guests directly from the Merida operation. Klaus told me that he was going to be forced to relocate the hostel soon, due to increasing rent on the property. I considered myself lucky, having found this fantastic place just in time.

The night in a hammock would have been very comfortable, if it hadn't been for the mosquitoes that had somehow found their way into our cabana. Eventually I wrapped myself into my sleeping bag to get a good night sleep, which was all right due to the wind coming off the shore.

The next day I said good-bye to Angela and Britta before joining the other two German girls, Ellen and Beate, on a tour of the San Crisanto Mangroves. The tour takes about ten tourists through a miles long channel by boat. It ends at a small cenote, a deep pond with crystal clear water. There were also some huge fish in it. We spent the better part of the day. Having reached the dock on my own, by bicycle, I was able to check out the village afterwards and grab a late lunch at one of the mom and pop restaurants.

When I returned to the hostel, most of the friends I had just met the night before were either gone, or preparing to leave. Angela and Britta had already taken a bus toward Cancun. The others were waiting for their ride back to the Merida hostel. The van from Merida arrived and I got to meet Susan, Klaus's mom. She was a youthful woman around my own age who was running the hostel in town with her Mexican boyfriend. To my surprise Susan was from Alabama. Klaus had grown up mostly with his Dad in Germany, but had joined his mom in the hostel business. The van brought a few new guests, among them young couple, Luz from Villahermosa and Jochen from Cologne, Germany.

Once again there was an excellent dinner that evening, which ended with a bonfire outside by the beach and a lot of beer and tequila. It turned out that Jochen was an engineer who was on assignment in Mexico for Pemex, the state controlled oil-company. He had met Luz only recently.

The next morning started out with a swim in the clear ocean water, after which I was intent on leaving the hostel to continue my voyage. Things turned out differently when I decided to some basic pre-trip maintenance on the bike and realized that one of the spokes had broken on my rear wheel. What was I going to do now? I decided that I couldn't ride like this. The weight of the panniers, plus my own, would only lead to more damage. There was a bus going to Merida each morning and it was cheap. Klaus reassured me that it would be easy to find a shop in town that could repair my wheel. It took only a few minutes to remove the wheel from my bike and walk up to the road with it to catch a bus ride back to Merida.

It was quite a change for me to be travelling by bus. The ride was enjoyable and took about an hour and a half. I ended up downtown, close to where I had stayed for one night. There was a bike shop near the market, which was not far, but hard to find for lack of signage. The shop was a well-organized family business. The lady who took my order assured me that my wheel would be fixed some time later in the afternoon. This meant I had time to explore the city during daylight hours, which was totally fine with me. Just as I was leaving the store, a voice called out for me: "Señor oye!"

I turned around and there was a bearded man who appeared to be inspecting my wheel. "We can't fix that", someone said in English. The problem was, once again, the wheel size, which had already caused me some grief months earlier, when I couldn't find a proper tire in Veracruz. I had totally forgotten about it, but my 700c wheel needed spokes that were slightly longer than the 26-inch wheels that were common here. What now?

I asked the mechanic if he knew of any shop in town that might carry the right spokes. His expression turned quite serious as he prepared to answer with a very convincing "no". I was out of luck, it seemed. Then it dawned on me that I had a couple of spare spokes somewhere in one of my panniers, which I had left at the hostel, beside my hammock. To say that I felt stupid would be an understatement. I must have looked devastated, because suddenly the bike mechanic in front of me seemed to have a solution. "We can do something, Sir." He told me in English. "Come back at five!"

Still feeling like an idiot and wondering why I hadn't attempted to switch out the spoke myself at the hostel, I left the market and started wandering the streets. Somehow I was quite comfortable with the bike shop doing the repair, even as I suspected that they were going to use a spoke that didn't really fit. At the time my skills for replacing spokes and truing the wheel were poor, at best. I had tried to true an old wheel at home once and the result had been so bad that the attempt had ended with a visit to a bike-shop. I had to learn more about bike mechanics!

I ended up spending a great day in Merida that even included a visit to Hostal Zocalo, the one that Susan was running. Several people I had met at the beach were hanging out in the lobby and it was fun to see them again. The hostel was in an old building that had recently been renovated, and appeared to be well cared for. I had the funny feeling that I might end up spending the night here, if my wheel wasn't ready later that evening.

Fortunately this didn't happen. The wheel was good to go at five, as promised. The mechanic had found a spoke that was longer than the on I needed and bent it at the end that hooks to the hub. This seemed like a good solution to me and I left the shop happily, only fifty pesos lighter.

I easily found my way back to the bus terminal and before long boarded a bus back to San Chrisanto. There was one minor problem however. Hostal Zocalo was not in walking distance of the town, nor was there an official bus stop in front of it. I thought I could rely on the bus driver to know where it was located, but it turned out that he had no idea. I was on my own now and it was pitch dark outside. Thinking I had recognized a landmark indicating close proximity to my destination, I asked to be let off. Minutes later I was standing in the dark with my bicycle wheel in one hand and the camera bag around my neck, at the side of a deserted highway in the middle of nowhere, wondering which way to go. I was reasonably confident that the bus hadn't passed the hostel, so I took a chance and walked on in the same direction. It didn't take long to adjust to the darkness and after a few kilometers I spotted the hostal sign. It was quiet at the main cabaña. Most of the guests had left, including my cabaña mate, The Pirate. I sat down for some tortilla chips, a beer and some conversation with the only two people present, Peter, a volunteer who was filling in for Klaus that night, and his girlfriend Gail. Both were Americans who hadn't seen their home states for over a year. "We just go to Belize on a daytrip and get another six months visa on our reentry to Mexico" Peter explained. A while later I returned to my cabaña, which I had to myself.

The next morning started, once again, with some bike maintenance. This time I only had to install the wheel. The new spoke stuck out like a sore thumb, but it was as tight as all the others and the wheel was perfectly true. I left the hostel around ten. My plan no longer was to go to Dzilam de Bravo. It had changed completely after some calculation had revealed that I was ahead of schedule. Someone had advised me to avoid Cancun at Easter and explore some of the lesser-known places on the Yucatan Peninsula instead. I had considered the advice and decided to visit Izamal next.

Izamal is an old town with an interesting history. Pretty much all of its buildings are yellow. There is an old monastery that may still be among the biggest in the world. What makes Izamal interesting historically however, is that it was built on an ancient Mayan city, reusing some of the same stone and building churches and the like on top of the old pyramids. To be honest, I did not spend a lot of time looking at the ruins. I ended up having dinner with a lady from Germany who told me that she spent her winters here. She explained that she loved how quiet the town was compared to the tourist hotspots on the coast and talked about Valladolid, a nearby city I could reach within a day's ride that was beautiful and not overrun by tourists.

In hindsight I regret not having spent a little more time exploring Izamal. It sure made an impression on me with all its yellow painted houses, but there also seemed to be something fake about it. Later I found out that a multi millionaire owned most of the town and had made sure all houses within city limits were painted yellow. Along with the ancient monastery this was meant to attract more tourists. I was out of there the next day and on my way to Valladolid, where I stayed in a very inexpensive hostel that featured hammocks in the dorms instead of beds. The dorms were basically cabañas, only larger and a bit sturdier, than the ones on the beach. The first night I had the men's dorm to myself, but there was a group of young Scandinavian girls, at least a dozen, sharing the women's dorm. The girls were noisy, some of them returned to their dorm drunk, in the wee hours of the morning. It was hard to get a good sleep. I heard voices singing, crying and vomiting, right next door. I had already paid for two nights and hoped those girls were going to leave the next day. I got my wish.

Valladolid was a beautiful town. Like most Mexican towns it seemed to have evolved around the main plaza with its cathedral and the town hall. I took a lot of pictures and enjoyed wandering around its streets, admiring the colonial architecture in various states of repair. After my extra day I was itching to move on.

The next major stop on my journey was Chichen Itza, the world famous Mayan ruins, which were not very far away. I found a cheap hotel in Piste, the nearest town and just a walk away from the archaeological area, where I spent the night relaxing. I walked to the ruins the next morning, so I wouldn't have to worry about my bicycle. The Mayan pyramids were astounding, but ironically there was going to be an Elton John Concert near the tallest one of them, a few days later. The stage that was being set up next to ancient Mayan structures looked out of place. There was also a lot of activity. Despite the disruptions, Chichen Itza was still worth the visit. The sheer size of the archaeological area is mind-boggling and it puts the accomplishments of Mayan culture into perspective.

After a morning of visiting ancient ruins, I was itching to get back to the ocean. Just as I was getting ready to leave Piste, a shirtless man who was hauling beer on a bicycle, advised me to avoid the main road to Tulum and take a less travelled secondary route instead. "You'll get killed by some bad driver if you take the main highway" he said, a cigarette dangling from his mouth. I liked the alternative he suggested, as it would lead me through some untouched jungle and a couple of villages that still held on to their Mayan routes, so I decided to follow his advice.

It took two days to reach Tulum. During that time I did not see many vehicles on the road. There were no obvious tourists. The villages I passed were quiet and untouched by commercial interests. I got to see some very old churches, taste some authentic traditional food and enjoyed conversations with people who still speak Mayan most of the time. Mexico's history is alive in the rural parts of the Yucatan Peninsula. To this day I'm grateful for that discovery. The ride through the jungle also didn't disappoint. The road was a bit rough, but free of cars for all but a few. Some of the vegetation that could be seen gave the illusion that I was on a different planet, especially the mangroves with their incredible root systems.

I made a stop in Coba before reaching the coast. All I did there was to eat, shower and sleep. At the time I had no idea that Coba actually had a larger pyramid than Chichen Itza and was also the gateway to Quintana Roo's National Park. Attractions like those are always worth visiting and a return to Coba remains on my bucket list to this day.

Tulum, which I reached a day later, turned out to be a bit of a tourist trap, which is typical for nearly all places near the ocean. When I arrived in town I realized that, riding on the main highway it would only take me two days to make it to Cancun. The deadline, my flight to Orlando, was still a week away. I made plans stay in Tulum for three nights, then move on to Playa del Carmen and spend another two nights there.

My first two nights in Tulum were at "The weary Traveler", a typical party hostel. It was my first experience in a mixed dorm. I thought this was awesome, probably for all the wrong reasons. I remember being the only male who was still in bed the first morning. Women, young and not so young, were getting ready for their day. Some were walking by my bed, wrapped only in a towel. The hostel had a shuttle to the beach, which was located about five kilometers away from town. I never took advantage of it because it was easy and more flexible to ride my bike. After spending two nights at the hostel, partying with people of different ages, from many countries and various walks of life, I was itching to get out. There were many hotels and even camping, closer to the beach zone of Tulum. I liked the idea of spending my last day near the ocean and the ruins I was planning to visit. Even in the beach zone, prices were generally pretty reasonable, yet significantly higher than in town. Staying right on the shore is always considered a bonus and it comes with a premium. The most expensive hotels and resorts are usually located on the side of the road that has direct access. For those with lower budgets, there is the other side of the road. Most of the time there is a public beach access within walking distance, so it is often a good compromise. I was looking for such a compromise; the right balance between affordability and proximity to the ocean.

I left "The weary Traveler" around lunchtime that day, in search of my bargain paradise on the beach. What did I find? - A lot of places that offered great accommodations at various price levels, and an empty lot with some guys drinking beer by a campfire. They had put up a banner that advertised fifty peso camping spots. Behind them, off to one side, was an older camping trailer where a woman, wearing only a bikini, was setting up her barbecue. She appeared to be the only guest and I was wondering where the rest of her family might be. With no facilities at all and rough vegetation in spots, the place could hardly be called a campground. But for the price, less than fife dollars, it didn't matter to me. If that woman was camping here it would certainly be good enough for me too, so I gave one of the guys fifty pesos, which was converted into a six pack of Corona at the nearby store without much delay. I picked a spot, set up my tent and unloaded my luggage into it, except for the handlebar bag that had my camera, my passport and a towel. It was time to take the short ride to the ruins, and visit the beach afterwards. I didn't think twice about security, even though my hosts didn't exactly seem hard working and trustworthy.

To me, the Mayan ruins of Tulum were easily the most memorable ones of the entire trip. While the remnants of pyramids and other buildings are by far not the largest, nor the most spectacular, their location on the shore, high up on a cliff, is simply stunning. There were lots of iguanas wandering around the pyramids, which seemed to have lost their fear of people. After taking plenty of pictures of both the ruins and the iguanas I joined dozens of other tourists and descended the stairs down the cliff to access the beach. A swim in the ocean was just what I needed to cool off. The water was crystal clear and warm.

When I finally returned to my tent it was almost dark. To my surprise, there were no other people campers, not even the guys who had taken my money for the spot. To this day I'm not sure if they even had any rights to the property. At the time I simply decided not to worry about it. All my stuff was where I had left it. Obviously no one was interested in my dirty laundry and a set of sun-worn panniers.

I was tired, but before I could get to sleep I needed to have supper. Once again I left my tent, this time on foot, with only a few essentials that I couldn't afford to loose. A neat little restaurant with outdoor patio was only a short walk away. The patio was empty, except for one guest. An attractive lady was sitting by herself, apparently waiting for her meal. We made eye contact and I could not help but ask her if she was dining by herself. It turned out she was, so we decided to have dinner together. Kate was from Rochester, NY, which was really close to home. We chatted as if we had known each other for a long time. It was her last night in Mexico and she was going to move to Spain permanently shortly after her return home. Sometimes good things are short lived. Even to this day, my dinner with Kate is by far my fondest memory of Tulum. We hugged good-bye before we parted.

The next day I was up relatively early, packed up my campsite and found a place to eat a quick breakfast, close to the highway. As I started my way toward Cancun, I saw a beat up car roll by in the oncoming lane. Some guy was waving to me. A closer look revealed that it was the same fellow who had taken my fifty pesos for the campsite. I waved back, but shook my head, still wondering if he actually owned the property, or if he had simply pulled off a stunt to get beer money. It didn't matter at this point. My last night in Tulum had turned out great and I had slept well.

Next stop on my journey was Playa del Carmen. I had read that it was the fastest growing community in North America and a tourist trap. When I finally got to "Playa", after a boring, straight ride on the shoulder of the main highway, I found a town that resembled places in the US far more than any other Mexican town. There was Walmart, McDonald's and even Hooters. The good thing was, that it was really easy to find a hostel in walking distance to the beach.

I spent three nights in Playa del Carmen. During that time I made some friends from all different corners of the world. We drank a lot of beer together, swam in the ocean and in a nearby cenote. Playa was a tourist and party town, but after months of riding a bicycle across much of the continent by myself, it made for a pretty good time. Reality was slowly starting to creep back into my mind, and spending two nights drinking and bullshitting with strangers was the perfect distraction. My flight to Orlando, Florida, was only days away now. I had just one more day of riding the bike on a Mexican highway. Next would be two days of flying on different airplanes. My return ticket from Orlando to Buffalo was via New Jersey. I was going to face a very different world and didn't feel ready for it. All kinds of thoughts crossed my mind. I could simply miss my flight and remain in in Mexico as an undocumented immigrant, living off low paid hostel jobs. Even starting a little business selling paintings to tourists seemed more attractive than returning to Ontario. In the end I decided to catch the flight, go home, wherever that was, and earn enough money over the summer to return the next winter.

   The ride to Cancun was much like the one to Playa del Carmen. On the way I passed plenty of high-end tourist resorts along the beach. To me they looked anything but inviting. Missing were any signs of the truly rich Mexican culture I had come to know. It was a positive surprise to see that the city of Cancun was actually quite ordinary, aside from the hotel zone, which I only got to see briefly on my way to a short trip to the beach. I stayed at a hostel in Cancun, a very quiet place with enough rules to keep away the hard partying crowd I had spent much time with in Playa. There was an interesting side to this too however. When I returned to my hostel on the last afternoon of the stay, plastic-wrap for my bike in hand, I met Dolores.

   Dolores was a rather quiet, and almost fragile looking girl. She was quite pretty, but her expression always seemed a bit too serious. We ended up having supper together since we seemed to be the only two guests of the hostel who actually spent time there before nightfall. Dolores had something to hide, and to this day I sometimes wonder what it may have been. The first version of her story was that she was from Ontario, Canada. That lasted only until she found out that I was from there as well. She than told me that she had been born in Ontario, but had lived in Michigan. She had had a dream of moving to Israel, but instead she had ended up in Texas and walked across the border without a passport. It seemed that her true story was probably a bit different from what little she told me, but I didn't care. We actually went grocery shopping and cooked dinner together, which was great.

After the dinner I took my bicycle up on the roof patio of the hostel to wrap it. I had a huge roll of plastic-wrap, but no bike box. I figured it would be good enough to wrap the bike really well, so that's what I did. The next step was to pack all my things into the panniers, except for a change of clothes, the laptop and toiletries, which went into my duffle bag. I tied all four panniers together and wrapped them until they looked like a suitcase. I was done, except for one thing. I still had to arrange for transit to the airport. That too was easy. There was a cabbie hanging out in the lobby, talking to the owner of the hostel. He was more than eager to come back in the morning to take me, but there was a problem: His car was too small to fit my bike. "No problem" he said and pulled out his cellphone. Minutes later he told me that his friend was going to show up at the door with his station wagon.

That was it, I had only a few hours left in Cancun and it was getting late. I was not looking forward to my return to Canada. Actually, I was kind of scared. I no longer had my truck, which had been my business. I had no home, except for a tiny cabin in the woods. I had no idea what I was going to do. The only thing I knew was that I wanted to return to Mexico, the following winter.

Chapter 28

Mechanics

Can you fix a bike?

You may have noticed that, in the last chapter, as well as some of the previous ones, I had to seek help for minor bike problems. As a matter of fact, the last repair was even a bit goofy. I actually had the correct spokes somewhere in my panniers, but had totally forgotten about it and taken hours long bus rides to solve the problem. When my derailleur got bent in Campeche I honestly thought that my tour might be over. Here is the truth, in case you haven't figured it out by now: Besides some minor maintenance, like oiling my chain and cleaning the bike, I had no clue about how to fix bicycles. Yet somehow, I managed to cycle across six US states and six Mexican states on a thirteen year old bike that wasn't perfect to start with. At a very young age I had learned how to fix a flat tire, but even at that I wasn't really good.

See, there goes another excuse not to start your own bike tour. Bikes are brilliantly simple, so even if you don't have a clue about mechanics, you will often be able to figure out why something doesn't work the way it should. When your own resources are exhausted, there usually is someone within reach who can help. Even seasoned bicycle mechanics would often rather help you for chump change or even free, than fix the bikes they usually see in their shop. Bicycle touring is exciting. Any tour that takes you across borders has the potential to be life changing. Those situations when you need help allow someone local to become part of something they probably view as significant. This is how lifelong friendships are formed, or at least some memories that you can look back on much later.

Would I recommend learning about bike mechanics before going on a major tour? You bet! I actually thought that as a former mechanic, I would have no problem fixing my bike, no matter what would happen to it. Bikes are simple, right? As you can see, this is just another lesson I had to learn the hard way. It took a 5,000-kilometer bike ride to accomplish that and that was just for understanding that studying bicycles more thoroughly might be a good idea. I learned about bicycles after my trip. As a matter of fact, I fell in love with bicycles to the point where I could no longer be ignorant about what makes them work. Have you ever heard someone say that they enjoyed their job so much that they would do it for free? Some time after my first major bike tour I joined Edmonton Bicycle Commuters as a volunteer. EBC is a non-profit organization that operates two volunteer run bicycle shops in Edmonton, Alberta, the city I now call home. Volunteering is a great way to learn about bicycle mechanics in a most hands-on way. At Bikeworks we accept donated bicycles, no matter what condition they may be in. The ones that are beyond repair get stripped for reusable parts before the rest gets recycled. The ones that can be salvaged get fixed up and resold at affordable prices. Fixing up old bikes is a fantastic way to learn about bicycle mechanics.

Another great resource is the Park Tool website and the catalogue by the same company. Park Tool is a company that has been specializing in bicycle specific tools for decades. While some of their tools can be pricy, they are among the best in the industry. They have the right tools and know how to fix any mechanical bike problem imaginable. If ever you're not sure about how to fix your bike, consult parktool.com. If you are traveling without Internet access for long stretches, it might be a good idea to get the park tool catalogue in book form and carry it with you. It weighs only a few grams and easily fits into your panniers.

Bicycles are essentially simple, but there are certain things that change as time goes on. Some parts you will find on newer bicycles are no longer compatible with the older bikes. Bicycle manufacturers are always striving to make their bikes better, lighter, more comfortable and faster. Some of the improvements they make can complicate your bike for no good reason other than a specific application that is totally irrelevant to you and your tour. It is for that reason, that for touring I recommend a relatively basic bike, which doesn't necessarily have to be brand new. What is important is that you carry the right tools to match your bicycle, so you avoid carrying anything unnecessary, but are prepared to work on all major components of your particular type of bike. As already mentioned, an older, simpler bike will often give you less trouble. For example; friction shifters hardly need adjustment, while index shifters have to be set just right or they may skip gears.

Parts that require specific tools that may look very different from one bike to another are the bottom brackets and the headsets. While the principle is always more or less the same, over the years different types of fasteners have been used to put those bikes together, which are not compatible. That's why it is important to familiarize yourself with your bike and make sure you've got the right tools.

In so called third world countries a lot of people depend on bicycles for transportation. Their bicycles are generally very simple and a lot of the parts they use have been designed decades ago. I have found that a 1980's mountain bike is ideal for touring in those countries. No mountain bike enthusiast in North America would even think about using a 1980's bike on single-track trails. Much better bikes are available for that, but there are still many good quality mountain bikes from the 80's around. Their relatively thick tires have definite advantages on rough roads or trails. They are also usually very easy to get off the rim in case of a flat. Those tires are among the most common in the world today. You won't have trouble finding a replacement. There are many other components on those bike that had been standardized and are still commonly available; anywhere. The tools required are also the most basic. It goes without saying that bikes of this kind are also easiest ones to learn inside out, mechanically. A fun way of accomplishing that is to overhaul your own old mountain bike before you take it on tour. Since most of those bikes never came with racks and fenders, you will have to ad them yourself. Again, old style bikes are generally the easiest ones to install racks to. While you're at this, make sure you have the right handlebars and a seat that allows you to ride for hours without pain in your butt. Both of these seem like simple things at first glance, but there is more than meets the eye. Handlebars have things attached. There are the brake handles, which have to be easy to reach when riding the bike. They also have cables attached which run along the frame, front and back, to where the brakes are. It is a good idea to inspect the entire brake system carefully before going on tour. On older bikes that haven't been ridden in a while, cables are often corroded to the point where replacing them is by far the best option. The best way to do that is to replace both the cables themselves and the housing, which is the flexible, plastic coated tube the cables run through where they are not guided along the frame. Both are inexpensive and you will not have to worry about them much once they are replaced and adjusted properly. The brakes have more items to check. There are several different types of brakes, some of which are harder to work on than others. Older bikes have rim brakes, which means that the brake pads are pushing against the rim when activated. Of course it is important that they are attached securely, and adjusted in a way that allows efficient braking. I recommend you consult one of the resources mentioned above to do this, as it would take up a lot of space here to describe the entire process. Also on your handlebars are the shifters, which operate in a manner that is very similar to the brakes. When it comes to gears, simplicity is the key to a good tour. Look at the sprockets on the rear wheel. There are usually six or seven, which is sufficient as long as they are the right size. The more you have, and some newer bikes can have up to ten or eleven, the harder they are to adjust.

    The cluster of sprockets is called a cassette. There are two types of cassettes. The first one is a freewheel cassette. A freewheel cassette has an internal mechanism that allows the sprockets to turn freely in one direction. This allows you to coast, down a hill for example, without moving your cranks. The other type of cassette doesn't have this mechanism and is essentially just a cluster of sprockets that slides onto a spline that's extending from the hub. In this case the freewheel- mechanism is part of the hub, which is called a freewheel hub.

Assembled both types look very similar and it can be hard to tell them apart, but the procedures to disassemble them are slightly different. There are two steps to determining if you have to do this. The first one is to take out your rear wheel and spin the axle by hand. Does it turn easily or does it feel rough? Set the wheel on a solid surface and hold both ends of the axle. Try to wiggle it, up on one side, down on the other! Is there play? Either of these conditions requires some overhauling of the hub. Sometimes all that's needed is some thorough cleaning, fresh grease and perhaps new ball bearings (they're cheap). In some cases more parts need to be replaced. For the exact procedures consult a bicycle manual, the Park Tool catalogue or a Youtube video! While you have the wheels out, take the time to check the spokes. Are they all equally tight? On a rear wheel, the spokes on the drive side will be slightly tighter than the ones on the opposite side. Put the wheel back onto your bike, or better, a truing stand. Spin it to see if it runs true. If there is significant wobble, the wheel requires truing. This is best done with the tire removed. The spokes are attached to the rim via nipples that have internal threads. The spoke tension is what determines the trueness of your rim and to straighten a slightly bent rim it is necessary to adjust individual spokes in key locations. To do this successfully you have to make sure all the nipples move freely. Sometimes it is a good idea to soak them in penetrating oil before starting. It would be a bit too technical to describe the entire truing process here, but here a re a few key points: If you are looking down on your rim, find a spot that is too far to the left. Identify the spokes on the right side of the rim in that area. They will need to be tightened, which will pull the rim slightly to the right. You will need a spoke wrench of the correct size to do that. It is best to go only about a quarter turn at a time. Also note that the threads are inside the nipple, so turning counter clockwise will tighten them. Once you tightened spokes on one side of the wheel, you will need to loosen the adjacent spokes on the other side of the rim by the same amount. Truing wheels successfully requires practice. It is best to have someone demonstrate the process and then practice on a scrap wheel, if you've never done it before.

Am I getting too technical in this chapter? Bare with me, you're almost done. The front hub and the bottom bracket of your bikes both have bearings that are similar to the ones of the rear wheel. After overhauling your rear hub you will find it easy to do the front one as well. For the bottom bracket, a few other steps come into play. You will have to remove the cranks before servicing the bearings, which requires a crank puller and sometimes a lot of patience. Once you get to the bearing itself you may find that the race, the thing that is threaded into the bottom bracket tube, on the drive side (where the chain wheels go), has a reversed thread. To loosen it you have to turn it clockwise, not the way you are probably used to. Again, the disassembly of the bottom bracket requires some special wrenches.

All of those bearings, wheel hubs and bottom bracket require plenty of grease and a similar way of adjusting, which involves tightening of the bearing parts just enough to allow them to move freely, then tightening a locknut to hold that adjustment. If you have never done this it is probably a good idea to have someone show you how, or perhaps attend a course. Even experienced mechanics do this by trial and error and sometimes it takes a few trials. The key is to know when to stop.

There is one more crucial bearing on your bicycle that is adjusted in that same manner. Your handlebars and the fork the fork are connected to the frame via a set of bearings called a headset. The headset only rotates back and forth as you're steering your bike, but wear and tear is also common because this mechanism is supporting much of your weight (and that of any luggage) when you're riding your bike. To see if your headset needs service, push your bike forward against a wall. Apply the front brake to lock the wheel. Now rock the bike back and forth lightly. If there is any movement of the handlebars or the fork, it means there is too much play in the headset. Adjustment procedures are simple, but when there is significant play it is always a good idea to inspect the parts of the headset more closely. Again, work on the headset requires special wrenches and some other tools.

Of course we must pay attention to the parts that make your bike move; the drivetrain. I already mentioned the cassette, or the cluster of cogs on you rear wheel, and the bottom bracket which your cranks and pedals are attached to. There are chain wheels attached to those cranks, which are connected to the cassette via a chain. All of those parts are subject to wear and tear. Usually the chain will wear out first. If your chain is rusty and does not move freely, it is probably a good idea to replace it. If it seems fine, but you are not sure how old it is, take a 12" ruler and measure 12 inches from the center of one of the pins. Is the 12" mark aligned with the center of another pin? If so, your chain is practically new. If the pin is about 1/16 of an inch past the 12" mark it is time to replace the chain. If the pin is 1/8 of an inch past the 12" mark it is time to inspect your sprockets. They will likely be significantly worn and it is best to replace them as well.

The chain is guided by derailleurs, front and rear. The derailleurs are also used to shift gears. They are operated by shifters, via cables. There are only two adjustments on the derailleurs themselves: High limit and low limit. You will see the tiny screws marked "H" and "L" if you look at them closely. Those adjustments ensure that your chain always stays on the sprockets, while providing access to the entire range of gears. Those are typically the first adjustments to be made when setting up a drivetrain. The adjustment is off when the chain can jump off, or when any of the outside sprockets can't be reached. The third adjustment crucial to shifting is cable tension. It is especially tricky to set up index shifters on a rear wheel with more than 7 gears. Friction shifters hardly require cable adjustment, except for a very rough one. How the rider operates those shifters determines how the bike shifts. Some skill is involved, but it is easy to acquire that. Friction shifters are less prone to trouble and I would definitely recommend them for a touring bike. Index shifters need special cable housings that ensure more precise operation and cable tension may have to be readjusted from time to time.

This breakdown is by no means complete, but covers some of the essentials you need to check before you take any bike on an extended tour. I'll be honest with you: When I set out to do my first extended bike tour I was not well prepared. I had no idea how to check or service even the most basic components of my bicycle. Please do me a favor and do better than that! This book is meant to help you with it. You will simply enjoy your trip more with a bike that is in great working order. If all you can afford is an old second hand bike and you don't have the means to overhaul it completely, by all means, work with what you've got rather than postponing your bike tour indefinitely. The worst that can happen is that you'll break down (I did) and learn a few things. Don't sweat the small stuff!

One last thing: make sure your seat is comfortable. Some bike stores let you try a new seat for a period of time. A comfortable seat can be the difference between a pleasant bike tour and a torture that will burn through the skin on your bum. Bicycle seats, or saddles, as some like to call them are very individual. We are all built slightly different and what works great for some may not work well for others. It is not always the most expensive saddle that's most comfortable neither. The only way to ensure a great ride is to try different saddles until you find one that feels right. You probably guessed it by now; I had to learn this lesson the hard way too, ouch!

Chapter 29

Returning Home

How the bike tour changed my life

I was not looking forward to my return to Canada. It meant that I would have to adapt to a "normal" life again and that in it self was scary. Before my tour, my normal life had been shattered by a divorce, the loss of my home and the sale of my truck, which had been my business for eight years. Going back into the trucking business was not an option; I had changed too much. The big questions were how I was going to earn a living, and where I was going to live.

All this was on my mind when I spent two days on airplanes in April of 2010 to return from Cancun to Buffalo, NY. It was a bit of a consolation that I still had about four days of cycling ahead, including one border crossing, to return to my little cabin near Parry Sound. I was going to enjoy every bit of that ride like it was my last one, even though I knew that this wouldn't be the case.

After arriving in Buffalo I spent another night at the same Days Inn hotel where I had first prepared my bike for a flight. This time I had to unwrap and partially reassemble my bike, which was more complicated than it should have been. On the flight from Cancun to Orlando my bike had only been wrapped in plastic wrap. The airline Jetblue had accepted the package to carry as a sport article, free of charge. A day after that flight I showed up with the exact same package at the check-in counter of Continental Airlines in Orlando for my return to Buffalo, expecting the same treatment. I was in for a bit of a surprise. United had very strict policies regarding oversize items. Not only was I forced to purchase a box from another airline, I also had to cut through the plastic wrap to further disassemble my bike when the box showed a minor bulge where the handlebars where pushing up the cardboard. I cannot stress this enough: Inform yourself about the policies of your airline and comply with them! Also; bring extra cash! It cost $ 100 plus tax to get the bike back to Buffalo on that Contiental flight. Good thing it wasn't going straight to Canada, because that would have cost double (probably more than the bike was worth).

I was not happy about going home, but there was a consolation. I had missed an entire winter and the weather was quite pleasant, if a little windy. The next day I left the hotel and headed back the same way I had come five months earlier; to the Canadian Border at Niagara Falls. The ride was uneventful. At the border I was asked how long I had been outside of Canada. When I replied that it had been just about six months I was asked if I had been detained somewhere because of trouble with the law. I had to laugh at this question, but it also made me wonder about my appearance. *Did I look like a delinquent?* In some way I actually was homeless. I had left Canada after signing my share of the house to my ex wife. All I had was a cabin up north with no running water or electricity. Both problems could be solved quite easily, but my adventure would not be over when I arrived there. My living circumstances were not the only thing that had changed significantly. I had changed myself. The bike tour had given me a new outlook on life. I was free like never before and I was going to try out ideas I had never even thought of before going on tour. I had seen so many different things, met amazing people, seen beautiful places I hadn't known existed and I was full of ideas. Besides optimistic I was also a bit scared. How would I earn a living and save enough money to do more bicycle tours? Where would I go? Was I going to settle in my tiny cabin or was there another place for me somewhere? I even thought of moving to Veracruz, but at the same time I was wondering what I could do there. Teaching English for the equivalent of four dollars an hour wasn't going to support me. All this and more was going through my head as I was riding through familiar terrain in Southern Ontario. Riding the bike was different here. I was hardly noticing my environment, focused almost entirely on my own thoughts. I was at a crossroads in life and I knew I wanted to make it count.

It was not long after arriving back in Ontario that I moved to Edmonton Alberta. I had found a job here and a very good friend. For the next six months my life was quite turbulent as my friendship grew more intimate and the lady I was with drifted deeper into old addictions she'd been battling. At some point I decided to part with her and live on my own for the first time in my life. It turned out to be one of the best decisions I'd ever made. Living in the city gave me access to many activities and resources. The best part of it was that I did not need a car to reach them. Even in the winter, at - 30 degrees, I'd use my bicycle. The first two bikes I had were freebies, donated by friends that really didn't ride or fit me very well, but I had wheels and it always got me where I wanted to go. It is a nice feeling when you can pass gas stations without even looking at the posted price.

After living in Edmonton for a while I discovered Edmonton Bicycle Commuters. Not only did I become a member and use their shop to fix my bike, but I also signed up as a volunteer. Rebuilding donated bikes was the best way for me to learn all the things I wish I would have known during my first big tour. Eventually I rebuilt two bikes for myself that I still own to this day. Both are old style mountain bikes from the 1980's. One is geared for getting around town. It looks like nothing special, but to me it is the most comfortable ride ever. The other is my touring bike. As I'm writing this I have already rebuilt this bike twice. The first time was for a tour across Central America, which I did during the first three months of 2013, the second time was to restore the bike to top condition after the tour.

I may not always be on a bicycle tour, but I am always thinking of the next time I will experience the total freedom of not having to be anywhere specific, the excitement of going places I've never seen and meeting people who live drastically different lives, simply because I took my bicycle out for an extended ride. A bicycle can get you pretty much anywhere. All you have to do is take the time. You will not regret it.

Chapter 30

The Dream

Safe cycling everywhere

This book is meant to inspire people of all walks of life to pick up their bicycle and use it, whether it shall be for a big tour, for commuting to and from work, or for recreational riding on weekends. In North America, bicycles are the most underrated mode of transportation. They have the potential to save millions in fuel cost, slash the health care budget dramatically and make people happier. Unfortunately there are still some obstacles to overcome. I basically have to ad a disclaimer each time I recommend cycling. We generally have to share the road with cars and trucks, except for a few places where short sections of bicycle trails exist. Enjoy cycling! You might end up getting killed by a careless driver.

There is only so much money for the development of new infrastructure. Road maintenance, as well as building new roads, definitely take priority over bicycle trails for cash strapped governments. The main reason is that most people don't even take bicycles seriously as a mode of transportation. Fortunately a trend is underway that is gaining momentum. It will probably take some time, but attitudes are shifting toward more cycling. Many people already know and understand the benefits of riding a bike regularly and every year more are discovering them. Many cities are already building more and better bicycle trails today than they ever thought of in the past. This trend needs to continue if we want to cut down on traffic fatalities, because unfortunately automobile traffic is also still on the increase. The idea that everyone needs a reliable car to travel wherever they want at any time has taken its toll on our cities and countries. Large roadways have changed the landscape and often they are too congested to make travel what it should be. While those roads may be one of the most efficient ways to transport people and goods over long distances, this is certainly not the case in any city during rush hour times. Why are we still using cars to get to work when the trip is often not even faster than it would be by bicycle? One reason I've heard over and over when talking to people, is that they are afraid to get hurt. They cannot imagine getting through the daily traffic on a bicycle. From their perspective they are right. To ride a bicycle on a busy main roadway at rush hour time is dangerous, if not suicidal. So instead of riding their bikes to work they are using their cars, adding more vehicles to the already huge traffic jam. What they don't realize is that in many places alternate roads already exist that may not be practical for cars, but would make perfect sense when riding a bike. Often those roads lead through residential areas and sometimes they don't connect in obvious ways, which can make it hard to map out feasible routes. To get a lot of people to try out cycling as a means of transportation more is needed, but for serious bike trails to be built a lot of demand has to come first. In many regions the winter season adds challenges. While lots of people ride bikes in the spring, summer and fall, in the winter you will only see a few hardcore cyclists.

  What would it really take to make cycling a great and safe alternative to cars and public transit, any season? Bicycle trails are relatively simple, compared to roads, automobiles, trains and the like. As we know, they have shortcomings, especially in harsh climate. However, compared to the money our governments are already spending on transportation, a weatherproof enclosure for all major bike routes would not be impossible to build. For some reason bikes are still generally considered inferior to other types of transportation, but with the right infrastructure this might change fairly quickly.

Of course, creating this infrastructure within our cities is only part one of a much bigger dream. Bicycles can go anywhere, and where there are oceans, bicycles can go on a ship. Yes, I'm dreaming of a worldwide network of bike trails that are maintained as meticulously as our roadways. Bicycle trails are where a large portion of our transportation budget should go. Bicycles are the only mode of transportation that can make us healthier and stronger, while not adding an ounce of pollution to our planet. When kept away from cars and trucks, bikes are very safe to ride.

For long distance cycling to catch on with more people, not only the infrastructure has to change. In our society of instant gratification attitudes would also have to change quite drastically. A trip that takes about a day by car, or a couple of hours on a plane can easily take a couple of weeks riding a bicycle. Who's got the time for that? Is it even realistic? In our jet set world of instant travel we have taken the best part almost entirely out of the equation. We are focused entirely on the destination and hardly anyone pays much attention to the journey itself. This is sad in a way. I hope the adventures in this book have shown how much value is to be found in extended journeys on a bicycle. We have a limited number of days in our lives. Even when we think we have a lot of time left, the best things should not be left on some "bucket list" and put on the backburner forever. It is a ridiculous idea that people should be working fifty weeks out of the year in jobs that few even enjoy, and get two weeks of vacation in exchange, along with a handful of public holidays. Life is too short and too precious for that. Often people get burned out to the point where they are no longer capable of contributing to society in a meaningful way. Most of us would indeed be more productive working less time and focusing more on enjoying our journey. Life is a gift, so why waste it by slaving away for corporations that are built around the idea of maximizing profits? Money was invented as a means of exchange and a measure of value, but has no intrinsic value of its own. Too many of us are chasing dreams that evolve around materialistic goals, like getting a bigger house or a brand new car. Ultimately those goals tend to disappoint when we reach them because they are hardly life changing. Some other shiny object always shows up on the horizon when we obtain something we wanted.

Traditional jobs are set up in way that are sure to get us stuck in a rut in exchange for a slow climb of the "corporate ladder". Touring on a bicycle for months at a time is for freaks, those who have no career ambitions or those who are already retired. Think about that! For most of us it is hard to find the time for a month long bike tour, when we have an average life expectancy of almost eighty years. In most western countries we have excess rather than lack of material goods. If you don't believe me on this one, go visit a landfill site! We do not need more productivity. What we need instead is a slower pace of life that allows us to take out time for what really matters, which of course is not just bicycle touring. This slower pace of life would allow us to take the proper time to go to places and experience the journey in a way that would be totally new for many of us.

My dream includes a network of bicycle "highways" that span the globe, regardless of what country. Bicycles would be recognized as a viable means of transportation because time would be valued in a different way. I have never been on a bike ride that I didn't enjoy at least in some way. I cannot honestly say that for any other mode of transportation. I hope this book inspires you to use your bicycle more and consider doing longer and longer tours. Perhaps one day there will be enough of us advocating together for better conditions and my dream will be a reality. Cycling may seem to be an insignificant activity in today's world, but bicycles are the greatest invention ever and they have the potential to help solve many of the problems we are facing today.

At the time of this writing some exciting news is circulating the Internet in Canada. "The Great Trail" as it is called now, is supposed to be fully connected by the summer of 2017. Will my next major tour follow the length of the Trans Canada Trail? Will it be possible to follow this trail from the Pacific shores of Vancouver Island, to the Atlantic? Apparently we are still a few years away from that. When I recently wrote to the information email of the Great Trail about my idea, I was told that some sections of the trail are actually on water. While I don't want to belittle the efforts that are under way, I don't agree with this definition of a trail. What bothers me equally is my very own experience with parts of the Trans Canada Trail in Alberta. There is a section of trail that carries the name Iron Horse Trail. It goes from the village of Waskatenau, north east of Edmonton, to Cold Lake. Most of the trail is designed for the use of ATV's. The gravel is so loose that it is almost impossible to ride on it with regular bicycle tires most of the way. Riding a bicycle with luggage on such a trail is even more difficult.

The Great Trail is a move in the right direction. However, there is a lot of work to be done before it will be suitable for cyclists. My goal is to contribute to this aspect of the trail in any way I can. My hope is that this book will inspire you not only to cycle, but also to respect cyclists more as you share the road with them and, ultimately contribute, in some way, to the dream of having a bicycle trail network across Canada.

Destinations are Fake. The ultimate destination of anyone's life is death. Everything that comes prior is part of a journey. I hope my book helps you make the most of yours.

Acknowledgments

I would like to thank everyone who contributed to this book, starting with the people who helped me make the tour a reality. There were countless strangers who welcomed me into their homes, helped me fix my bike and obtain the right parts for it to keep going. All the persons in this book are real, but names have been changed to protect their identity.

It took years to actually put this book together and it would not have been possible without the strong support of my wife, Barbara Derrick. Barbara gave moral support when it most mattered and she helped me with editing.

Special thanks also goes to Sherry Heschuk, Barbilee Hemmings, Jessica Schlagheck and Zaza Chand for volunteering to proofread chapters and making suggestions on how to improve them.

CPSIA information can be obtained
at www.ICGtesting.com
Printed in the USA
LVOW10s1103300417
532746LV00009B/615/P